| DATE DUE | | | |
|---|---|---|---|
| SEP 2 8 1988 | | | |
| 8 1 | | | |
| JAN 28 '9 | | | |
| AUG 16 199 | | | |
| APR 4 199 | | | |
| | | | |
| | | | |
| | | | |
| | | | |
| | | | |
| | | | |

# MODERNIZATION OF
# THE ARAB WORLD

# MODERNIZATION
# OF THE ARAB WORLD

Edited by
## JACK H. THOMPSON
and
## ROBERT D. REISCHAUER
for the
*Journal of International Affairs*

NEW PERSPECTIVES
IN
POLITICAL SCIENCE

## D. VAN NOSTRAND COMPANY, INC.
PRINCETON, NEW JERSEY

TORONTO　　　　　　MELBOURNE　　　　　　LONDON

# Editors' Foreword

AFTER CENTURIES OF IMPERIAL DOMINATION, MOST OF THE emerging nations of the Arab world are now responsible for their own destinies. With varying degrees of wisdom and success, each has been forced to grapple with the complex problems of modernization—political, social, and economic. The divergent, and often conflicting, solutions that now characterize the area reflect not only differing interpretations of what modernization involves, but also the peculiarities of national institutions, historical experiences, and resource bases—as well as the ever-present influence of the external world powers.

It is yet too early to speculate about the characteristics of a modern Arab world. This volume only attempts to shed some light on the processes of change now at work in the region—on the interactions between the traditional themes of the past, current realities, and future expectations. Insofar as tradition contains elements which are incompatible with aspirations for the future, the legacy of the past impedes modernization. However, in the Arab world the positive aspects of tradition are evident also. Islam has provided an element of cohesion and continuity in the inherently disruptive and destructive processes of development. The memory of a glorious past also has served as inspiration for the future, however little it can do to alleviate the pains stemming from current problems. Reality—economic backwardness, intra-Arab and Arab-Israeli tensions, social instability, and population pressures—must be met by today's leaders for solutions cannot be found by appeals to millennia gone by nor empty promises for the years to come. How this reality is to be met and with what tools is the theme of this book.

The articles included reflect a diversity of opinion and approach.

They are not intended to be definitional, but rather provocative. The background of each contributor is unique, but all possess an expertise that demands close attention. The majority of the articles was taken from *The Journal of International Affairs* ("The Arab World: Paths to Modernization"). These have been supplemented by additional contributions and several reprinted essays. If the articles together do not constitute a complete coverage of the Arab world, taken singly they represent some of the most original writing done in the field.

J.H.T.

R.D.R.

# Acknowledgment

THIS VOLUME IS PUBLISHED UNDER THE AUSPICES OF THE *Journal of International Affairs,* a non-profit periodical issued by the School of International Affairs, Columbia University. A number of the articles herein contained originally appeared in Volume XIX, number 1 of the *Journal.*

# Contents

EDITORS' FOREWORD     v

ACKNOWLEDGMENT     vii

BIOGRAPHICAL NOTES ABOUT THE CONTRIBUTORS     xi

I. THE ARAB WORLD IN QUEST OF A FUTURE
   *by John S. Badeau*     1

II. THE ARAB WORLD'S HEAVY LEGACY
   *by Charles Issawi*     13

III. ISLAM AND MODERNIZATION IN THE ARAB WORLD
   *by Hisham Sharabi*     26

IV. FROM RELIGIOUS TO NATIONAL LAW
   *by Majid Khadduri*     37

V. THE RÔLE OF THE ARMY IN THE TRADITIONAL ARAB
   STATE
   *by Sir John Bagot Glubb*     52

VI. BASIC CONFLICTS OF ECONOMIC DEVELOPMENT IN
   THE MIDDLE EAST
   *by Oded I. Remba*     61

VII. THE POLITICS OF RAPID POPULATION GROWTH IN
   THE MIDDLE EAST
   *by J. C. Hurewitz*     87

VIII. THE ECONOMICS AND POLITICS OF OIL IN THE MID-
   DLE EAST
   *by Stephen H. Longrigg*     102

IX. SAUDI ARABIA: THE ISLAMIC ISLAND
   *by George Rentz*                                      115

X. KUWAIT: A SUPER-AFFLUENT SOCIETY
   *by Fakhri Shehab*                                     126

XI. SOCIAL STRUCTURE AND IDEOLOGY IN IRAQ, LEBA-
   NON, SYRIA AND THE UAR
   *by Charles Issawi*                                    141

XII. PALESTINE: THE BROKEN TRIANGLE
   *by Erskine B. Childers*                               150

XIII. ISRAEL AND THE ARAB NATIONS
   *by Don Peretz*                                        166

XIV. ARAB SOCIALISM
   *by Gordon H. Torrey and John F. Devlin*               178

XV. THE OBJECTS AND METHODS OF NASSERISM
   *by George Lenczowski*                                 197

XVI. U.S.A. AND UAR: A CRISIS IN CONFIDENCE
   *by John S. Badeau*                                    212

XVII. THE U.S.S.R. IN THE NEAR EAST: A DECADE OF
   VICISSITUDES
   *by Uri Ra'anan*                                       229

# Biographical Notes
## about the Contributors

JOHN S. BADEAU is Director of the Near and Middle East Institute at Columbia. From 1961 to 1964 he was United States Ambassador to Egypt and previously he was President of the American University in Cairo and President of the Near East Foundation. Dr. Badeau is the author of *The Emergence of Modern Egypt* as well as numerous articles on the Middle East.

CHARLES ISSAWI, Ragnar Nurkse Professor of International Economics at Columbia University, is the author of *Egypt in Revolution* and the co-author of *The Economics of Middle East Oil*. His book *The Economic History of the Middle East, 1800-1914* has recently been published.

HISHAM SHARABI, Associate Professor of History and Government at Georgetown University, is the author of *A Handbook on the Contemporary Middle East* and *Politics and Governments of the Middle East in the Twentieth Century*. His forthcoming book is entitled *Introduction to Politics in the Arab World: The Middle East and North Africa*.

MAJID KHADDURI is Director of the Near Eastern Center of the School of Advanced International Studies of The Johns Hopkins University. He is the author of *Islamic Jurisprudence, Modern Libya,* and *War and Peace in the Law of Islam*.

LT. GENERAL SIR JOHN BAGOT GLUBB, K.C.B., C.M.G., D.S.O., O.B.E., M.C., was Chief of General Staff and Commander-in-Chief of the Arab Legion from 1939 to 1956. Widely known as Glubb Pasha, he is the author of a number of books, including *Britain and the Arabs, War in the Desert, The Great Arab Conquests,* and *The Empire of the Arabs*.

ODED I. REMBA, a specialist on economic development, is Associate Professor of Economics at Staten Island Community College of the City University of New York. He has published many articles on economic problems of the Middle East.

J. C. HUREWITZ is Professor of Government in the Near and Middle East Institute of Columbia University. He is the author of *The Struggle for Palestine, Middle East Dilemmas,* and *Diplomacy in the Near Middle East,* and is currently completing a book to be entitled *The Military in Middle East Politics.*

BRIGADIER-GENERAL STEPHEN H. LONGRIGG is an expert on the Middle Eastern oil industry and government administration in Africa and Asia. A Doctor of Letters of Oxford University, he was awarded the Lawrence of Arabia Medal in 1962 by the Royal Central Asian Society. He is the author of numerous works, including *The Middle East, A Social Geography* and *'Iraq, 1900 to 1950.*

GEORGE RENTZ, now the Curator of the Middle East Collection of the Hoover Institute on War, Revolution and Peace at Stanford University, worked in Saudi Arabia with the Arabian American Oil Company for seventeen years. He has contributed numerous articles on Arabia to learned journals.

FAKHRI SHEHAB is currently a lecturer in economics and a Fellow of St. Antony's College, Oxford University. Previously, he was an advisor to the Government of Kuwait and the United Nations Secretariat. He is the author of *Progressive Taxation.*

ERSKINE CHILDERS is an author and broadcaster specializing in Arab and Afro-Asian affairs. The author of *Common Sense about the Arab World* and *The Road to Suez—A Study in Western-Arab Relations,* he is currently completing a major book on the Palestine conflict.

DON PERETZ is the Associate Director of the Office of Foreign Area Studies of the University of the State of New York. He is also the author of *Israel and the Palestine Arabs* and *The Middle East Today.*

GORDON H. TORREY is the author of *Syrian Politics and the Military, 1945-1958*. He is currently a Visiting Professor at the School of Advanced International Studies of The Johns Hopkins University.

JOHN F. DEVLIN is a Middle East expert who has lived and worked in the Arab world for a number of years.

GEORGE LENCZOWSKI is Professor of Political Science at the University of California, Berkeley, and a member of the Governing Body of the American Research Institute in Turkey. He is the author of *Russia and the West in Iran, Oil and the State in the Middle East,* and *The Middle East in World Affairs.*

URI RA'ANAN, Senior Fellow of the Russian Institute on Communist Affairs at Columbia University, is the author of *Frontiers of a Nation.* In addition, he has written a number of articles dealing with Soviet tactics in the Third world. He has spent many years in political journalism and diplomacy in the Near East.

# I. The Arab World in Quest of a Future

## by John S. Badeau

MANY TERMS ARE USED TO SPECIFY THE FORCES OF CHANGE which are altering so profoundly the character of the post-war Arab world. Sociologists speak of "modernization," political scientists of "nationalism," while the Arabs themselves call it *nahdha*[1] —the Awakening. Through such diverse terms runs a basic implication: there is a widespread shift in the center of attention away from the familiar past to the modern, if nebulous, future.

To be sure, that familiar past is far from disappearing. An Arab proverb frequently quoted in the Middle East has it that "What is past, is dead." Obviously, the past of the Arab world is not dead. Islamic institutions, social patterns, popular mores and folkways are still powerful influences in modern Arab life. Yet, for all its force and ubiquity, the past no longer commands the stage and *bida* (innovation) is no longer the great heresy. "Men resemble their days more than they resemble their fathers"—to quote another Arab proverb—and it is the aspirations, achievements, institutions and challenges of modern life which are becoming the vital goals of Arab development.

This is to say that, both for the Arabs and the outside world, the post-war Middle East is in many ways a new creation. This newness involves both the internal character of Arab states and society and their relation to the outside world. The process of change and innovation is not yet complete, and the new patterns

[1] Note on the English spelling of Arabic words: the transliteration of Arabic words and proper names throughout the issue has been retained in the style preferred by each author.—Eds.

1

which have emerged are not yet final. They are part of a current of change of which it is only possible to indicate the general direction. While the old order—political, economic and social—is being eroded and destroyed, it is not possible to predict what new shape will finally replace it. The Arab world is still in quest of a future.

One of the primary factors in this newness is the emergence of fully sovereign states in the Middle East. At the beginning of the nineteenth century, when European interests began to penetrate the area, there were only two sovereign entities—Iran and Turkey —which controlled most of the Middle East. This control was eroded and reduced by the European powers through direct colonization, spheres of influence and the mandatory system which made France and Great Britain the dominant influences in the area after the First World War. By 1939 there were eight sovereign and independent Middle East states, though the larger part of the area was still under the direct or indirect control of European powers. In contrast, there are today eighteen sovereign states (stretching from Morocco to Pakistan) while European control has shrunk to the southern littoral of the Arabian peninsula and a few sheikhdoms on the Persian Gulf. For the first time in many centuries, the Arab people are fully responsible for their own destinies.

With the emergence into sovereignty, internal change is burgeoning in the Arab world. States are now free to choose and develop their own forms of government, society and economic life without the guiding hand of a mandatory or colonial master. They are no longer under direct pressure to accept and adopt the institutions of the West—political, cultural or economic. The Western-trained and European-oriented elite, under whom the beginnings of modernization and nationalism started, is being replaced by a new and more independent nationalist group. This group frequently feels that it has little personal stake in continued cooperation with the ex-colonial powers of the West.

Moreover, under the new condition of sovereignty the Arab world has accelerated its attempt to modernize economic and social life. It is discovering that independence is more than a political condition; it involves meeting popular demands for a higher living standard and bringing about economic developments more rapidly than during the colonial period. In pursuing these goals, many Arab states gravitate toward systems of state economy, steadily reducing the area and influence of foreign investment and control.

One evidence and focus of such elements of newness is the tension, suspicion and clashes which have been occurring between Arab states in recent years. In the past three years, there have been alarms and excursions involving Jordan, Syria, Iraq, Kuwait, Saudi Arabia, Yemen and the United Arab Republic. Some of these resulted in broken diplomatic relations, some in a near military confrontation, all in continuous and bitter propaganda.

Such clashes were exceedingly rare in the past when there was a single controlling power holding the reins behind the façades of the various national governments. When Britain's right hand was in Baghdad and her left in Kuwait, it was inconceivable that Iraq should directly threaten Kuwait's existence. With such controls gone and the Arab states now fully sovereign, each government can pursue its own national interests, cultivate its own ambitions and make its own bid for Arab leadership without any direct, external restraining hand. Under these conditions, it is inevitable that there should be a degree of tension and difference between sister Arab states.

Within this framework, many claim that the chief cause of difficulty is the ambition of the United Arab Republic and its President, Colonel Abdel Nasser. In a report to the Senate in 1963, Senator Gruening accused President Nasser of "pouring oil on whatever brush fire breaks out, seeking his own and his country's aggrandizement—and in that order." Evidence can be cited to document this view. Except for the Iraqi drive on Kuwait, the United Arab Republic has been a partisan in most of the Arab world's internal disputes, using both open and covert activities to support the more radical side. The clearest case of this is in Yemen, where the UAR role was overt and obvious, involving military occupation, armed support for a civil war and sharp conflicts with both Jordan and Saudi Arabia.

But the conclusion that the Middle East is tense and troubled because Nasser is a "compulsive meddler in his neighbors' affairs," is both shallow and dangerous. Of course personal and national ambitions play their role—as they do within our own society. Yet throughout its long history, Egypt has always "meddled" in the affairs of certain of her neighbors whenever she was free and strong. This reflects basic considerations of national security (as Egypt sees it) and geopolitics, neither of which Nasser invented and whose operations will not cease with his demise.

Today something new has been added to this historic situation making the UAR a particular focal point in current area tensions. This new factor is a latent cold war which intermittently separates the Arab world into opposing camps. The cold war is not a tidal inlet of the larger East-West struggle, although that struggle affects and complicates the situation. Rather, it is an indigenous affair, reflecting both the problems and the aspirations of Middle Eastern people. Were there no United Arab Republic, no Arab Socialism, no Nasser, tension would still be there, making matters difficult both for the Middle East and the international community.

The Middle East's cold war is born out of the question "How shall we, the ancient peoples, yet new nations, of the area modernize ourselves and our society?" There is the memory of a glorious past, when Islamic countries were the full equals, often the superiors, of the Western world. There is also the obvious fact of a recent colonial past, social impotence, poverty, ignorance and backwardness that is a reproach both on the tongue of the West and the conscience of the Middle East. To walk with dignity among the community of nations, to be in reputation and fact progressive, to bring the fuller life of modern men to the underprivileged masses of the area; these are aspirations found in some form in every country of the Middle East.

They are aspirations which began over a century ago when the Middle East started to move back onto the stage of world affairs, only to find its political power gone, its culture static and despised and its social life backward as compared to the modern world. Leaders such as Jamal-ed-Din el Afghani in Iran, Mohamed Abdu in Egypt and the young Turks in Turkey pondered this humiliation and sought some program that would cure it. Their conclusions, differently phrased but in essential agreement, were that the Middle East must become politically free (both from Oriental despotism and Western colonialism), religiously revived and socially modernized. They therefore urged the adoption of much of Western civilization, which they believed could be absorbed into the native and inner Moslem spirit of Islamic civilization.

In this soil of reform and progress, the movements of Middle East nationalism and modernization took root. Beginning with small elite groups, they gradually spread downward through the population until, in the aftermath of the last war, they represented popular forces found in every country. Both the effect and evidence of this is seen in the rising tide of expectation with which the masses of Middle East peoples look to their leaders and governments. Whether in the more sophisticated and experienced societies such as the Egyptian and the Syrian, or the traditional tribal areas such as Saudi Arabia, there is a demand for some form of modernization to which no government can be permanently indifferent.

But while there is a ubiquity of social discontent, there is no ubiquity of solution. By what process and in what form can the transformation from backwardness to the modern age be accomplished? It is in this question and its differing answers that the Middle East's own cold war is rooted. On one hand, there are those who believe that salvation will come by a wedding between the forms of nineteenth century Middle East society and liberal Western institutions. This view was the first to emerge. Seeking to explain why Europe was able to overrun and control so much of the East, nationalist leaders of the late nineteenth and early twentieth centuries concluded that the answer was to be found in the constitutions, parliaments and social organizations of the European states. They therefore sought to introduce these institutions into their own societies. At the end of the First World War, in the fluid aftermath left by the collapse of the Ottoman Empire, the Mandatory European Powers in the Middle East were thus able to find wide support for the introduction of many features copying current political and social organization of Europe. Constitutional monarchies were created, the party system appeared, government services of education and public health developed and agricultural reform was started or expanded. The Middle East proposed to solve its problems by adopting the ways of Western Europe.

In this process, many new elements were introduced, but many old centers of power remain unchanged. The combination of landowning families, urban merchants and tribal leaders who had run the political business of the Middle East during the nineteenth century continued, although operating behind a different façade of government organization. Egypt, for example, had a functioning parliament under a constitutional monarchy, yet the practical government of the country was tightly held by a minuscule part of the population. Even those in revolt against Western occupation objected to foreign political control rather than the institutions for which such control had been partly responsible.

This traditional-liberal ideal is still being followed in the Middle East. States like Jordan, Iran, Morocco—and trailing far in their rear, Libya and Saudi Arabia—believe that they can retain the forms of monarchy and landlordism or tribal leadership while gradually introducing modern and liberal programs which will eventually answer the popular demands for a more progressive society with a better standard of living for the masses. Especially in Iran and Jordan, the monarchy is making vigorous efforts to identify itself with the rising tide of expectation, and seeks to use its authority to diminish the power of the landed aristocracy. In both countries considerable progress has been made.

But there is another, and more radical, program of modernization. This is based on the conviction that there must be a total change in the social structure before a truly progressive modern state can emerge. The framework of the past is too outmoded, rigid and shot through with privilege to be adopted as the basis for a modern state with a higher standard of living for the common man. Proponents of this view believe in a revolutionary repudiation of the past as the prelude to nation-building in the modern world. They would say, with Omar Khàyyám, that it is necessary to "grasp this sorry scheme of things entire . . . shatter it to bits, and then remold it nearer to the heart's desire."

The first revolution came when Atatürk overthrew the traditional Ottoman state in the aftermath of the First World War. The result was the repudiation of a system which had sustained Turkey through some 400 years of political life. The Sultanate and its shadowy Caliphate were abolished, the power of religion in state circles was broken and even the alphabet was changed. By the end of Atatürk's life, the political organization of Turkey had been transformed beyond recall.

Both the success of the Turkish Revolution and the infection of its ideas have been spreading through the Middle East ever since. During the 1920's Reza Pahlavi started on the same path in

Iran, although with less drastic results. After the Second World War Egypt followed a similar pattern, to be followed in turn by Iraq. In greatly diluted form the impulse reached Yemen, causing a *coup d'état* for the overthrow of the Imamate in 1962. Since winning its independence from the French, Algeria has taken the same line, although its revolt was against the foreign *"colon* system," rather than a traditional Arab government.

But the devotion to revolution is not confined to the countries mentioned above. In practically every country of the area there are groups, usually among students and young technicians, who believe that only a radical solution will suffice. Often their objectives are not clear and their programs largely nebulous, but of one thing they are sure—the old order with its political and social elite must be done away with before their generation can enter the new world. Long before Colonel Nasser and the Egyptian Revolution, these ideas were being discussed in many an important Middle Eastern circle. In 1938 I heard a sober history professor in Beirut argue passionately that the traditional forms of Arab government were hopeless and that only by their overthrow could modernity be achieved.

It is obvious that these two answers to the problem of modernization are not only radically different, but also in sharp conflict. If the revolutionaries are right—and they can demonstrate that their wholesale onslaught on traditional society will solve the age-old problems of a depressed peasantry, low standard of living and political impotence—then the traditional-liberal answer will be discredited. Not only so, but the people leading the traditional-liberal movement (such as the King of Jordan and Shah of Iran) may well lose their thrones and possibly their heads. It is not essential for the UAR, Algeria and Iraq to undertake direct action against the traditional monarchies—their success can activate and encourage radical forces in these countries until the collapse of the present system becomes inevitable.

On the other hand, if the traditional-liberalists are right, and demonstrate that, without the vast upheaval and wastage of a revolution, they can accomplish the purposes of modernization, dignity and mass well-being, the revolutionary camp and its leaders are placed in peril. They, too, may well lose their thrones and their heads. For the radical answer, dramatic as it is and effective as some of its first fruits appear, generates a significant amount of internal hostility. While the masses of the countryside want a better way of life, they are by nature and instinct suspicious of change and often must be driven down the road of revolution by harsh measures. Then there are always the remnants of the dissolved old order who struggle to regain their possessions and position and who seek to mount, either directly or through family and group connections in the new army and state, a move to unseat the current rulers. Added to this is the rising generation of post-revolutionaries who are seeking greater rewards for themselves and their class and for whom any significant failure of lasting economic progress under the revolution might well be the signal for a change of loyalty. Thus, revolutionary leaders like Abdel Nasser cannot yet be sure that their position is permanently established or that the changes they have brought about will necessarily endure.

President Nasser admitted this publicly in the spring of 1964 when he said at a popular rally, "A failure of the Arab revolution anywhere is a failure everywhere—and a failure anywhere is a failure in the United Arab Republic." This was not mere histrionics for the crowd—it is an accurate observation of the still fragile position of the revolutionary movement. That movement has been successful in smashing the institutions of the past, probably beyond any hope of their rebuilding. But it has not yet succeeded in erecting a firmly knit and institutionalized order which satisfactorily solves the basic questions of economic well-being, political organization and popular participation. Everywhere throughout the area the forces of destruction are strong—but the forces of construction lag far behind. While the accomplishments of the revolutionary regime in Egypt are indeed dramatic and have resulted in raising living standards, the movement has yet to pass its critical period and prove that it has indeed the answers to Egypt's perennial problems. Nasser is probably right in thinking that the collapse of sister revolutionary regimes would have a profound effect upon the Egyptian and his position.

Thus the Middle East is beset by recurring tensions between the revolutionaries and the non-revolutionaries. The division is both internal and external. Internally there are groups within every traditional state who either are in direct contact with outside revolutionary forces, or are motivated by similar objectives. These pose a continuous security problem to their governments, for their agitation may be activated by an apparently trifling event— as witness the student disorders in Khartoum set off by the government's refusal to allow a public rally. Externally, foreign policy toward neighbors in 'the opposite camp is difficult to maintain because even minor differences may be viewed in the context of the cold war struggle.

Yemen is a clear and current example of this. The Imamate under which it was governed was one of the most venerable—and medieval—political forms of the Arab world. Since 1948 there were spasmodic moves of revolt against it, generated partly by Free Yemen Movements outside the country, and partly by discontent among tribal leaders and forward-looking *sayyids* within. When the *coup d'état* of September 1962 occurred, it quickly generated the involvement of Saudi Arabia, Jordan and the UAR. None of these had vital interests *per se* in the Yemen. But the appearance of a revolutionary regime in that country might, if successful, stir up similar movements in Jordan and Saudi Arabia, each of which had its own indigenous discontents. King Saud and King Hussein moved to the support of the Royalist forces primarily as a matter of self-protection, lest a revolutionary Yemen mean in the end a revolutionary Jordan and a revolutionary Saudi Arabia. The pro-Royalist British reaction in the Colony of Aden was largely motivated by the same consideration.

The UAR's involvement was in part for the same reason, except that Egypt was interested in supporting the revolutionary view which Nasser and his associates believe is the ultimate destiny of an awakened Arab world. There is no evidence to show that the UAR caused or controlled the Republican movement at its beginnings. Immediately after the *coup d'état,* the Yemen Republicans appealed to Egypt for aid as a "revolutionary brother." Egypt responded without any clear idea of the magnitude of the task or the difficulties involved. Before long Yemen became the focal point for a clash between revolutionary Egypt and traditional Jordan and Saudi Arabia. Each side supported different parties in the Yemen struggle and all engaged in raucous propaganda warfare appealing to each other's citizens to rise up against their respective regimes.

The result came close to a military confrontation between the UAR and its Arab rivals, which was averted partly by strenuous efforts put forth by the United States.

Whenever traditional states in the Middle East come to a period of crisis or weakness, the Yemen pattern may repeat itself. Libya is a particular concern. Somewhat artificially constructed of three regions with a strong sense of localism, led by a respected but aging king, penetrated by the ferment caused by the ever swelling oil industry and near enough to Egypt so that malcontents can be infected with the revolutionary virus, its future may well be precarious. A revolutionary movement in the country could call in assistance from Egypt and Algeria who would consider their own revolutionary prestige at stake in Libya's internal struggle.

No one can predict what the future course or final outcome of these clashing paths to modernization in the Middle East will be. Like the larger cold war, the Middle Eastern cold war has its periods of thaw and compromise, with at least temporary adoption of the principle of coexistence between the two camps. Recently there have been a number of hopeful signs of lessening tension. The Yemen dispute is on its way to solution, with the UAR withdrawing its troops from the country and Saudi Arabia acquiescing in the establishment of a non-royalist government. The overthrow of Ben Bella has not signaled Algeria's retreat from the path of "Arab Socialism," but it has made Algeria less active outside its own borders, with a greater concentration on internal problems. Diplomatic relations between the UAR and Morocco, as well as between Jordan and Saudi Arabia, have been restored. Three meetings of the Arab chiefs-of-state under the aegis of the Arab League have revived the inter-Arab dialogue that was badly shattered in the aftermath of Syria's withdrawal from the UAR. For the moment coexistence, even limited cooperation, seems to be the ruling spirit.

There are several reasons for this. One is that both camps are being influenced by their rival's successes and problems. The traditional monarchies have been pushed into a more vigorous attack on the problems of modernization by the presence and threat of their revolutionary neighbors. It is no accident that the deposition of Arabia's King Saud by his more progressive brother Feisal occurred during the Yemen crisis, when discontent in Saudi Arabia was being fanned by the threat (or hope) of an expansion of the revolutionary camp through UAR backing of the new Yemen regime. Morocco has adopted several "revolutionary" procedures to speed up its modernization and meet the popular demand for improvement.

On their part, the revolutionary brotherhood—especially the UAR—has had to revise its estimates of the vitality and strength of traditional regimes. They are not as moribund and lacking in popular support as was assumed. The fact that "medieval" Saudia Arabia could successfully stalemate the UAR's efforts in Yemen, forcing Nasser to come to terms with a rival on whom his propaganda machinery had poured scorn for three years, was a lesson carefully read by the surrounding Arab world. Jordan has shown surprising resilience and has outlasted the pressures on it from Baathist Syria and revolutionary Egypt.

Added to this is the fact that the revolutionary brotherhood has not proved to be as united as its proponents had hoped. Although the program of the Baath party and the Egyptian revolutionary regime are closely similar, Syria has remained aloof from Egypt after its secession in 1961. All Egyptian efforts to win at least a friendly Syrian regime have thus far failed. Revolutionary Iraq continues to be a weak reed and the UAR (judged by its deeds) has been reluctant to make effective moves toward consummating the over-discussed Iraq-UAR union. Through its President, Tunisia has spoken up strongly for a separate North African "personality" which does not invariably follow the UAR line. Thus, the capacity for coordinated action by the revolutionary sector of the Arab world (which means in fact action under UAR leadership) has diminished, making a larger degree of coexistence possible and necessary.

Allied to this is the alarming degree of fragmentation in the Arab world in the aftermath of the Syrian secession. Viewing the separation, the UAR concluded that its basic cause was a lack of shared national goals by Egypt and Syria. President Nasser therefore announced a new foreign policy for the UAR, based upon a "unity of purpose" with sister states. This was to say that the UAR could only have close relations with states having the same revolutionary goals—suggesting the possible formation of a "revolutionnary bloc" in Arab affairs. But the result of this policy was not to create such a bloc, but increasingly to isolate the UAR from most of its Arab neighbors. Diplomatic relations were strained or broken with Morocco, Tunisia, Jordan, Saudi Arabia and Syria. Relations with Libya and Kuwait were correct, but scarcely warm. Iraq proved a weak and problem-ridden partner and even Algeria sometimes caused the UAR embarrassment.

This fragmentation affected not only the UAR but all the Arab world. As one Arab statesman put it, "We are out of step with the times. While other parts of the world are drawing closer together, we are drawing apart. The Arabs are trying to swim against the tide."

The implication in this is not simply that the UAR felt itself isolated, but that the Arab states (whatever their character) found themselves weakened by disunity and tension. It was partly reaction to this which led to the first Arab chiefs-of-state meeting in 1964, followed by two subsequent meetings, in which the role of the Arab League was revived. The UAR discarded its "unity of purpose" policy and announced in its place a new line of "unity of work"—i.e., its readiness to cooperate with any Arab state seeking progress, modernization and support for the Arab cause, whatever its particular program of reform and development might be.

Whether such shifts are permanent or only tactical remains to be seen. Certainly, neither party to the dispute over modernization has yet demonstrated that it has found all—or any—of the answers. While it seems unlikely that the traditional system, even under enlightened leadership, can permanently survive in its present form, it is by no means certain that Arab Socialism will take its place as the wave of the future. Conditions among the various Arab states are markedly different and it may be that different programs of modernization are inevitable. Moreover, elements of radicalism and traditionalism may combine in some new form not now envisioned. Of only one thing can we be certain—that with or without the UAR and its President, the Arab world will be restless and unsettled, sometimes at strife with itself and with us, while its people strive to find their way through the maze which leads from a medieval past to a modern future.

# II.  The Arab World's Heavy Legacy*

## by Charles Issawi

NO OBSERVER OF PRESENT TRENDS IN THE ARAB WORLD CAN FAIL
to be impressed by the strength of its revulsion against Western
political and economic values and ideologies. To take one example among many, a recent book by a prominent Egyptian publicist
starts with two propositions which he not only believes to be self-
evident but obviously assumes are accepted as such by his readers:
present-day capitalism does not work; and Western democracy is
a sham, since all power is concentrated in the hands of the owners
of the means of production. Judging from pronouncements at the
recent Cairo conference of non-aligned nations, such views are
widespread in Africa and Asia.

The revulsion of the Arabs is not difficult to understand in
view of their grievances—many real, more fancied—against the
various Western peoples. But the matter is more complex. It is
not just a question of a whole society turning against an alien
civilization. It is also a process in which some parts of a society
turn against other parts, and in so doing against certain alien
values which the latter represent. In other words, the ideological
changes taking place in the Arab countries today reflect deep
structural changes in their society. The principles and institutions
that held together the traditional Arab society have broken down;
a desperate search is under way for new bases of integration; and
it is felt that the traditional Western ideologies and institutions
do not provide these bases.

Arab society in the eighteenth century had very few virtues. Its
economy was not only stagnant but actually retrogressing. Its poli-

* Reprinted by special permission from *Foreign Affairs*, April 1965.
Copyright by the Council on Foreign Relations, Inc., New York, New York.

tics were characterized by venality, rapacity, insecurity and oppres-
sion. Its intellectual and artistic life was barren. Worst of all, it
lived in a smug, self-satisfied lethargy, completely isolated from
the outside world—"we do not hear of a single Egyptian who had
visited Europe in the sixteenth, seventeenth, and eighteenth centuries." [1] But it had one redeeming feature, the obverse of some
of its defects: it was a stable, integrated society, i.e., practically
all its members believed in the prevailing values and had a strong
loyalty to a small group and at least passive acceptance of existing
institutions.

Of the sedentary population, perhaps four-fifths consisted of
peasants, whose condition was hardly idyllic. Their exploitation
by the tax-farmers cannot but have aroused deep resentment. The
constant feuds between village factions added their share of misery.
Bedouin raiders, famine and plagues were frequent visitors. But
the prevailing communal systems of land tenure (*musha, dira* and
*ard al-fallah*) provided both security and a rough measure of
equality, since the land of the village was periodically redistributed
among its members in more or less equal shares. This meant that
there were no landless peasants. It also meant that within the community there were no great differentiations of wealth. Lastly, it
meant that each individual knew that he belonged to two closely
knit units, the family and the village, which would stand by him
in case of need.

The handicraftsmen, who probably constituted the majority of
the urban population, were bound together by guilds (*asnaf*) and
religious brotherhoods (*turuq*). The former regulated production
and doubtless formed strong barriers against technological and
economic progress. But, in alliance with the brotherhoods, to which
they were closely tied, they did provide the craftsmen with security
and an object of loyalty. A further integrating factor was the tie of
kinship binding the inhabitants of each quarter, which often con-

[1] G. al-Shayyal in *Historians of the Middle East,* Bernard Lewis and
P. M. Holt (editors), London, 1962, p. 410. By way of contrast, by the
end of the eighteenth century, a group of Japanese scholars had achieved
—through the small chink provided by the Dutch settlement in Deshima—
a much clearer picture of contemporary Western civilization. They had
accepted the Copernican cosmology and understood the system of the
circulation of the blood. See Donald Keene, *The Japanese Discovery of
Europe,* London, 1952.

stituted a self-contained unit with its own gates, baths and place of worship.

The merchants, who in Europe were for several centuries a dynamic and even revolutionary class, certainly did not constitute a threat to the existing order. For one thing, their wealth was small and their social and political power very limited—the Islamic world never had city-states with independent, self-reliant bourgeoisies. For another, they had practically no contacts with the outside world which might have inspired them with new ideas. Lastly, in many areas and branches their activity was largely regulated by custom, which meant that the driving force of competition was greatly attenuated.[2]

Another group which in the West and Russia has been both dynamic and subversive of existing régimes is the intelligentsia. Its nearest counterpart in the Arab world were the *ulama,* men trained in religion and jurisprudence. But because of their religious background the *ulama* were almost necessarily bound to be loyal to any society based on Islam. Moreover, for many centuries Muslim political theory had stressed the principle of obedience to any government that both had military power and promised to respect the *sharia,* or religious law of Islam. In the absence of an intellectual ferment and of a group that could utilize it to further its own ends, the various disturbances that occurred in the Arab world—army insurrections, conquests by one ruler or pasha of another's territory, bedouin raids, local revolts, etc.—could not lead to any important modification in the social structure, but only to a change in the composition of the ruling group.

Of course Arab society was not completely static. Economic and social changes occurred in Syria and Iraq in the eighteenth century. The Egyptian scholar, Shayyal, already quoted, states that: "Towards the close of the eighteenth century we detect the first signs of a spontaneous cultural revival. It was an internal movement which emerged from within Egypt away from any outside influence whether from the East or from the West." The Wahhabi movement was a challenge that might have revitalized Islam. A Soviet scholar has discerned the beginnings of "capitalist produc-

[2] A friend told me that as a young man in Damascus, in the 1860's, wanting to buy some cloth, he was told by the shopkeeper: "I have sold quite a bit today—try my neighbor, who has done very little business."

tion" in the larger textile and other establishments in Egypt at the
end of the eighteenth century. It is just conceivable, though highly
improbable, that left to itself Arab society might have evolved into
a healthier state. But in fact it was violently thrown into the mainstream of world history.

The chief responsibility for this may well lie, as Toynbee, Gibb
and other Western writers claim, with those monarchs and statesmen—Muhammad Ali in Egypt, Mahmud II and Reshid Pasha in
Turkey, Khaireddin in Tunisia—who realized that, without some
thoroughgoing modernization their countries could not survive a
European onslaught. But an equally important factor was the quest
of the Western countries for raw materials, markets, bases and
spheres of political, religious and cultural influence. This led them
to open up the Ottoman Empire to Western traders by such measures as the Anglo-Turkish Commercial Convention of 1838, to
back with diplomatic and other means those of their citizens who
were hunting for concessions, and eventually to impose their rule
over practically the whole Arab world. And it was certainly the
presence of the West in the region that caused the latter's development to take the peculiar form that it did. To put the matter con-
cisely, Western influence accelerated the transformation of the
Arab world from a subsistence to a market economy, and the dissolution of its communal and organizational ties and their replacement by individual, contractual relationships; at the same time, it
inhibited the growth of an Arab bourgeoisie.

II

The process of transformation, and the consequent dislocations,
took much the same form as in other parts of the world. In the
first place, Western medicine and hygiene eliminated the plagues
and many of the endemic diseases prevalent in the region, while
improved transport and increased food supplies prevented the oc-
currence of famines. The result was a sharp reduction in the death
rate which, since the birth rate remained at its previous high level,
led to a rapid increase in the population. For a long time the
annual rate of growth averaged about 1 percent, but in recent years
it has risen to between 2 and 3 and may soon go over the latter
figure, which would mean a doubling of the population every 20-25
years. The vast growth that has already taken place, unaccom-

panied by either massive industrialization or a commensurate extension of the cultivated area, has led to great pressure on the land and, in recent years, to an exodus to the cities. The social consequences have been the appearance of two new phenomena: the landless peasant, and a large, underemployed, amorphous, urban proletariat.

The emergence of a landless peasantry was also promoted by another important transformation: the change-over from a subsistence to a market-oriented, cash-crop agriculture. The economic consequences of this change were predominantly beneficial—a large increase in agricultural productivity and output, greatly expanded exports and a substantial growth in the national product. But the social consequences were far less favorable. Thus the dissolution of the village community—without which no progress could have taken place—eliminated the security formerly enjoyed by all peasants. Production for the market meant exposure to price fluctuations, which often led to indebtedness and loss of land. Economic progress produced a rapidly widening gap between the able, cunning or lucky members of the village on the one hand and the inefficient, simpleminded or unfortunate on the other; and such inequalities tended to be self-perpetuating and cumulative. The adoption of Western law codes and their application to land worked in the same direction. Moreover, much of the land was appropriated by former tax-farmers, tribal chieftains, city notables or others, and since rents soon came to absorb a large and growing portion of the total product, the benefits of agricultural progress accrued primarily to a small number of landlords, often absentees. Again, in some countries, notably Algeria, Libya, Tunisia, Palestine and Morocco, a large fraction of the cultivated area passed—partly by expropriation or chicanery, partly by purchase—into the hands of foreign settlers, thus reducing still further the area available to Arab farmers. Lastly, it should be noted that agricultural techniques showed little or no improvement. The only exceptions were Egypt and such enclaves as the European farms in North Africa, the Zionist settlements in Palestine, the Gezira scheme in the Sudan, and parts of Lebanon. The cumulative effect of all these factors—coupled with the lack of industrialization—was that the Arab countries did not acquire a prosperous, conservative peasantry. Instead, there was an ever-growing number of landless peasants, or of land-hungry farmers with steadily shrinking plots, envious of the neighboring estates of native landlords or foreign planters. Where, as in Egypt and Algeria, the level of living of the rural populations actually declined, the explosiveness of the situation was greatly increased.

Meanwhile, the towns were passing through an even more acute crisis. The handicrafts, which had occupied the greater part of their population, received mortal blows from the competition of machine-made European goods and, in Egypt, from Muhammad Ali's state factories and monopolies. The disruptive effects of this shock went deepest in such towns as Aleppo, Damascus, Baghdad, Cairo and Tunis, which had previously supplied the adjoining regions with manufactured goods.[3] And with the ruin of the handicrafts came the dissolution of the guilds that had bound together their members. In their place emerged a mass of unemployed or underemployed workmen, constantly augmented by influxes from the villages and—again in the absence of industrial development—unable to organize and raise its level of living.

The processes so far described do not differ basically from those that took place in Western Europe in the eighteenth and nineteenth centuries, or in many other parts of the world somewhat later. But the crucial difference lies in the fact that Western Europe industrialized. This greatly strengthened its bourgeoisie, which had already become a significant force thanks to the earlier development of trade and finance. And in the course of the nineteenth century the bourgeoisie became the dominant power in society. But the Arab countries began to industrialize only during the last few years, and their economic and social structure was such that—with the exceptions noted below—no native bourgeoisie developed until very recently. This delay, and the consequent weakness of the bourgeoisie, prevented the latter from playing a significant part until hostile forces had developed to the point where they could overwhelm it. And, since the political and economic values and institutions of the West—liberalism, constitutionalism and free

[3] The above is an oversimplified account of a long-drawn and complicated process. Some handicrafts gained a new lease on life by using cheaper imported materials, e.g., cotton yarn. Others managed to survive by drastically reducing the earnings of the craftsmen. A handful improved their processes, thus raising their productivity.

enterprise—are essentially middle-class ones, the crushing of the Arab middle class has meant the elimination of the one class that could still have defended these values and institutions.

The factors that impeded the industrialization of the Arab countries, and of other underdeveloped areas, have often been described. Some would have existed under any political régime: the narrowness of the market, because of low agricultural productivity; the unfavorable social structure; the scarcity of iron and coal, until very recently almost indispensable to industrialization; the dearness of fuel, until the discovery of petroleum and natural gas in the last few decades; the very poor transport systems; the paucity of investment capital; the absence of industrial credit; and the lack of technicians and skilled workmen and, still more, entrepreneurs. But it is no less true that some of these difficulties were greatly aggravated by the nature of the relationships between the Arab countries and the West. Thus the shortage of capital was accentuated by the heavy service charges on the debts contracted—often at usurious rates—by spendthrift monarchs.[4] Industrial credit facilities could have been expanded by goverment pressure on the banks, which confined their activities almost solely to trade. The lack of skills could have been partly remedied by an appropriate educational policy. But the absence of Western interest in Arab education may be illustrated by the fact that in 1955, after 125 years of French rule, the literacy rate among Algerian Muslims was about 15 percent and only one-sixth of the children of school age (6-14) were attending school. Similarly in Egypt during the first 20 years of British rule government expenditure on education was under 1 percent of the total.

Moreover, the little that was done in education was misdirected, from the point of view of economic development. Thus whereas under Muhammad Ali (1813-1848) 327 of the 339 students who were sent abroad on government missions studied industrial technology, engineering, medicine or agriculture, and under his successors (1849-1882) 270 out of 279, during the British Occupation (1883-1919) the figure was 74 out of 289. But the most

---

[4] At the beginning of this century, interest and service charges on the public debt absorbed nearly a third of the Ottoman budget, in Egypt nearly a half and in Tunisia a quarter. The £5,000,000 thus paid out annually by Egypt represented perhaps 4 percent of its gross national product.

important point is that a sympathetic government could have given the encouragement and protection without which no industry could possibly have established itself against foreign competition: tax exemptions, rebates on transport rates, preferential purchases and, above all, tariff protection. Instead, local industries were exposed to the full blast of foreign competition. Thus French goods entering Algeria and, with few exceptions Tunisia, and Italian goods entering Libya were exempt from duty, and all imports into the Ottoman Empire and Egypt paid a flat rate of 8 percent, no distinction being made between raw materials, capital goods and consumer goods. Indeed hostility to local industrialization went further: when a small cotton textile industry did develop in Egypt it was subjected to an 8 percent excise duty, i.e., the rate levied on imports.

Lack of industrial development and the weakness of the bourgeoisie are closely interconnected. On the one hand, industry has everywhere been one of the main sources of middle-class strength. And, on the other hand, in most countries capital and entrepreneurship have flowed into industry from other sectors of the economy dominated by the bourgeoisie, notably trade and finance. But the fact that Arab handicrafts were under such great pressure meant that few if any could expand and develop into workshops and factories, and industrial recruitment from this source was negligible. And in the Arab world all the main sectors of the economy, with the partial exception of agriculture and petty trade, were largely or wholly controlled by foreigners.

This situation comes out most clearly in Arab Africa. In Algeria and Libya almost every single urban activity—finance, transport, trade, real estate, manufacturing and the professions—was controlled by Europeans, who even provided most of the skilled labor; in addition they ran most of the "modernized" agriculture. In Tunisia and Morocco, the bulk of urban activity and a significant part of agriculture were similarly controlled by Europeans. And the same applied to Egypt until the 1950's, with the not very important difference that here Europeans shared their control, to a certain extent, with various minority groups. In Arab Asia, except for Palestine under the Mandate, foreign investment and immigration were insignificant until the recent expansion of the oil industry. But in several of these countries the middle class consisted to a large extent of minority groups—Jews in Iraq and Christians in Syria and Jordan.

The effect of this phenomenon was that for about a century the entrepreneurial middle class (as distinct from the salaried middle class) became identified with foreigners or minority groups. Of course a Muslim bourgeoisie did eventually develop but, except in Lebanon and to a lesser degree Syria, it came too late and was too weak to meet the onslaught of the hostile forces that had emerged. In Egypt, the bourgeoisie developed as a result of the efforts of the Misr group, of the 1930 tariff, of the abolition of the Capitulations in 1936, of various government measures to "Egyptianize" business, of the weakening of the Europeans during and after the Second World War and of the Arab-Israeli War of 1948. In the Arabian peninsula the small middle class that arose owed its existence to the oil boom of the 1940's and 1950's. The same cause was at work in Iraq, supplemented by the exodus of Jews after the Arab-Israeli War. In Libya the sequence was reversed, the withdrawal of the Italians after the Second World War being followed by an oil boom. In Tunisia and Morocco French withdrawal enabled the local bourgeoisie greatly to increase its strength. And in the Sudan a small middle class is being slowly formed, thanks to the country's relatively undisturbed development.

Given sufficient time, these bourgeoisies might have been able to get control of their societies and reshape them in their image. Unfortunately for them, and for the West, the fabric of their societies was already being torn by the various stresses to which they were being subjected. Among such stresses were the population explosion, the hypertrophic urbanization, the agricultural revolution and the industrial revolution referred to above. Two other processes deserve more detailed treatment: the cultural changes and the political struggles.

The discovery of the West, and the consequent cultural transformation of Arab society, has had the revitalizing—and intoxicating—effect of a renaissance. Its over-all consequences have of course been incalculably beneficial. But it has had a very unsettling effect on Arab society by bringing into being a new class of intellectuals. And whereas the old "intellectuals," the *ulama,* were deeply loyal to the basic values and institutions of their society the new ones did not owe it any such allegiance and looked right and left, East and West, for new sources of inspiration and loyalty. Thus, for the first time in many centuries, new ideas began to corrode the fabric of Arab society.

Meanwhile political strife was being added to social discontent and stirring up the masses. In the Arab East there were the struggles against the British and French, the traumatic Arab-Israeli War and the Suez attack of 1956. In North Africa there was the shattering effect of the Algerian Revolution. All these struggles could be waged only by calling on ever wider sections of the population to participate, by digging into ever deeper social strata. The increased participation of the masses meant that new leaders, of more humble origins, soon took command. And these leaders represented not the hitherto dominant upper- and middle-class values but radical ideologies.

### III

In the light of the above analysis, the shift in Arab ideologies becomes quite intelligible. For a long time, until the 1920's or '30's, the dominant ideas were those of moderate nationalism, constitutionalism and political and economic liberalism.[5] The reasons for this are obvious. First, these were the dominant ideologies of the leading powers—Britain, France and the United States—and to them was given full credit for the prosperity of these countries and their victory in the First World War. Second, Arab cultural contacts were almost entirely restricted to these three countries. Third, liberalism and constitutionalism suited the Arab upper and middle classes, since they controlled parliaments, parties and the press. And economic liberalism, in addition to being fashionable, was the only policy open to governments whose hands were tied by the Capitulations, Commercial Conventions and other bonds. But, given the Arab social structure, these ideas made practically no impact on the masses.

During the 1930's and '40's Arab society passed through an acute crisis, caused by such factors as the drastic fall in agricultural prices during the Depression; the presence of hundreds of thousands of Allied troops during the war and the consequent sharp inflation; the growth of unemployment among both unskilled work-

---

[5] Even as late as the mid-1940's, the two heroes of my students at the American University in Beirut were Mazzini and Frederich List.

ers and high school and college graduates; and the unending struggles against foreign occupation. But at the same time the world climate was changing, with the emergence of the Soviet Union and, subsequently, China as major powers and with the rapid growth in the "developing" nations of the belief in socialist planning and one-party dictatorship. The result was the collapse of the fragile Arab parliamentary systems and the replacement of the landowner and bourgeois élite by one of army officers, bureaucrats and technicians drawn from lower strata.

And now, as in so many other underdeveloped countries, an attempt is being made to reconstruct society on the twin bases of nationalism and socialism.

The nationalism consists of an attempt at self-affirmation, primarily against the Western countries which formerly ruled the area and still dominate its economy. But the question immediately arose as to whether that nationalism was to be based on Islam or Arabism. Islam, the religion of 90 percent of the Arabs, had been for centuries the traditional, and is probably still the strongest, bond holding them together. This fact was clearly seen by the Muslim Brotherhood who, in the 1940's and early '50's, achieved great success by appealing to the sense of Muslim solidarity of the masses and by promising radical changes which would bring down the rich and improve the lot of the poor. But such an approach was open to serious objections. First and foremost, the greater part of the educated classes realizes that the ideology and organization of the Brotherhood cannot cope with the complex modernization required by Arab society. Second, the Brotherhood's approach presupposes an essential identity of interests between the Arabs and their Muslim neighbors—the Turks, Iranians and Pakistanis; but in fact there has been considerable tension between them because of conflicting territorial claims (Alexandretta, Bahrain and Khuzistan) and opposed international alignments. Third, in the mid-twentieth century it is no longer fashionable to proclaim religion as the official basis of society. Lastly, it created unnecessary difficulties with the Christian minorities, which had played an important part in the development of Arab nationalism and still have a minor contribution to make to Arab society.

Instead, the army groups that crushed the Muslim Brotherhood worked out an alternative, Arab Socialism. Like the socialist nationalism which is sweeping so many underdeveloped countries, it is an amalgam of intense nationalism (with a strong Muslim component), militarism, state ownership and egalitarianism. In other words, the essential ingredients were the same as those of the Brotherhood but the doses different. The nationalist aims of this movement are the achievement of full independence, which implies the elimination of all foreign military, political and economic positions in the area; cultural independence, which is deemed to require close regulation of the entry of outside influences and the suppression or strict control of foreign schools and other institutions; and Arab unity. Its socialist aims consist essentially of the desire for greater equality and rapid industrialization, since industry is regarded as the main hope for economic development and military and political power. In view of the failure of the native bourgeoisie to carry out sufficiently rapid industrialization, this is to be brought about by state ownership of the principal means of production and by socialist planning. This, it is rightly believed, should reduce private consumption and increase the amount available for investment, though little thought has been given to the concomitant rise in public consumption and the sharp reduction in the efficiency of capital investment under bureaucratic socialism and increasing militarization. Nationalization and planning are also favored because they are expected to eliminate the influence of all private individual or group interests, foreign or local, and give the new rulers full control over their societies.

For it goes without saying that the socialism in question is an authoritarian or perhaps even a totalitarian one, resting on army rule or one-party dictatorship. It is one that gets much more inspiration from Russia, China or Jugoslavia than from Western socialism. As for Western political and economic liberalism, its influence and appeal have practically disappeared. It may be added that the new socialist ideas have been spread by, and the new leadership has been recruited from, not the working classes but mainly the lower middle class. In the words of Hisham Sharabi: "It is significant that just as parliamentary democracy had been established without a middle class, revolutionary socialism under army control is now instituted without the firm base of a working class or proletariat."

Of course, the ideological shift described above has not taken place everywhere. Lebanon is still committed to parliamentary democracy and economic liberalism. Morocco, Syria and Tunisia are struggling hard to find their way. In all four countries a native bourgeoisie had the time to develop, and is not inclined to give up its power without a struggle. Several Arab countries have not yet reached the stage where either liberal or socialist ideologies are meaningful. But all this is less important than the fact that both Egypt and Algeria are engaged in revolutions to implement their slightly differing versions of Arab Socialism; with the nationalization laws of July 1964, Iraq also seems to have chosen the Arab Socialist way. For well over a hundred years Egypt and Algeria have been the seed beds of change in the eastern and western halves of the Arab world. Because of the reforms started by Muhammad Ali in Egypt and the activity created by the inflow of French capital and settlers in Algeria, economic and social developments in these two countries have, in the past, had deep repercussions on their neighbors. It is hard to believe that this will not also hold in the immediate future.

# III. Islam and Modernization in the Arab World

## by Hisham Sharabi

UNTIL MODERN TIMES ISLAM HAD NO KNOWLEDGE OR EXPERIENCE of civil society. Arab society had always been theocratic, its political and religious associations always one and the same. The objects of politics and society had been defined solely in terms of an Islamic system of ideas and rendered intelligible only in terms of an "Islamic awareness." In this respect and speaking in the strictest sense, the contemporary states of the Arab world can no longer be categorized as "Muslim" states, except in that the majority of their populations is Muslim. With the exception of Turkey, Islam has not been *officially* dethroned or its institutional structures openly abolished: in the contemporary Arab world Islam has simply been bypassed.[1]

It is perhaps useful to recall that the relaxing of Islam's grip on Arab society in the nineteenth and early twentieth centuries did not result, as did that of Christianity over European society in the fifteenth and sixteenth centuries, in the gradual replacement of "a religious morality" by "a social morality" and in the restriction of religious jurisdiction to a clearly delimited area. On the contrary, it resulted in an inner collapse and a withering away of its position and effective power in social and political life.

By the post World War II period, Islam in the Arab world had survived in three main forms. First, in the spontaneous, instinctive beliefs of the common man; an unarticulated attachment to inherited attitudes and modes of behavior and a psychology beyond

[1] Except in the states and principalities of Arabia.

26

the reach of certain external ideas and influences. Here Islam presents itself in its vaguest but most tenacious form. Secondly, in the articulate urban Arab intellectual's intuitive self-image we find the same *état d'esprit,* but now compounded with an intellectual awareness sufficient to free the intellectual from the bonds of popular piety. Though he may be an unbeliever, a "non-practicing Muslim" on the religious plane, his ultimate sense of identity firmly rests upon an inner sense of belonging to Islam, of simply "being Muslim." Thirdly, Islam has survived in the shape of the moulds in which thought and evaluations are cast. Apart from the formative influence which the Koran-rooted Arabic language exerts on the content of thought—lending even to the most foreign of concepts a color and a flavor all its own—there is a certain type of "logic," a kind of mental attitude and approach which is exclusively Islamic.

The decline of Islam in the twentieth century as an organized institutional force capable of exerting direct influence on society and the state cannot be explained or accounted for by a simple or unitary diagnosis. The attempt here is to trace and define the main developments and the principal factors leading to this decline, bringing into focus characteristic Muslim responses to the many-faceted challenge of modernization.

## IMPACT OF ECONOMIC CHANGE

To begin with, the introduction of rationality and technique into the sphere of economic activity, beginning with the military reforms of Selim III and Mahmud II in Turkey and Muhammad Ali in Egypt, effected not only a lasting breakthrough in the traditional system of organization and method but also an intellectual revolution that was irreversible. General economic growth and expansion of transport and communication in the course of the nineteenth century had by World War I brought about the breakdown of the autarkic economy of the countryside as well as the social and religious patterns of authority and organization on which it was based. Simultaneously, urban centers, which were more directly exposed to the process of economic change, saw the dissolution of traditional craft corporations and guilds and the collapse of the old system of socio-economic association. In North Africa, particularly in Algeria and Tunisia, this process was enhanced and given an especially strong character by French colonization, which hastened the rise of a North African proletariat and, by the 1920's, the development of labor movements.

The social imbalance resulting from the disintegration of the traditional economic system brought in its train other significant transformations, perhaps the most important of which were the weakening of tribal and family ties and the breakdown of traditional attitudes and loyalties. On another level, Muslim society experienced a different and subtler transformation. The sense of insecurity and contingent existence which only the lower classes had experienced began to engulf the higher status groups, bringing about radical changes in social relations, especially in the outlook and orientation of the elite.

BREAKDOWN OF THE ISLAMIC SYSTEM OF LEGITIMACY

The retreat of Islam on the legal and institutional fronts began with the introduction of the Ottoman *tanzimat* (legal and administrative reforms) in the second and third quarters of the nineteenth century. The religious institution, strictly Erastian both in theory and in its development under the Ottoman Sultanate, was rendered increasingly subservient to the state and was forced to accept a series of major compromises from which it was never able to disentangle itself; and its autonomy and effective authority suffered in proportion to the inroads made on its once exclusive area of jurisdiction. Even under the Hamidian retrenchment (1876-1908), return to former positions and restoration of lost prestige proved impossible. It is important to note that the religious hierarchy refused to come to grips with the problems presented by *de facto* innovations. Indeed, it precisely devised methods to evade head-on confrontation and provide ways and means whereby merely the theoretical validity of the *shari'a* (Islamic Law) could be preserved. It could not have been otherwise. For the Law, with its origin in prophecy and revelation and its communication of the precise will of God to man, could not itself be adjusted to conform with the new exigencies. The ulema could only defend and preserve the Law at any cost.

It was a matter of time before Muslim society began to move from the old system of legitimacy toward one of more pragmatic validation based on interest and practicality. In this light the Kemalist "revolution" of the 1920's—abolishing the Caliphate and divorcing Islam from the state—was not so much a revolution as a logical conclusion of a process which began long before the collapse of the empire. In the Arab nation-states of the Fertile Crescent and Egypt a similar revolution took place in the interwar period, but it went largely unnoticed because it was carried out gradually and because it lacked the dramatic breakaway which was effected in Turkey. But there, no less than in Turkey, Islam as a legal and constitutional system was overthrown and a Western-type legal and parliamentary system was gradually established. Though lip-service was paid to it, it was evident that Islamic Law had been superseded and that society was well on the way to secularization. In recent years even the narrow area of "personal status" —marriage, divorce, inheritance—left under the jurisdiction of the *shari'a* courts has been breached and for all practical purposes brought under civil jurisdiction. Indeed, by mid-century the ulema in most Arab countries had been reduced to a small ineffectual body dependent on the toleration of the state and on a meager income from the rapidly dwindling pious foundations.

Closely connected with the decline of Islamic Law was the ulema's failure to maintain their monopoly over education, particularly on the primary level. The secularization of education began with the introduction of the technical schools in the first half of the nineteenth century and the subsequent establishment of Christian missionary schools in Syria and Egypt. By the time of the last Ottoman generation both the substance and structure of education were transformed;[2] and by the early 1920's the ground was laid in the new nation-states to establish a secular school system on both primary and secondary levels. Thus by the end of the First World War the religious hierarchy had not only lost its position as the defender and interpreter of the Law in society, but also its function as the upholder and transmitter of Islamic learning and tradition had been irreparably undermined.

## POLITICAL DISINTEGRATION

Perhaps the disintegration of the Islamic hold was most rapid and decisive in the area of political activity. In the Arab world

[2] Cf., Muhib al-Din al-Khatib (ed.), *Safahat min tarikh al-nahda al-'arabiyya fi awa'il al-qarn al-'ishrin* (Memoirs and other Writings by Salah al-Din al-Qasimi), Cairo, 1959, p. 8.

until roughly 1900 allegiance to the Ottoman Empire was more than loyalty to a state or to a set of political ideas; loyalty was rooted in the concept of the Caliphate and in the unity of the Islamic *ummah* (community). Reform on the social and political planes was still viewed as taking place within the Islamic framework under "the banner of the great Caliphate" for the benefit of all Muslims from India to Morocco.[3] The secular intelligentsia saw no necessary distinction between national revival and the resurgence of Islam. Indeed, no revival seemed possible without Islam as a fundamental part of it. As Mustafa Kamil (d. 1908), leader of the Egyptian nationalist movement, put it, political and social backwardness have only "one cause: our abandonment of religion."[4] Nevertheless, within a little over a decade the loyalties of the Arab and Egyptian secular elites had shifted; the concept of nationalism came into its own and religious considerations were thrust into the background. This was already evident by the outbreak of the First World War. When in 1914 the Ottoman Caliph proclaimed the *Jihad* against the "infidel Allies," his call went unheeded in the Arab provinces and Egypt. And in 1916, when the Arab revolt was launched, it was Ottoman Turkey that represented the enemy, not Britain or France. By the war's end the Caliphate had lost its sway even in Turkey. A captive of the Allies in Constantinople, it became the willing instrument in putting down the nationalist revolution of Mustafa Kemal. When the Caliphate was abolished in 1924, Islamic theocracy came to the end of a continuous existence of nearly fourteen hundred years. Islam as an institutional political force had finally succumbed.

FAILURE OF THE WAHHABI AND MUSLIM BROTHERS REVIVAL

For a while in the interwar period Islamic traditionalism took heart from the resurgence of Wahhabism in Arabia. By the late 1920's Ibn Sa'ud (d. 1953) had succeeded in building in Arabia the greatest kingdom since the death of Muhammad. And to many leading traditionalists, such as Sheikh Rashid Rida (d. 1934), the new Islamic state represented the realization of what the *salafiyya*

---

[3] Jamal al-Din al-Afghani, *Khatirat* (Reflections), Muhammad al-Makhzumi (ed.), Beirut, 1931, p. 84.

[4] Cited in Louis Shaikho, *al-Adab al-'arabiyya fi al-rub' al-awwal min al-qarn al-'ishrin* (Arabic Literature in the First Quarter of the Twentieth Century), Beirut, 1926, p. 45.

movement had been calling for all along. Puritan Islam appeared triumphant in the only Arab country (besides Yemen) to emerge independent after the war, and Arab leadership seemed firmly grounded in Islamic revivalism. But the ideal which Wahhabism represented was soon shattered. The traditional virtues of patriarchal society were not a strong enough shield against the corrosive impact of newly-discovered wealth. The moral disintegration and social corruption of the Saudi ruling class became the object of harsh attack by the younger generation of ulema, who were finally no longer able to view the Wahhabi state with anything but anger and bitter disappointment.

> Many infidel nations are more just and righteous in the exercise of their rule, and their peoples enjoy a higher standard of living, than those of [Saudi] Arab lands. How then can chaos, injustice, and oppression of [these] lands be called Islamic rule? The truth is that those lands are only a collection of masters and slaves.[5]

Perhaps the last refuge of Islamic traditionalism in the twentieth century took form in the activist political party, *al-ikhwan al-muslimun* (Muslim Brothers). Founded in Egypt in the late 1920's by Hassan al-Banna (d. 1949), a graduate of al-Azhar and a man of exceptional ability and great personal magnetism, the movement became by the end of World War II one of the largest mass parties in the Middle East. Its aim was nothing short of the reinstatement of Islam and the restoration of the Caliphate. The tremendous appeal which the movement exercised served to show the extent to which Islam could still move the masses of the people. But it came too late to stem the tide of secularism, and its fate was sealed with the triumph of Abdul Nasser's secular revolution. The Muslim Brothers may well be the last serious effort of traditional Islam to regain its position in Arab society.

The "socialist" revolution which now arose first in Egypt and Syria, and later in Algeria and Iraq, was the culmination of the movement of secular modernization that had its roots in the late nineteenth century. It had embarked upon a road which inevitably divorced Arab society from the remnants of its religious past. The attitude of uncompromising reformism which characterized the

[5] Muhammad al-Ghazzali, *Min huna na'lam*, Cairo, 1951, p. 22. Eng. trans. Isma'il R. el Faruqi, *Our Beginning in Wisdom*, Washington, 1953.

Kemalist "revolution" in Turkey a few decades earlier was now fully taken up by the Arab revolutionaries of the mid-twentieth century.

## CHARACTER OF THE "ARAB AWAKENING"

How did Islam fail to renovate itself and to achieve in the name of the old, something new and vital that could have meaning and value to the "westernized" generations of the twentieth century? Why is it that after the long-drawn agony of "reform" and "revival" the Islamic system of values and ideas was abandoned by the mid-twentieth century revolutionary modernizers? While it is impossible to provide any final or satisfactory answers to these questions, the following considerations may highlight some vital aspects of the problem.

The "Arab awakening" of the nineteenth and twentieth centuries did not constitute a renaissance. It may again be helpful to recall that the European renaissance of the fifteenth and sixteenth centuries was only in part religious and "reforming;" it was primarily an intellectual revolution spearheaded by an awakened intelligentsia that succeeded in transforming its world by a radical adjustment of its relations to its past. The movement of reform in nineteenth century Islam, the "awakening," was not an intellectual awakening but a *reaction* to the military and political threat of Europe. Even after the European impact had been transformed into a cultural challenge, response to it remained largely defensive and negative. It focused in an effort to show that Islamic civilization was just as great as modern European civilization and that Islamic society in adopting this civilization was in effect no more than re-appropriating what was originally its own. This attitude, however, tended to inhibit the development of self-criticism and contributed to the growth of an apologetic and propagandistic frame of mind which persisted from Tahtawi in the early 1830's well into the twentieth century. (Thus: "The various sciences which seem to be Western are in fact Islamic sciences;" [6] and "it is well-known that the civilization which was passed on to Europe was transferred

---

[6] Rifa'a Rafi' [al-Tahtawi], *Manahij al-albab al-misriyya fi mabahij al-adab al-'asriyya* (The Paths of Egyptian Hearts in the Joys of Contemporary Arts), 2nd ed., Cairo, 1912, p. 373.

through the Arabic tongue." [7]) This attitude provided the best justification for the process of borrowing from Europe. For by showing that in its essential structure European civilization was really nothing more than "Arab civilization improved upon by new discoveries and inventions," [8] it became not only legitimate to borrow from it but a "duty to retrieve it." [9]

This effort went to great pains to prove that Islam's decline was a temporary accident of history, that Islam contained within itself all the elements for a powerful resurgence in the modern world.[10] The ulema insisted that only by a return to the Koran, the source of all wisdom and strength, could Islamic society overcome its "sickness." [11] Their line of thought was simple: since history shows that Islam reached its highest peak during Muhammad's life and under the stewardship of his "orthodox" successors, it was by resurrecting the spirit and ideals of early Islamic society that the decline could be halted and moral and political strength restored.

By this vision Islamic traditionalism was hypnotized until its fall. It was never seriously able to attend to the task of reformulating doctrine or of reinterpreting Islam in modern terms. The *salafiyya* (ancestral) movement, in which this attitude became intellectually immobilized, was the parting point between the secular and religious branches of the Muslim intelligentsia. Indeed, under the growing influence of Western positivism (from Comte to Spencer), the secular intellectuals adopted the position that the range of the static traditionalist view was insufficient for comprehension of the

[7] *Al-Jawa'ib,* Constantinople, May 12, 1868, editorial by Ahmad Faris al-Shidyaq.

[8] Jurji Zaydan, *Tarikh adab al-lugha al-'arabiyya* (History of Arabic Literature), Vol. IV, Cairo, n.d., p. 165.

[9] Khayr al-Din Pasha, *Muqaddimat kitab aqwam al-masalik fi ma'rifat ahwal al-mamalik* (The Road Most Straight to Know the Conditions of the State), Constantinople, 1876, p. 6.

[10] For a typical argument, see Muhammad Ibn Rahhal al-Jaza'iri, "Mustaqbal al-islam" (The Future of Islam), in *Majallat al-majallat al-'arabiyya,* Vol. II, Cairo, January 1962, pp. 68 ff. From the Arab point of view after 1916, the main causes of decline were attributed to Ottoman domination. "The achievements of the Arabs were present in every age until the coming of the Turkish state . . ." See Lutfi al-Haffar, *Muthakkirat* (Memoirs), Vol. I, Damascus, n.d., p. 151.

[11] "Every Muslim is sick and his cure lies in the Qur'an." Afghani, *op. cit.,* p. 88.

fullness and depth of modern life.[12] Progress, the key emphasis of their thought, was a process of constant improvement of the human lot made possible not by the invocation of old ideas and values but by the application of human intelligence and will. In the end, however, the secular-oriented intellectuals failed, as did the reformist ulemas, either to effect a breach in traditionalist inertia or to bring an intellectual awakening which could lead to a genuine revival of an ethical-religious inner life.

## INTELLECTUAL RETREAT

In this atmosphere of contradiction and "double-mindedness" the opportunity to admit doubt and to grapple decisively with it was never seriously allowed. In controversy, ambiguity replaced mystery, and doctrine remained enshrined in traditionalist terminology. The approach of a genuine critical system of thought thus never developed in modern Islam as a tool of valid intellectual research. By the beginning of the twentieth century, as the material and spiritual pressure of Europe increased, the trend of striving to "repossess" modern civilization veered into a headlong drive toward attaining and securing the conditions of survival in a world that had suddenly become dangerous. Both the values and ideas of a whole intellectual generation and the position of the elite for fifty years from about 1875 were in the grip of this psychological condition. Knowledge (*'ilm*) came to be viewed with a new kind of awe, and insistence upon its possession assumed a desperate urgency. For *'ilm* was seen not only as the basis of truth and validity (in theological or philosophical contexts), but primarily as the source of power and strength in a concrete political and material sense. Europe came to be respected and feared in terms of its science and industry, the means of its vast power. Afghani echoes a widely shared conviction in his remarks that "the nations of Christendom are able to overrun the nations of Islam by their science, the source of all power, and Islam is vulnerable because of ignorance, the

[12] Indeed scepticism and refusal to accept the "old philosophies" was already apparent in the last Arab intellectual generation of the Ottoman Empire. See, for example, Shibli al-Shumayyil (d. 1917), *Majmu'a* (Selected Works), Vol. II, Cairo, 1909-1910, pp. 85-88. He was able to declare publicly that "good and evil are not absolute but relative values, depending on the circumstances of time and place." *Ibid.*, p. 7.

origin of all weakness." [13] In this context the desire to acquire knowledge and to modernize society became a self-conscious act with the primary objective of self-preservation. To achieve this end, it was obvious to the Westernized intelligentsia that the cautious legalistic approach of the traditionalists could never be sufficient. The authority of religious sanction inevitably lost its power and was gradually replaced by the utilitarian principle of *maslaha* (interest or efficacy). Secular lawyers, not the learned ulema, undertook to elaborate new criteria of validity.

The basic point underlying the new pragmatism, which by the end of the first decade of this century began to pervade society, is illustrated by the following excerpt from a lecture delivered in 1909 at, significantly, the Shari'a Courts School in Cairo, by the young Syrian lawyer Rafiq al-'Azm.

> Since laws are made to prevent evil and to bring about the good . . . [proper] legislation stipulates that [a given] legal text may be made nonoperative if interest [*maslaha*] requires it. [This is to be done] in cases of genuine necessity, when interest is established beyond any doubt—that is, when interest is better achieved by abandoning the text [of the Law] than by adhering to it.[14]

Doubt and despair had already penetrated the very heart of the Islamic reform movement. Shiekh Muhammad Rida, a leading disciple of Muhammad Abdu, reports the following conversation, which must have taken place shortly before Abdu's death in 1905.

> We were at the home of the Imam [Abdu] talking about what we had just heard concerning the desire of the Japanese nation to adopt the religion of Islam. Sheikh Husain al-Jisr exclaimed: 'Now there will be hope for Islam to regain its true glory!'
>
> [Sheikh Salman (d. 1918), another disciple of Abdu's] answered: 'Leave [the Japanese] alone. I am afraid if they became Muslims like us we will corrupt them before they have a chance to reform us . . . We shall yet see the result of your hopes in this dead [Muslim] nation and the outcome of the reforms you have attempted in these corrupt [Arab] people. . . .[15]

[13] Afghani, *op. cit.,* p. 225.
[14] *Al-Muqtabas*, IV, Damascus, 1909, p. 611.
[15] Cited by Shaikho, *op. cit.,* p. 94.

The voyage from despair to secular revolution was short. Soon after the end of the Second World War the older generation was overthrown, and modernization and reform became the monopoly of the secular state.

## THE FUTURE ROLE OF ISLAM

To determine the role that Islam can still play in the process of modernization, we must first find answers to a number of questions: what new classes and social groups have emerged since the end of World War II and the coming of mass society? What traditional groups have survived? What divides these from the new classes and social groups? What psychological and functional values, if any, are still operative that may bind the older with the younger generation? If, on the political and economic levels, Islam and traditional values no longer possess meaning or relevance to social planning and political organization, what frame of reference now determines the choices in the drive toward political centralization, in the effort to establish social justice, and in the striving to build modern economic systems? It is primarily for the psychologist, the sociologist and the economist to investigate and try to answer these and other related questions. The historian can supply no final answers; his task is to try to render intelligible the problems of the present in terms of their historical developments.

# IV.   From Religious to National Law*

## by Majid Khadduri

LAW IS A SYSTEM OF SOCIAL CONTROL HAVING THE OBJECT OF regulating human conduct in accordance with a certain set of rules. Different societies tend to develop different systems of social control; but law, which may be regarded as the "control of controls," is probably the best measure designed to protect what society honors. The magnitude of the legal edifice reflects the genius of its architects, but its survival down the centuries depends less on the legal structure than on the ability of succeeding generations to adapt it to new conditions of life. The attempt to change Islamic law, despite its notorious rigidity, which still has a strong hold on the Muslim society, is worthy of close study.

The Middle East is renowned for the oldest legal systems known in recorded history, and Islamic law, a part of its surviving cultural heritage, is one of the great legal systems of the world. Many of these systems had been exposed to foreign influences, but Islamic law has preserved its basic character. The greatest challenge in recent years has come from the West, under the impact of which Islamic law is bound to change. Perhaps it is too early to hazard a prediction; but there are signs which indicate that this impact may well mark a new milestone in the development of the Islamic legal system. It is proposed in this paper to study the process of change and the forces operating to transform the law from a medieval to a modern legal order.

### NATURE OF ISLAMIC LAW

Muslim thinkers, following their Greek predecessors, have taken it for granted that by nature "man is a social animal." Not only

* Reprinted by special permission from *Mid-East: World Center* (Ruth Anshen, editor), copyright © 1956 by Harper-Row.

can man not live alone save as a member of society, but society itself cannot survive without authority. For although man is a social animal by nature, he is not a well-behaving animal. The restraint upon his social relations was enforced by authority and regulated by law; the latter was to show the track to be trodden (and indeed the word *Shari'a* bears this meaning) and the former was to sanction the enforcement of law.

Islam, probably more than any other religion, has the character of a jural system which regulates life and thoughts of the believer according to an ideal set of rules regarded as the only correct and valid one. This system, unlike positive law, proceeded from a high divine source embodying God's will and justice. As the expression of the will of God, the divine law is regarded as most perfect, eternal, and just, designed for all time and characterized by universal application to all men. The ideal life was the life in strict conformity with this law.

In Muslim legal theory, the divine law preceded both society and the state; the latter existed for the very purpose of enforcing the law. But if the state failed to enforce the law—in such a case the state obviously forfeits its *raison d'être*—the believer still remained under the obligation to observe the law even in the absence of anyone to enforce it. The sanction of the law, which is distinct from the validity of the law, need not exist. For the object of the law is to provide for the believer the right "path" (*Shari'a*), or the standard life, regardless of the existence of the proper authority charged with its enforcement.

If the divine law is regarded as the source of governing authority, the Islamic state must possess a special character. It has been maintained that such a state should be called a theocracy—a term coined by Josephus—on the assumption that God is the head of the state. It is, however, not God but God's law which really governs and God was never regarded, as under Shintoism, as the direct ruler of His subjects. Only God's representative (in the capacity of a prophet or caliph), deriving his authority from the divine law, was charged with executive powers. Hence the state must be called a nomocracy, not a theocracy, as the law is the real source of authority. Since this is a divine law, the state would be a "divine nomocracy."

The law comprises the believer's devotional obligations to God as well as rules regulating his relations with fellow believers. It is essentially a set of duties which the believer must obey; if he consummates his obedience, he realizes his ultimate objective in life, namely, the achievement of salvation. This fulfillment of the law would constitute his "happy" life—hard as it may seem—by giving him an inner satisfaction that his next life would be assured in Heaven.

Islamic law is not all to be found in the Qur'an, as the Qur'an is often too brief and vague on matters of law. The Qur'an is regarded as the basic and the most fundamental source of law. The details of the law, however, were worked out later by jurist-theologians, who developed elaborate doctrines and schools of law which constituted the *Shari'a* or the system of Islamic law.

The jurists agreed that the Qur'an, embodying the infallible revelations, was an unquestionable source of law. But here agreement ended, as the Qur'an provided no clear guidance for further legislation. As a result, the controversy that followed was essentially one on the use of the sources, rather than the essential substance, of legislation. The character of this controversy was not, strictly speaking, legal; fundamentally, it was theological, since an inquiry into what would constitute an authoritative "supplement" to Qur'anic revelations is a doctrinal, not a legal, argument.

The jurists made use of Traditions, comprising precedents based on Muhammad's own decisions and utterances. These in turn were based on local custom, which were later compiled in digests of Traditions and which supplied material for further legislation. On the basis of both Qur'anic and Traditional citations the jurists, by applying reason or personal opinion, made legal decisions. This method of legislation, providing a fresh source of law, was called *qiyas,* or analogy. The jurists had to resort to still another source of law called *ijma',* or consensus. This was based on a Qur'anic injunction, which stipulated: "Follow the way of the believers" (Qur'an, IV, 115) and on a Tradition which runs as follows: "My people will never agree on an error." *Ijma'* or consensus was so highly regarded that it ranked next in importance to Traditions, but no precise method was ever agreed upon as to how consensus was to be reached. In practice, however, consensus was a matter that only the jurists exercised; when they agreed on a matter of law, their agreement constituted *ijma'*.

The controversy over the "sources" of law resulted in the rise of various schools. But it was also owing to geographical variations and local precedents that various schools were bound to develop. The so-called 'Iraqi schools perhaps made more use of analogical reasoning, which reflected the new conditions outside Arabia, than the Hijazi school, which claimed to represent the home of Traditions. Of the 'Iraqi jurists, Abu Hanifa (A.D. 699-767) distinguished himself as the most liberal in using analogy, while Malik (A.D. 717-795) in the Hijaz emphasized Tradition and advocated *ijma'*. Shafi'i (A.D. 767-820), the founder of a third school of law, laid down a precise method of reasoning concerning the use of sources and systematized the body of law that had been provided by his predecessors. Although the tendency to develop various schools of law continued, it was perhaps Shafi'i's successors who initiated the movement to limit the number of schools.

By the tenth century of the Christian era only four were recognized as orthodox, namely, the Hanafi, the Maliki, the Shafi'i and the Hanbali schools. The Shi'a heterodox sect developed its own school, or schools, of law. The opinions and writings of the founders of these schools and their disciples became the standard textbooks for all students of law. But there was, and still is, no restriction on the Muslim against changing his allegiance and practice from one school of law to another. Allegiance to the Hanafi and Shafi'i schools was dominant in 'Iraq, Syria and Egypt, but later, under Ottoman rule, the Hanafi school was adopted as official. The Maliki school, shrinking in the Hijaz, spread all over North Africa and Spain, before the latter was restored to Christian rule. The Shi'a doctrine spread widely in southern 'Iraq, central Asia, India and the Persian Gulf, and it became official in Persia in the sixteenth century.

DECADENCE

The divine law flourished at a time when Islam was still on the move and the jurists, aware of the need for further legislation, followed the principle of *ijtihad* or independent reasoning. *Ijtihad* was not in itself the cause of legal growth, but it helped to maintain the flexibility of the law. Opinion was then in favor of *ijtihad* and the Muslim took a tolerant attitude toward disagreement among the jurists, believing that although the *ijtihad* of a single jurist was by no means infallible (only the combined *ijtihad* of all the jurists, constituting *ijma'*, was infallible) each jurist sought the truth in his own way. The Muslims regarded the various opinions of jurists, as Sha'rani has it, as various routes, all leading to the truth. Thus during the eighth and ninth centuries of the Christian era the Muslim world abounded in schools of law, major and minor. Each school had its followers, although the believer could change his allegiance from one school to another, provided he did so with moral conviction, not to fit his own interests or conveniences.

In the tenth century of the Christian era only four schools were recognized as orthodox. Their lawbooks became the standard textbooks and any attempt to depart from them was denounced as innovation. As a result *ijtihad* was gradually abandoned in favor of *taqlid* (literally, "imitation") or submission to the canons of the four schools. At first *taqlid* reflected a tendency to reduce the differences among jurists and limit the number of schools, but the growing intolerance of the Muslims to legal reasoning rendered *taqlid* an obstacle to legal development. Thus the door of *ijtihad* was shut and *taqlid* became the dominating rule. During succeeding generations there were occasional protests against *taqlid* by such leading jurists as Juwayni (d. 1283), Ibn Taymiyya (d. 1328) and Suyuti (d. 1505), but the Muslims had become so habituated to *taqlid* that no serious efforts were made to abandon it. In fact, the more the Muslims became conscious of their weakness the more the rule of *taqlid* was tightened. Thus *taqlid* reflected the apprehension of a society in decline, resorting to the imposition of "imitation" in the hope that it would check the evil influences of "innovation."

During the period of *taqlid* the jurists gave undue importance to details and particulars of the *Shari'a*. Lacking the initiative and broad understanding of the classical jurists, their efforts, restricted by *taqlid,* found an outlet in discussions on matters of detail and formalism which shifted the emphasis from the principles to the particulars of law. As a result the believers tended to adhere rigidly to obscure details while often abandoning or even violating the spirit implied in the principles of the law.

IMPACT OF THE WEST

A fresh impetus for the development of the law was received when the Ottoman Empire was established. Not only was the liberal Hanafi school adopted as official, but the Ottoman sultans followed an old Turkish practice of issuing decrees, having the force of law, based on custom and precedent. These decrees were often compiled in statute books known as *qanun-namé,* which supplied valuable additions to the *Shari'a.*

With regard to the treatment of non-Muslims, the Ottoman sultans followed a liberal policy to attract Western merchants and to revive commerce with the West at a time when the new route to India via the African Cape was threatening the commerce of the Levant. Thus French merchants were given liberal terms when Sultan Sulayman the Magnificent signed a treaty with the King of France in 1535. Not only were favorable customs duties, protection of life and property and freedom of religion accorded to them, but judicial privileges were granted (renewed and extended in 1740) permitting Westerners to be tried in their own consulates by their own laws. The poll tax, imposed on all non-Muslims (except visitors for a period less than one year), was suspended for Westerners. To this treaty the King of England, as well as other Western monarchs, were invited to adhere (Article 15). But England signed a separate treaty in 1580 and was followed by other powers, including the United States, which signed such a treaty in 1830. These Western commercial arrangements were not considered harmful to Islam, for Islamic law is not binding on non-Muslims, and the Sultan, in giving such judicial privileges, did not violate the law of his country. Furthermore, the sultans were quick to adopt from the West new weapons and military skills which were not only permitted but encouraged by Islam since any weapon or skill strengthening Islam against its enemies was in accord with Islamic law. But the Ottoman sultans were not prepared to adopt Western legal concepts which would compromise or materially change the *Shari'a.* When Ottoman power declined the sultans could still with relative ease replace the outmoded military weapons. However, when certain admirers of the West voiced their praise of Western legal and administrative institutions and suggested their adoption, the cry was at once violent and unanimous that this was impossible as they were contrary to the principles of the *Shari'a*.

The process of social change, however, pays no attention to abstract doctrines. The Muslim legal system had either to change or to fall to pieces. Facing a threat from within and without, the Sultan could no longer afford to please the conservatives and was forced, by liberal Muslim thinkers as well as Western sympathizers, to introduce Western concepts of law and justice. In solemn proclamations, he issued the *hatti-sherif Gulhané* of November 3, 1839, and the *hatti-humayun* of February 18, 1856. These decrees provided certain limitations on his own authority, such as respect for the lives, honor and property of all subjects, and promised the enactment of laws for the organization of courts and the promulgation of commercial and penal codes. For the first time, Muslims and Christians were declared equal before the law; the poll tax was no longer required from non-Muslims and the apostate's life was to be spared (although in practice this proved hard to enforce). As a result, a commercial code was promulgated in 1850, a penal code in 1858, a code of commercial procedure in 1861 and a code of maritime commerce in 1863, based in the main on French models. In the meantime new courts, called Nizamiyya Courts, were set up to apply the new laws together with mixed courts to deal with cases between Muslims and foreigners. These codes were carefully phrased lest they would infringe on the *Shari'a* and arouse the hostility of the *'ulama'*. It was pointed out that the new laws provided additional—not contrary—rules to the *Shari'a,* and the government made no move to repeal any provision of the *Shari'a* relating to the new position of equality attained by non-Muslims, such as the ineligibility of non-Muslim witnesses in a Muslim lawsuit. With the possible exception of the principle of equality of all the subjects before the law, which raised the status of the non-Muslims to a position of equality with Muslims, the Sultan adopted codes which were merely designed to regulate the life of Muslims in fields not covered by the *Shari'a*. Nonetheless, these enactments were denounced by the *'ulama'* as inconsistent with the *Shari'a,* and their authors were called *gavur* (infidel).

Shortly after these enactments, perhaps inspired by them, a movement to modernize and codify the *Shari'a* was started. Beginning in 1869 it aroused interest among Muslim jurists who resented the adoption of Western codes without recourse to the *Shari'a*. When Sultan 'Abd al-Hamid came to the throne in 1876 and assumed the title of Caliph and advocated Pan-Islamism, he sought to satisfy the conservative elements by reviving interest in the *Shari'a*. During his reign the *Majalla,* as a Muslim civil code (although by no means covering all aspects of a civil code), was promulgated. Derived in the main from the Hanafi school (although there was also recourse to other schools), it marked a significant landmark in the development of the *Shari'a*. The Western influence is shown particularly in the form in which the *Majalla* was made. A similar attempt, made in Egypt by Qadri Pasha in his *Kitab Murshid al-Hayran,* codifying the law of contract, according to the Hanafi school, was not unlike the *Majalla* in its content or a European code in form. Although this was an unofficial codification, it was regarded authoritative by the government of Egypt and the Mixed Courts, and the Ministry of Education approved its use as a textbook in its schools. The Mixed Courts, established in 1875, were set up to deal with cases between Egyptians and foreigners, while native civil and *Shari'a* courts were to deal with the civil and personal-status cases of native Egyptians. Instead of the *Majalla,* however, a civil code based on the *Code Napoléon* was applied in the civil courts.

Neither the *Majalla* nor Qadri Pasha's *Murshid al-Hayran* concerns itself with the law of personal status. Matters relating to the family have been considered too closely linked with religion, and the hold of conservatism was nowhere stronger than in this domain. No fundamental changes had been made before the First World War, although a few *fatwas* (legal opinions) were issued to alter certain minor practices. It was not until 1917 that the bold step was taken of the enactment of a law of family rights (with special sections dealing with the family rights of non-Muslim subjects), in which all matters relating to marriage, dowry, divorce, etc., were codified in the same form as in the *Majalla*. Occasional recourse was had to early jurists, but the law may be said to be a codification of the Hanafi law of personal status. This code, although no longer in force in Turkey, is the basis of the laws of personal status of Syria, Lebanon, Jordan and 'Iraq. Egypt has probably deviated from the traditional law more than any other Arab country. Although the substance of its law has been derived from the *Shari'a,* with adaptations as far as possible to modern needs, Western influence is apparent at least in the techniques and methods of drafting.

Toward the end of the Hamidian period many a Muslim thinker became impatient with the Sultan's despotism, enforced in the name of Islam. In the meantime the new generation had been influenced by Western constitutionalism and nationalism and many young Turks hoped that their adoption might create a strong Turkey. The liberals argued that religion was no longer adequate as a basis for a modern state and demanded that it should be replaced by nationalism as the mode of allegiance. The Young Turks sought to restore the short-lived Constitution of 1876, based on European models. This constitution placed authority in the hands of a responsible cabinet and provided that laws were to be enacted by parliament in accordance with the needs of the people. It also stated that no discrimination was to be permitted on the basis of race or creed, and all subjects were declared free and equal before the law. The Young Turks finally succeeded in deposing Sultan 'Abd al-Hamid (1909), and thus the era of Pan-Islamism came to an end.

The change in the character of the state from "Islamic" to "national" marked a significant landmark in the development of Islamic law. For nationalism, the product of Western thought brought with it the secular conception of government and introduced the doctrine that the "nation" is the source of authority. As a result, the *Shari'a* ceased to be the sole sanction of legal decisions or the authoritative source of legislation. The nation became the ultimate source of authority, acting through its representatives in parliament and the government. But no attempt was made at this stage to separate the religious from the secular powers, nor in fact was serious thought ever given to reconciling Islam with the new concepts of law and authority. Perhaps a liberal interpretation of Islam might have proved a more salutary approach to reform in view of the subsequent conflict that developed between the "religious" and "secular" institutions. The nationalists were not prepared to compromise with the conservatives and were determined, especially after the peace settlement of World War I, to accelerate the movement of national reconstruction.

Nationalism, in so composite a society as the Ottoman Empire, proved to be a disintegrating factor and speeded the breakup of the Ottoman structure. The successor states, still under the spell of nationalism, made further strides to part with the *Shari'a*. The degree of their emancipation varied from complete break with the *Shari'a,* as in the case of Turkey, to its maintenance almost intact, as in the Arabian peninsula. The Fertile Crescent, following a *via media,* proceeded to set up new national regimes, paying only lip service to Islam as the official religion of the state and recognizing the jurisdiction of the religious courts and foundations in matters relating to personal status and *waqf* (pious endowments). During the interwar period the importation of Western secular laws and institutions reached the flood mark without regard to their consistency with an adaptation to Muslim law and institutions. As a result, the religious elements took a negative, though at the outset a passive, attitude toward such a movement, denouncing it as "secular" and incompatible with Islam. Apart from the slogan "Return to Islam," however, they had little to offer in the way of a constructive legal reform which might modernize the *Shari'a* and bring it up to date.

Nor was the experiment of the nationalists with "secular" law a happy one. For the new laws could command neither the respect nor the allegiance of the people in the same way as God's law had done in the past. The new legal order appeared too vulgar and too worldly in the eyes of pious Muslims, who have habitually revered the awe-inspiring *Shari'a*. Thus a conflict inevitably ensued between two extreme schools: the new denounced the old as incompatible with modern life, and the old, witnessing a sudden break with the past, demanded the restoration of the *Shari'a*. A new approach combining the best of the two was therefore needed.

### SYNTHESIS

Although the importation of Western legal concepts continued with ever increasing celerity, a few modernists paused to take stock of the enormous changes that had taken place during their life-time. It is not an unhealthy sign to look back at one's own achievements, whether to iron out certain mental doubts or to gather momentum for further strides. Some modernists took a critical attitude toward the adoption of Western law without regard to existing conditions, and their views gained support in certain quarters because the results achieved by Western law did not measure up to expectations. Such critics began to re-evaluate Western law; they could see that Western legal concepts, transplanted into a new social milieu, were not expected to achieve results similar to those achieved in the West. Western law, even though it did not interject itself uniformly into society, came into direct conflict with Muslim law in fields in which the latter had a strong hold. But this very fact raised the question as to whether Muslim law could not be modernized to avoid conflict with Western law. Perhaps the adaptation of Western law and the modernization of Muslim law might bring the two systems into harmony and work out a coherent synthesis of the two.

Thinking along these lines first took place when the Muslim world was faced with the issue of the abolition of the Caliphate in 1924. The Kemalist reformists made a decision to part with Islamic law and institutions and to reorganize Turkey along national and Western lines. A year later a book was published in Egypt, entitled *Islam and the Sources of Authority,* by 'Ali 'Abd al-Raziq, in which the author argued, in support of the abolition of the Caliphate, that Islam was not designed by the Prophet Muhammad as a political institution but, like Christianity, as a system of religion for the regulation of the spiritual life of the Muslims. Thus he saw no reason why the Caliphate should be tied to religion and could not be abolished, as it was instituted, by the Muslim community. Although Raziq's theory was officially rejected by the *'ulama'* and his name dropped from their ranks, no constructive criticism was then offered by them.

At the time of the Raziq controversy a young Egyptian was studying law in Paris. He chose the subject (later published in book form) for his dissertation, *Le Califat: son évolution vers une Société des Nations Orientales* (Paris, 1926). Dr. Sanhuri rejected Raziq's theory that political authority was not an integral part of Islam, but saw no reason why Muslim public law could not develop to fit conditions of modern life. He suggested, accordingly, that the Caliphate, which had undergone many changes in the past, was still capable of further changes and might develop into an Oriental League of Nations. No response was then made to Sanhuri's constructive criticism, but his approach bore fruit when he began to apply it to other branches of Muslim law.

The first attempt to adopt Sanhuri's approach of modernizing the *Shari'a* took place in 'Iraq, when Sanhuri was a visiting professor of law at the Baghdad Law College in 1936. A committee was appointed by the 'Iraqi government, of which Sanhuri was a member, to prepare a draft civil law. Although the work was interrupted, the committee approved Sanhuri's proposals regarding a synthesis of Muslim law and Western law, and work was resumed when Sanhuri, back in 'Iraq in 1943, completed a draft Civil Code for 'Iraq. Before this law was formally enacted in 'Iraq, it was adopted, with modifications, by the Syrian government in June 1949. Meantime a new civil code for Egypt was enacted in October 1949, in the preparation of which Sanhuri took the leading part, when the Egyptian national courts assumed full jurisdiction following the abolition of the Mixed Courts. Profiting from the two new civil codes of Syria and Egypt, the 'Iraqi government, making a final revision, formally adopted in June 1951 Sanhuri's draft as the 'Iraqi Civil Code. In these codes Sanhuri tried, as he stated before the Committee of Civil Law set up by the Egyptian Senate, to adopt all sound provisions of the *Shari'a* and to harmonize them with sound principles of modern legislation. In form, if not in substance, the codes resemble Western rather than Muslim law; but the substance may be said to be the product of various sources, including the *Shari'a* itself. The decisions of the national courts, national as well as comparative legislation, were no less heavily drawn from the *Shari'a*. In the Egyptian and Syrian codes the *Shari'a* figured less in substance than in the 'Iraqi code, but all have been drafted on the same pattern and they accepted the *Shari'a* as a basic source.

Sanhuri's remarkable success may be attributed to the fact that he started to apply his approach to that part of the *Shari'a* where it aroused little or no opposition from conservative elements. He wisely abstained from discussing controversial issues which might have brought him into conflict with the *'ulama'* and interrupted his work. Without going into a theoretical discussion on how the *Shari'a* generally should be modernized, or even trying to give a rationale of his scheme, Sanhuri proceeded in a practical way to show how a synthesis between Muslim and Western law could be achieved. This may seem much like Muhammad 'Abduh's (d. 1905) reform approach, which aimed at combining the best of

Islam and modernism. Like 'Abduh, Sanhuri emphasized the principle of modernization, rather than secularization, of the law and avoided discussion of the feasibility of the latter. Sanhuri, however, has gone farther than 'Abduh by trying to achieve a "synthesis" between Muslim law and Western law which may be adapted to modern Arab life. But Sanhuri's process of selection, adaptation and synthesis of Islamic and Western law may well raise the question as to whether some sort of "secularization" is not implied in his "modernization."

Owing to the action of the Kemalist movement in separating religion from the state, often referred to as the "secularization" of Turkey (which in turn has been an imitation of a Western movement in separating church from state), the term "secularization" has acquired the connotation of undermining religion. As a result, Sanhuri and other Muslim thinkers have avoided the use of this term for fear of wrecking schemes of reform which would be opposed if identified as "secularized." But does "secularization" necessarily aim at the separation of religion from the state (or the spiritual from the temporal authority), and could this not be achieved in fields which have nothing to do with religion? Has not Sanhuri in the new civil codes of Egypt and 'Iraq introduced a "secular" element (i.e., Western secular law) into the *Shari'a* by his synthesis of Western and Islamic law? Has he not made free choice in the selection and adaptation of Muslim law to fit certain Western principles deemed necessary for modern life? It is significant, therefore, to argue that there are various forms of secularization other than that of the separation of religion and state.

Secularization may take the following forms: first, the adoption of Western legal rules and principles which are either not adequately covered by the *Shari'a* or not mentioned at all by the *Shari'a;* second, the adoption of Western law which is in principle in conformity with the *Shari'a* but is not dealt with in such detail as would fit the conditions of modern life as influenced by the West (Western law may be adopted to cover such new phases of modern life as are not in conflict with the *Shari'a*); third, the adoption of Western law which may take the place of certain *Shari'a* rules that have become obsolete; fourth, the separation of the devotional and religious provisions of the *Shari'a* from those regulating daily life.

Although Sanhuri has implicitly recognized the principle of separation, he advanced no argument for it; but Subhi Mahmasani, a Lebanese jurist, strongly argued in favor of it in an address given at the Colloquium of Islamic Culture, held at Princeton University on September 14, 1953, in which he said that early "Muslim jurists made a differentiation in certain cases between the legal and religious rulings, a differentiation similar to that made today between civil and natural obligations." In support he cited a Tradition from the Prophet Muhammad to the effect that a differentiation between religious and daily matters must be made and that the Muslims were not required to follow Muhammad's opinion in daily as in religious matters (Muslim's *Sahih,* VII, 95).

Finally, modernization on a national basis, in the form advocated by Sanhuri and other Muslim thinkers, must inevitably carry with it some sort of secularization. The fact that several new civil codes have been enacted for Egypt, Syria, 'Iraq, Jordan and Libya (although they have many features in common) seems to emphasize the national character of the law. These codes, combining Western and Islamic principles of law, are national laws, making no distinction between subjects on the basis of religion, and are strictly territorial and not personal in character. Except in such matters as personal status and devotional duties, the national laws of these Muslim countries make no distinction among subjects on the basis of creed.

CONCLUSION

In view of the great strides that have been made in the law of the Arab states, a few Muslim thinkers in Turkey have raised the question: Are not the Arabs slowly doing what Turkey has done by revolution? To this question it may be replied that it was easy for Turkey to discard a system of law which it never regarded as part of her national heritage, but to the Arabs, the *Shari'a* is an integral part of their cultural heritage which could not so easily be disclaimed. To modernists it is a matter of national pride that the *Shari'a* should be preserved, in order to maintain the continuity of the national heritage. Thus the modernization of the *Shari'a* is not looked upon merely as another way of transforming Arab legal systems into Western secular systems. The Arabs are consciously trying to preserve those elements of the *Shari'a* capable of survival by adapting them under the impact of Western law to conditions of modern life. No attempt is made to copy the Kemalist experiment and abolish the *Shari'a in toto*.

Nor is the complete break with the past in the life of a nation, whether in the field of law or in any other system of social control, always a happy one. New regimes set up by revolutions must be maintained by force in order to prevent continuity of past influences, but once such force or external control is relaxed, as recent experiences in Turkey have shown, the people are likely to have recourse to past concepts and customs which are not so easy to obliterate in the life of a nation. A system of law survives because it has become adapted to the social, economic, and psychological conditions of life. These conditions may be modified by a government guided by some new ideology or philosophical ideas, but such a government can safely follow them only if it makes concessions to traditions and local conditions. Social change by its very nature is slow and requires a nexus with the past in order to insure healthy progress. A sudden break with the past may not always be the sure way for a nation to leap into a modern phase of progress.

# V.   The Rôle of the Army in the Traditional Arab State

## by Sir John Bagot Glubb

BEFORE DISCUSSING THE SUBJECT OF THE RÔLE OF THE ARMY IN the Arab state, I would like to draw attention to two attitudes common among Western nations which render such a study difficult. The first of these is the commonly held conviction that so-called "Western democracy"—the system of government at present in vogue in the United States and Britain—is the best of all forms of government. If we, whether consciously or unconsciously, hold this view, we inevitably tend to judge all other systems by this yardstick. We approve those institutions which most closely resemble our own and condemn those which differ from them. In discussing the traditional institutions of other nations we should, I believe, divest ourselves of these opinions, a task by no means easy.

The second point which I wish to emphasize is that the character of all nations has been formed by their past history, reaching back through many centuries. Unless we have some knowledge of their history, therefore, we are unable to appreciate the behaviour of different nations today. One of the most powerful factors which has moulded the character of various races over the last two thousand years has been their religion. I propose, therefore, to begin with the origins of the religion of the Arabs, namely Islam.

The Prophet Muhammad began to preach in his native town of Mecca in A.D. 613. His message met with little encouragement on the part of his fellow-citizens. After eight years of his ministry, he had only made some seventy converts, and opposition, even persecution, was increasing. As a result, the Prophet and his handful of converts were obliged to escape from Mecca and to take refuge in the town of Medina, two hundred and fifty miles to the north, where they arrived, destitute for the most part, on June 28, 622.

Hitherto the Prophet had behaved with remarkable patience towards his persecutors, but in Medina he announced a change of policy. God, he said, wished the Muslims to fight against unbelievers. Beginning with small scale raids against the people of Mecca, the operations were gradually extended until, in A.D. 630, Muhammad captured Mecca at the head of an army of 10,000 men. Within the next two years, the whole of the Arabian Peninsula acknowledged the suzerainty of the Prophet who, having begun his career as a religious reformer and having then become a military commander, ended his life as the political head of the state.

So greatly was Muhammad revered by his followers that his successor, or caliph, sought only to imitate the Prophet's example in every detail. Thus he too, like his model, became religious leader, military commander and political head of the state, all at the same time. The incidents of Muhammad's life gave birth, therefore, to a tradition to which Muslim countries have conformed ever since.

The United States is peculiar among independent states in that its Constitution was deliberately planned, though the planners were themselves, of course, strongly influenced by the traditions which they had brought from Europe. The majority of nations, however, have not developed their governmental institutions systematically. Under the stress of circumstances, measures adopted to meet various emergencies have become incorporated into the complex of the national life and are now accepted and indeed almost unperceived.

In the West, for example, we tend to separate religion from politics. If the clergy speak for or against any political party, we tell them to confine their activities to their spiritual duties. The successors of Muhammad, however—the caliphs—ruled for centuries after his death, combining religious and political authority; they were Pope and Emperor in one. To this day, in Muslim countries, religion and politics are continually intermingled. Politics, to the traditional Muslim, were a part of his religion.

The fact that the caliphs enjoyed both religious and political authority tended to make their rule authoritarian, for to resist them in the political sphere could be interpreted as irreligious.

In the same manner, the position of the army in the state dated from the time of the Prophet, for Muhammad himself established his religion in Arabia by force of arms. After his death, the Arabs emerged from their desert peninsula and conquered an immense empire extending from the Atlantic to the frontiers of China. As a result of these military conquests, Islam was established as the dominant religion over the whole of this vast area. Therefore, while the Arab tradition was that of one-man rule, combining religious and political leadership, the whole imperial structure depended on the army.

The difficulties encountered by Muhammad in the propagation of his religious teachings had led him to proclaim military service against unbelievers to be a religious duty. In the Arab Empire it was assumed that every able-bodied Muslim was a soldier. With the progress of civilization, wealth and culture, however, the practice of using mercenary armies became general, but the army nevertheless continued to occupy a vital and highly honoured position in the country. Later on, after the Turkish conquests, the armies were no longer Arab but Turk, but this fact did not destroy the honourable position occupied by soldiers. Emphasis was not laid on the racial difference between Arabs and Turks but in the unifying force of their common Muslim religion. Thus a Muslim Arab could honour a Turkish commander as being a soldier of Islam.

Yet even these traditions were in a way obvious and superficial. We should perhaps look deeper for an explanation of the honour accorded to soldiers in Arab countries and indeed in all Muslim areas. As we have seen, the original propagation of Islam was largely due to the employment of military force. Moreover, this method was used by the Prophet Muhammad, the founder of the Muslim faith. This point is surely of essential importance. Christians also have constantly used armed force in the service of religion but we are, to say the least, free to criticize their action because Christ did not use force. If He had done so, Christians could not criticize those who do.

It is quite possible that this original use of force, legitimized by the Prophet himself, has resulted in the evolution of a more authoritarian system of government in Muslim states than is now regarded as desirable in the United States and Britain. Authoritarian forms of government inevitably rely more on the loyalty of the army than do those systems which base their power on the complete consent of the governed. Relying on the army, they cause it to be held in honour, and soldiers enjoy a privileged position in the state.

This is one of the questions on which we have to endeavour to divest ourselves of many Western ideas with which we have been brought up. Our first reaction is to say that it is obviously only right to govern with the consent of the governed. Many would go much further and say that to govern contrary to the wishes of the governed is morally reprehensible—but by what system of morals?

The economic, financial, military and diplomatic aspects of government are extremely intricate and complicated and require great experience and expert knowledge. Not one person in a hundred, perhaps in a thousand, can possess such knowledge or experience, nor is it possible for them, when obliged to earn their living, to acquire such knowledge. Those responsible for governing should possess these abilities, but if they do so, they will probably frequently see it to be their duty to follow a course to which the majority of their fellow-citizens might not consent. This dilemma, however, arises only in questions of expediency.

In moral questions, the ruler's sanctions are even clearer, for Islam states that two books alone, the Koran and the Traditions, lay down all the rules necessary for government and individual conduct. This is the corollary of the statement already made that under Islam religion and politics are interwoven. The head of the state is the head of religion. The duty of the head of the state is to enforce the laws laid down in the Koran and the Traditions, which Muslims believe to have been the laws given by God to man.

Where God has already spoken, the opinions of men are obviously valueless. Thus the consent of the governed in the Muslim traditional state is irrelevant. There can be no need whatever for elections, for congress, for parliament or for the approval of the public. The duty of the government is to enforce God's laws as stated in the holy books. In the moral sphere, this mentality is illustrated today in nearly all the Arab countries. In the majority of such countries, cinema films, television, books and periodicals are liable to censorship, and indecency and promiscuity are prohibited by law because it is accepted that the government is responsible for public religion and morals. In the Western democracies it is the people themselves who are supposed to decide. If the public wishes to encourage promiscuity, they have a legal right to cause laws to be passed to that effect. In Muslim states it is believed to be the duty of the government to enforce the laws of God and not the will of the people, who may well be immoral and will certainly be ignorant.

It may be said that these are civilian questions of law and government which do not seem to concern the army, but in fact they are at the root of the whole problem of the army. For if the government is responsible to God and not to the majority of voters, then it must have the power to coerce the public to follow the way of God. Thus the army becomes not only the defence of the country against foreign injury, but also the guarantor that the general public obeys the government, the duty of which is to enforce the laws of God.

In practice, of course, these theories are not always observed. The head of the state may be a man who deliberately breaks God's laws and encourages the public to do the same. In such circumstances there is no constitutional method, such as an election, by which he can be peaceably removed. It may be necessary to remove him by revolution or even assassination. To the citizens of the Western democracies, the absence in the traditional Arab state of any peaceful machinery for the removal of a bad ruler appears to be a serious drawback to the system.

Yet the essential point for us to realize is that when a military dictator assumes control of an Arab country, he does not necessarily do so against the will of a public who are yearning for democratic institutions. Far from it. The majority of Muslims consider it to be the duty of the ruler to govern the country in accordance with the laws of the Muslim religion, not in accordance with the wishes of the mob. In order to do this, in view of the fickleness and wickedness of men, he must have at his disposal adequate physical force which it is the duty of the army to provide. Thus the army becomes the guardian of the nation's morals.

Apart from religion, we are faced with an almost insoluble problem when investigating the peculiar institutions of any nation. Are we to attribute their institutions to the natural peculiarities of the people in question or are they due merely to the stage which they have reached in the march of progress? Let us take an example. The Arabs, we have seen, show a predilection for one-man rule. Is this because they are merely "backward" or because their emotional nature makes such a system more congenial? The governments of the Western democracies seem to hold the first opinion. They do not hesitate to express the hope that the peoples of Asia and Africa will soon reach that stage of "progress" when they will adopt methods of government similar to those now in use in Western nations.

The alternative theory, however, has much to be said for it. It can be urged that the inhabitants of hotter climates have more lively emotions than the north European stock. They are more cordial, genial and affectionate, but also more violent. They are less patient than Northerners, but also less lethargic. Their emotions can be more easily aroused and may lead to outbreaks of violence, which will subsequently be regretted. They visualize everything in terms of personality rather than of theories or organizations.

Thus we speak of the policy of the United States or the British governments, but nine Arabs out of ten will talk of Nasser or King Husain, not of the Egyptian or Jordanian governments. This personal approach penetrates every sphere of life. In any Arab country, employees, domestics or gardeners soon become one of the family and often remain in the same employment all their days or as long as their employer is alive.

If we admit that people with such warm emotions are more likely to be loyal to individual leaders than to abstractions like "democracy," then it may well be that personal rule will always be the most suitable to them, whatever stage of "progress" they may achieve.

This problem is indeed at the very root of the rôle of the army, which, as we have seen, in the traditional Arab state is not merely a force maintained to repel foreign invaders but is the very foundation of the state itself and the guardian of the nation's morals.

It is not suggested that every Muslim Arab has thought out the system in so logical a manner, any more than the man in the street in the United States or Britain can trace the historical steps by which Western democracy has been built. On the contrary, many Arabs are anxious to adopt "modern" systems of government.

The powerful are always imitated by the weak. A thousand years ago, when the Arab Empire dominated a great part of the world, much of Europe endeavoured to copy its institutions. Now that the situation has been reversed and Europe and America have been dominating the world for two hundred years, the Arabs tend to imitate the methods used in the West, the nations of which are so much more powerful than they are. Young men who have been educated in Europe or the United States return home filled with enthusiasm for what they have seen.

In most cases, however, the opinions which they have absorbed are somewhat superficial. They fail to appreciate that the institutions of Western democracy have been built upon the basis of rule with the consent of the governed, whereas Arab civilization was built up on a system of authority based on the commands of God. To cite a simple example, young men educated in the United States may be profoundly impressed with the benefits of democracy and return home determined to introduce it. When they reach their own countries, however, no one is really interested in their theories. Faced with this deadlock, their instinctive reaction is to use authority to introduce reforms. They accordingly subvert the young officers of the army, who stage a *coup d'état*. A military dictatorship is established, and the inauguration of "democracy" is proclaimed by edict. But this is like trying to build a brick house onto the hull of a ship. The superstructure cannot hold together on such unsuitable foundations. Soon we find the young "democrats" ruling by edict and using the army to compel the nation to accept what they think is good for it.

Here again, more often than not, we find the Arab proclivity for one-man rule unconsciously asserting itself. The most forceful of the young "democratic" officers assumes control and in a few weeks the new "democratic republic" has become a military dictatorship. No one particularly planned that it would be that way; it just happened because that is the most suitable structure for the existing foundations, which were laid many centuries ago.

It may well be objected, however, that military intervention in politics does not lead to stability, as witness the continual *coups d'état* in Syria and Iraq. Here it is, I think, necessary to define what we mean by "military intervention in politics." In the conventional Arab state ruled by one man, there were no politics. To oppose the ruler was not politics, but treason. The army was the traditional support of the ruler. (The weak point of the system, the lack of any peaceful means of disposing of a wicked ruler, has already been referred to.)

When, however, we introduce the theories of Western democracy we find ourselves in a dilemma. The whole basis of government is changed. The Muslim ruler was responsible for enforcing God's laws and the army was his instrument for doing so. But under democracy it is not God's laws we have to enforce but those of a portion of the nation, while another portion of the nation alleges these laws to be wicked, oppressive and unscrupulous. The army no longer has a straightforward brief to safeguard the nation's morals. It is perplexed by the clamour, propaganda, accusations and hypocrisy of rival politicians, few if any of whom are interested in the laws of God. Western democracy has dealt with this situation by declaring that none of this has anything to do with the army, which is solely intended to defend the country from outside attack. "No military intervention in politics" thus becomes the very basis of democracy.

But the Muslims are not accustomed to regard the army thus. To them the army is the very backbone of the nation. If attempts be made to introduce democracy, rival politicians hasten to convert army officers to their theories and to enlist their support. The army, confused and bewildered, is divided against itself, some supporting this candidate to rule and some that one. The result will be the repeated revolutions which we have witnessed in recent years.

We may, therefore, conclude that frequent military *coups d'état* are the result of attempts to introduce democratic party politics into a country in which there is no traditional foundation for such institutions, but in which the army has always traditionally been employed as much in the internal affairs of the state as in external defence. The cessation of such military *coups* (or at least a respite from them) can only be secured when the emergence of some outstanding personality restores one-man rule, the traditional form of Arab government. Under such circumstances, the army, once again united, will play its traditional rôle of supporting the authority of the ruler.

On the other hand, to insist on the maintenance of democratic and representative forms of government and at the same time to forbid the army to interfere in politics is unlikely to succeed. The

citizens of Arab states may be intellectually persuaded of the bless-
ings of Western democracy and may endeavour to introduce them
with genuine enthusiasm. But the deep, instinctive emotions of the
nation have for over a thousand years been developing on quite
another pattern and only endless revolutions and confusion will
result.

We are thus obliged to confess that much of the recent instability
in the Middle East has been due to the misguided enthusiasms of
the Western powers—to our unfortunate efforts to erect our own
superstructure on other men's foundations. It is interesting to note,
moreover, that in nearly all these Arab revolutions we find the old
idea that the army is the guardian of the nation's morals. In Britain
and America, on the other hand, we regard military rule with a
detestation which is quite foreign to Arab traditions.

It is true that army officers are not normally the most suitable
candidates for administrative posts, nor as financiers, economists
or educationalists. This, however, was also the case in the early
Arab states. Army officers did not fill posts in the civil departments
of government. The head of the state might be, and probably was,
a soldier, but, apart from that, the army did not intervene in
day-to-day administration. It was, however, the foundation of the
state and the executive arm of the government.

It will be seen that these ideas of government, based as they are
on authority wielded to enforce the laws of God, are very different
from the foundations on which "Western democracy" has grown
up. It is impossible, in my opinion, to declare one of these systems
to be better than the other. But any attempts on our part to persuade other nations to adopt the outward forms of our system of
government may well lead only to confusion and misery. They will
almost certainly administer their own forms of government more
successfully than ours. The poet Pope, two hundred and fifty years
ago, may have shown greater insight than we possess when he
wrote:

> *O'er forms of government let fools contest,*
> *Whate'er is best administered is best.*

# VI.  Basic Conflicts of Economic Development in the Middle East[1]

## by Oded I. Remba

NO REGION ILLUSTRATES MORE DRAMATICALLY THAN DOES THE Middle East the full range of issues inherent in economic development. The area has attained a remarkable record of economic progress in the postwar period. Economic growth, living standards, food production and consumption have advanced more rapidly than in any other developing area. The 155 million people of the region—nearly 100 million in Arab countries and 56 million in non-Arab countries—are considerably better off than a billion other people in Asia and Africa. Average per capita income more than doubled from less than $100 at the end of World War II to $200-$250 by the mid-1960's. This is more than twice as high as the per capita incomes of $85-$110 in South Asia, the Far East and Africa. While Latin America led the underdeveloped world with individual income of $300-$325, its rate of growth has lagged behind that of the Middle East.

[1] The emphasis of this essay is on the 13 independent countries of the Arab world. Where relevant, the three non-Arab nations which are generally included in the Middle East—Iran, Israel and Turkey—are also covered.

Regional statistical data are rarely given either for the 13 Arab countries or for the 16 Arab and non-Arab countries combined. Various sources not only use diverse terms to designate the region (Middle East, Near East, West Asia), but also delimit the area differently, indeed if it is delimited at all.

All definitions include the seven Arab countries of Asia (Iraq, Jordan, Kuwait, Lebanon, Saudi Arabia, Syria and Yemen). But the practice varies widely, even among United Nations publications, regarding the six Arab countries of Africa (Algeria, Libya, Morocco, Sudan, Tunisia and the United Arab Republic).

The area's potential for development is impressive—not only because of its immense oil reserves. On the whole, the Middle East has not been afflicted with the hopeless imbalance between human beings and physical resources (i.e., man-land ratios) which distinguishes most of Asia, and its economic structure is not as backward as that of sub-Sahara Africa.

But as a result of constant turmoil, particularly in the Arab world, the area has already forfeited at least as much as it has gained. Future success of its ambitious development efforts will hinge on the choice of goals and priorities. Economic development programs have been caught in a maze of conflicting claims against critically short foreign exchange and limited resources of trained manpower and capital equipment. For better *and* for worse, development plans have also become entangled in the contradictory national goals arising from the larger ideological, political, social and psychological forces which are shaping the area's destiny. While the problems of the Middle East cannot be explained primarily in terms of economics, the fundamental but related economic concepts which form the basis of this essay apply to these problems only too forcefully. The use of scarce production factors and foreign currency in one direction, whether essential or not, precludes their use in another direction. And no two opposing goals can be simultaneously attained.

POPULATION GROWTH VERSUS HIGHER LIVING STANDARDS

The most serious dilemma of economic development is posed by rapid population growth. The goal of raising living standards or per capita income cannot be reached even partially if present demographic trends continue. Until World War II, population grew by 1 percent a year. During and immediately after the War, the rate of growth climbed to 2 percent. In the mid-1960's it is ranging between 2.5 and 3 percent and is expected to reach 3-3.5 percent during 1970-90 before starting to decline. Assuming a medium projection, the population of the 13 Arab countries will rise to 165 million in 1980 and that of the three non-Arab countries to 85 million.[2]

The exploding population has already significantly offset past

[2] United Nations, *Provisional Report on World Population Prospects, As Assessed in 1963,* 1964, p. 143.

economic gains. Although food production during 1952/55—1962/65 rose by 3.1 percent annually—the highest among all developing regions—after allowance is made for the 2.5 percent rise in population, per capita food production advanced by only 0.6 percent annually.[3] Similarly, from 1950 to 1960 annual growth of total national income was 5.2 percent, but only 2.7 percent per head.[4]

Most Middle Eastern countries seek to double national income in ten years, an effort which requires an annual growth rate of

TABLE 1. *Population and Per Capita Gross National Product*

| | Population (1964) | | Per capita Gross National Product[a] (in dollars) |
|---|---|---|---|
| | Total in millions | Rate of growth | |
| *Arab countries* | | | |
| Algeria | 10.8 | 2.5 | 185 |
| Iraq | 7.0 | 1.6 | 228 |
| Jordan | 1.9 | 3.2 | 199 |
| Kuwait | 0.4 | 9.0 | 3,300 |
| Lebanon | 2.0 | 2.5 | 383 |
| Libya | 1.3 | 1.5 | 359 |
| Morocco | 13.1 | 3.0 | 173 |
| Saudi Arabia | 6.4 | 1.0 | 175 |
| Sudan | 13.1 | 2.8 | 100 |
| Syria | 5.6 | 3.6 | 148 |
| Tunisia | 4.6 | 2.5 | 185 |
| UAR | 28.7 | 2.5 | 139 |
| Yemen | 4.0 | ... | 90[b] |
| *Non-Arab countries* | | | |
| Iran | 22.7 | 2.5 | 216 |
| Israel | 2.5 | 4.0 | 1,111 |
| Turkey | 30.8 | 2.9 | 233 |

*Source:* Agency for International Development, *Proposed Mutual Defense and Development Programs FY 1966. Summary Presentation to the Congress,* Washington, D. C., March 1965, pp. 239-43.

[a] Per capita Gross National Product data (generally in 1963 prices) are unadjusted for inequalities in purchasing power among countries. The terms national income, Gross National Product and Gross Domestic Product are used interchangeably in this study to show general orders of magnitude for economic growth and living standards.

[b] The United Nations *Yearbook of National Accounts Statistics 1963* (p. 323) estimates per capita Gross Domestic Product for 1958 at $50, probably a more realistic figure for 1963 too.

[3] Food and Agriculture Organization of the United Nations, *The State of Food and Agriculture 1965,* 1965, p. 16.
[4] United Nations, *World Economic Survey 1963. I. Trade and Development: Trends, Needs and Policies,* 1964, pp. 19-21.

7.2 percent in output of goods and services. Only some of the oil-producing countries (Saudi Arabia and Kuwait) and Israel have consistently achieved comparable or higher rates. Most of the other countries, including oil-rich Iran and Iraq, have not been able to improve upon the average growth rate of 5 percent achieved in the 1950's. With population rising at 3 percent yearly, per capita national income will advance at best by 2 percent a year. At this pace, it will take 35 years for individual incomes to double.

Population growth has imposed other severe social and economic burdens. According to the 1960 census, more than two-fifths of Egypt's 26 million people were under the age of 15. This group contributes little to production but requires heavy government expenditures on health and education. Underemployment in rural areas and overcrowding in urban centers have become increasingly acute problems. The number of inhabitants in Cairo grew from 2.7 million in 1957 to 4 million in 1964. The mushrooming cities need high rates of capital investment for streets, water supply, electricity, waste disposal, mass transit and markets. But such investment has received low priority in development programs,[5] even in such a country as Lebanon which has one of the highest living standards in the Arab world.[6] This neglect is particularly acute in the squatters' settlements of peasants—the *bidonvilles* in Algiers, *barrakas* in Tripoli, *sarifas* in Baghdad and *gecekondus* in Istanbul.

Middle Eastern countries have not incorporated family planning as an integral part of development planning. The only exception is Tunisia, the first Arab country to commit itself to birth control on a national scale. Following a pilot project in 1963, Tunisia has experimented with a variety of family planning techniques. Special clinics have been established in maternal and child welfare centers, with birth control supplies provided free. The Health Ministry launched a nationwide information campaign, followed up by visits of field workers. The Population Council of New York administered a grant of $200,000 from the Ford Foun-

[5] United Nations, *Report on the World Social Situation,* 1963, p. 97.

[6] "The population of Beirut has doubled in the last ten years, outstripping the water supply, sewage disposal and telephone service—government enterprises in which no one, least of all the taxpayer, wants to invest." The New York *Times,* November 20, 1965.

dation to support the program for 1964-65.[7] The only other two countries to begin preliminary family planning programs in the early 1960's have been Egypt and Turkey, also with the support of the Ford Foundation and the Population Council.

Widespread illiteracy, socio-economic attitudes toward family size and the belief of the masses that religion forbids birth control (even though Muslim theologians have declared that Islam contains no such doctrinal prohibition) make acceptance of family planning a slow process. But more nations might well emulate Tunisia's systematic long-term approach.

## CONSUMPTION VERSUS INVESTMENT

In common with other developing countries, Middle Eastern nations face a set of choices specifically related to the content of their development schemes. The most significant conflict is between current consumption and capital formation—between more consumer goods now or more investment in basic facilities which will make possible greater production five or ten years hence. The countries of the area cannot raise living standards and promote economic growth without stressing long-term investment, yet they cannot fail to meet at least some of the rising expectations for more immediate benefits.

Still in their initial stages of development, Middle Eastern countries must allocate a large share of expenditures to infrastructure—dams, roads, railways, ports and telecommunications. Even Egypt and Iran, which have relatively well-developed transportation and communications networks, are devoting one-fourth of all public investments to that sector alone. The establishment of directly productive facilities—such as industrial plants, mines and new farms—must await completion of the costly pre-investment projects. The 55-mile-long Mecca-Taif road, which opened up previously inaccessible areas in Saudi Arabia, took nine years (1956-65) to build at a cost of $40 million; the country's projected 6,200-mile highway system will be completed in 1970 at a total cost of $250 million. After eight years (1956-64) and an investment of $67

[7] The Population Council, "Tunisia: Proposed Family Planning Program," *Studies in Family Planning*, New York, December 1963, pp. 3-4, and *Report for the Calendar Years 1962 and 1963*, New York, pp. 22-23.

million, the Khuzestan Project—Iran's TVA—made possible the irrigation of an initial 50,000 acres, benefiting 12,000 people.

Some countries such as Morocco have tried to shorten the waiting period by emphasizing more immediately productive schemes—expanding the production of sugar beets and other commercial crops and installing minor irrigation networks. But there are definite upper limits to the extension of such short-term projects, as the resources (e.g., irrigated land and electric output) supplied by the major projects reach full utilization.[8] These were the major considerations which induced the UAR to build the Aswan High Dam, the world's largest rock-fill dam. The project will increase acreage by 30 percent and greatly increase electric output for industry when completed in 1969 after ten years of work and an investment of $1 billion. But in the meantime, it has tied up vast amounts of materials and equipment as well as 24,000 workers, including 3,000 Egyptian technicians.

The results of Egypt's first five-year plan (1960-65) fully exemplify the conflict between consumption and investment. The government acknowledged that the production sector (agriculture, industry and mining) fell 33 percent short of its goal, while the money supply and private consumption were far in excess of the plan's estimates. During 1964 and 1965, Egypt suffered from critical shortages of food and consumer goods; rising prices and black markets appeared even on the village level. At the same time, many of the 835 industrial enterprises established during the plan period operated far below capacity due to scarcities of raw materials and spare parts caused by lack of foreign exchange.

Some aspects of this conflict, notably the rise in disposable income without a corresponding increase in the output of consumer goods, are inherent in the development process. But the Egyptian government accentuated the clash by pursuing contradictory goals. By giving factory workers and civil servants new benefits under the 1961 socialization laws, the government increased current consumption. But by carrying out a multi-billion dollar plan based on investment in the Aswan scheme and heavy industry, it decreased current consumption in favor of future increases.

[8] In developing human rather than man-made resources, the short-term solution is even more questionable. After vainly trying to turn out technicians quickly, the Moroccan government decided that training courses should last several years.

As the first five-year plan came to an end in June 1965, both consumption and investment had to be curtailed. A system of forced savings was imposed on civil servants and employees of nationalized enterprises, and instalment buying of consumer durables was halted. As for the second five-year plan, at first it was to be extended by two years to mid-1972, but then in October 1965 the government announced that the cost estimates of the plan would be more realistically based. Even as Egypt was struggling with the 1960-1970 overall plan, the deputy premier for culture and national guidance proclaimed: "We have another bold plan for doubling the national income within ten years." [9]

Some of the oil-producing countries have also had to contend with the consumption-investment clash. In the 1950's Iraq and Iran allocated as much as 70-80 percent of oil revenues to government investment. However, the share was progressively reduced to less than 50 percent; the other 50 percent went to burgeoning ordinary budget expenditures (i.e., current government consumption). In Saudi Arabia much of the oil income was squandered through conspicuous consumption by the royal family. The decisive switch in the use of oil revenues for development did not occur until Faisal replaced Saud as King in November 1964 and cut the allotment for the private treasury from 17 percent in the 1957/58 budget to 5.5 percent of the 1964/65 budget.

INDUSTRIALIZATION VERSUS AGRICULTURAL DEVELOPMENT

Another major conflict of economic development is agriculture versus industry, i.e., given a particular allocation between consumer and capital outputs, should capital facilities go for the expansion of farming or manufacturing? While all Arab countries are committed to industrialization, only in Egypt have investments in industry outstripped those in agriculture. Egypt's first five-year plan allocated 31 percent of expenditures to industry (plus 6 percent to power), compared with 24 percent to agriculture.

Industrialization has great popular appeal in many developing countries for it is felt that this is the surest way to diversify one-crop economies, build up national power, create employment and transform static agrarian societies into advanced and progressive economic systems. But the industrialization drive has given rise to

[9] *Arab News and Views,* April 15, 1965.

several paradoxes and problems. In the first place, while contributing substantially to productivity, industrialization has done little to ease the massive unemployment-underemployment problem. Industrial development in Egypt during 1952-63 provided work for 350,000 persons;[10] however, in a single year population grew by 650,000. Automation in the big Egyptian cotton mills and in some newly established industrial plants provided very limited employment opportunities. As one UAR official put it: "If more workers are hired for employment's sake, we lose the efficiency benefits of automation." [11]

Another problem is that industrialization has been accompanied by growing food imports. Arab world imports of American surplus food, which were $276 million in the fiscal year 1964 alone, have totaled $1.5 billion since 1946. Some of the major reasons for the growing food imports were unrelated to industrialization. They were the rising population and consumption levels, drought and the initially disruptive impact of land reform on agricultural production (e.g., in Iraq and Syria). But industrialization also contributed to the apparently paradoxical situation whereby countries could not feed themselves, even though 60-75 percent of the labor force was engaged in farming.

The relatively well-paid industrial workers, constituting about 10 percent of the work force, created a greater demand for food products. Previously many of them were underemployed peasants who at least met their own minimum requirements. In some countries, notably Iraq during 1958-64, agriculture was actually neglected as a result of overhasty industrial development. Even in Egypt—where the case for industrialization was more compelling than elsewhere due to the scarcity of arable land—*planned* investment in agriculture lagged, while industrial investment exceeded the target rate.[12] In Libya employment opportunities opened up by

[10] An extreme but increasingly more characteristic example is that of the Eregli steel mill in Turkey. Completed in 1965 at a cost of $280 million, it provided work for less than 3,000 workers.

[11] The New York *Times,* May 21, 1962. An example of still another conflict—between efficiency in government administration and social welfare aspects of employment—is shown in the following report: "On the day that efficiency was being urged by Premier Mohieddine, the Government was announcing plans to make room for most of the 26,000 new university graduates in need of work." The New York *Times,* November 14, 1965.

[12] Food and Agriculture Organization, *op. cit.,* p. 128.

the booming oil industry and soaring oil revenues led to migration from the rural areas and to the decline of the subsistence agriculture on water-deficient lands.

Still another problem concerns the direction of industrialization. In most countries, the emphasis has been on light industries such as food processing, textiles and building materials, all of which utilize local raw materials. More recently, enterprises assembling consumer durables (cars and refrigerators) and packaging pharmaceuticals have been started. Egypt and Turkey also have moved into heavy industries producing steel, railway freight cars, engines and machinery. Several other countries—including Algeria, Iraq and Saudi Arabia—are implementing plans for steel mills and petrochemical complexes. In the long run, some of these industrial plants may justify themselves on economic grounds. In the meantime, many are "national monuments" rather than creators of competitive commodities as in the case of Turkey's aircraft engine factories and steel mills,[13] and heavy drains on resources as evidenced by Egypt's Helwan steel mill.[14] Industrialization can make important contributions to development, but only to the extent that it is carried out in close interrelationship with agricultural development and in directions which are economically feasible.[15]

PRESTIGE VERSUS NECESSITIES

The conflicts between consumption and investment, agriculture and industry are essentially economic. But even in these areas, choices and priorities are often dictated by other considerations: steel mills are wanted for the sake of national power, short-term projects are pushed to hasten benefits to restive masses. In another set of conflicts, the non-economic factors—ideological, political,

[13] A. J. Meyer, "Economic Modernization," *The United States and the Middle East* (edited by Georgiana G. Stevens), Englewood Cliffs, New Jersey, 1964, p. 61.

[14] "Coke is imported, through Alexandria, and iron ore is carried from Aswan, nearly 1,000 km. away; owing to these high transport costs, to the relatively small scale of the plant, to operation below capacity . . . , to the inexperience of management and workers, and to the inadequate use of by-products, costs of production are twice as high as those of imported goods and quality is inferior." Charles Issawi, *Egypt in Revolution: An Economic Analysis,* London, 1963, pp. 329-330.

[15] See World Bank and IDA, *Annual Report 1964-65,* 1965, p. 54, for a particularly forceful statement on this problem.

military, social and psychological—are decisive, with economic considerations largely cast aside. It is not the main concern of this particular study to inquire why Arab nations have made certain choices of goals—a question best left to historians, political scientists and sociologists—or to express value judgments as to whether the choices made are good or bad, desirable or undesirable. What is relevant is that the non-economic decisions involve both visible and hidden costs which are cumulatively enormous.

Preoccupation with external affairs leads to neglect of domestic problems. The opportunity cost of growing military establishments is the sacrifice of constructive civilian projects. Likewise, essential development schemes compete with dubious prestige projects for use of resources and foreign exchange. The "showcase" projects take several forms. While they are common in heavy industry, they occasionally also occur in agriculture. One example is the costly Tahrir (Liberation) Province reclamation scheme, an early showpiece of the revolutionary regime in Egypt, which ran into technical difficulties due to inadequate preparatory study, inefficiency and corruption.[16] Another type can be found in the mass communications media. Radio and television fulfill important educational and informational purposes, but in some countries the facilities built far exceed functional requirements. Networks have been widely used for domestic propaganda campaigns and Arab propaganda wars. Cairo's *Voice of the Arabs* is estimated to have a budget comparable to that of *Voice of America*. Its medium-wave transmitting station with a power of 1,000 kilowatts, completed in 1963 at a cost of several million dollars, was said to be the strongest in the world at the time.[17] In 1965 Saudi Arabia signed a $3 million contract with a French firm for construction of two transmitters with combined power of 1,200 kilowatts.[18] National airlines too build up prestige, but operate at losses due to low load factors.

Luxurious structures in and around the capital comprise still another category. In its third year of independence, Algeria engaged in this type of superfluous spending: a $20 million international fairground, a 100,000-seat Olympic stadium and a $30

[16] Issawi, *op. cit.*, p. 132.
[17] *Ibid.*, p. 217.
[18] *Le Commerce du Levant—Beyrouth-Express*, May 8, 1965.

million convention site built for the (indefinitely postponed) 1965 Afro-Asian Summit Conference. The various prestige projects not only were intended to develop national identity at home and a better image in the Arab world; they also served countries such as Egypt and Algeria in their bid for leadership in the Afro-Asian bloc.

## CIVILIAN VERSUS MILITARY

Costly as the prestige projects are, they do not compare with the amounts lavished on the military establishments. In a majority of countries, 10 percent of the Gross National Product and as much as half of ordinary budget expenditures go for military purposes. Military budgets in Arab countries absorb more than $1.5 billion in local funds each year, exclusive of Soviet and Western military aid. In a speech marking the thirteenth anniversary of the Egyptian Revolution, President Nasser claimed that Egypt's military budget for 1965/66 totaled £E220 million or $506 million (including aircraft, rockets and military factories). This sum compared with an average annual investment of $686 million during the first five-year plan and exceeded 10 percent of total national income ($4 billion). In the 1961/62 fiscal year, Egypt spent £E100 million or 7 percent of the GNP on defense, a figure higher than found in most NATO or nonaligned countries (6.5 percent in Britain, 4.3 percent in Turkey and 2 percent in India).[19]

The three year war in Yemen cost Egypt a minimum of $30 million a year in hard currency.[20] The development of missiles and jet aircraft has absorbed about $50 million in hard currency a year since 1960.[21] Despite these huge expenditures, former President Amin Hafez of Syria taunted Egypt that Syria spent 60 percent of its budget on the armed forces, whereas Egypt spent only 11 percent (an invalid comparison in view of the entirely different budget systems in the two countries).

The reasons for the mounting diversion of resources to military ends have had little to do with the global cold war or with membership in Western military alliances. The contributing factors were regional and domestic: chronic internal instability, Arab-Israeli ten-

[19] Issawi, *op. cit.*, pp. 277-78.
[20] *The Christian Science Monitor*, August 24, 1963.
[21] The New York *Times*, August 1, 1965.

sion and inter-Arab squabbles. In Syria all three factors operated
at the same time, thus explaining why a larger share of the
ordinary budget recently has been allocated to defense than
in any other Arab country. In Saudi Arabia the inter-Arab confrontation over the Yemen civil war was largely responsible for
swelling defense spending from $58 million in 1961/62 to $162
million in 1965/66. As a result of Egyptian bombings of its territory at the height of the Yemen war in 1964, Saudi Arabia signed
agreements with Western powers for the purchase of supersonic
planes, antiaircraft missiles, radar equipment and supporting facilities which would cost an estimated $400 million.

Military conflicts of one type or another, lasting even longer
than the Yemen war, took place in almost every part of the area:
rebellions of Kurds in Iraq and southern tribesmen in Sudan; ter-
rorism in Aden; and border clashes between the Arab states and
Israel. The list of short-lived conflagrations is much longer, including, in the Maghreb alone, the Berber revolt in Algeria and
the brief Algerian-Moroccan war. The true economic costs involved were far higher than indicated by military outlays. Most
Iraqi cotton production was suspended during the Kurdish rebellion. State experimental farms in southern Sudan were abandoned. Yemen in particular suffered heavy general damage.

## STABILITY VERSUS INSTABILITY

The question of political stability or instability—no less than
that of war or peace—has crucial implications for development.
Frequent *coups* and unresolved power struggles inflicted inestimable
economic losses. Few examples parallel the economic setbacks
experienced by Iraq as a result of successive convulsions since the
July 1958 revolution. Long regarded as the Arab country with the
greatest development potential, Iraq saw its economy come to a
virtual standstill. Its development program—viewed as a model
before 1958—was drastically revised several times; it became little
more than a list of unrelated projects without priorities. Many
schemes were neglected. A huge abandoned agricultural project
near Baghdad supported only six families. Irrigation canals near
the Euphrates River vanished into the desert. Agrarian reform
made little headway. Political purges eliminated experienced technicians. Wholesale nationalizations in 1964 frightened away local

investors. Each regime did little more than blame its predecessors.

Syria's political instability—punctuated by such extreme shifts as union with Egypt in 1958, secession in 1961 and a Ba'th *coup* in 1963—was only slightly less disastrous. Successive *coups* reversed government economic policy, altered economic relations with neighboring Arab countries and jeopardized loan negotiations with both Western and Communist countries, particularly regarding the Euphrates dam project.

## DOMESTIC VERSUS EXTERNAL

Both in Iraq and Syria, internal instability has been closely tied with regional instability. Due to the overriding questions of Arab nationalism and Arab unity, domestic and external affairs are not as clearly separated in the Arab world as in other parts of the world. Yet the domestic-external clash is very real, for the external issues—be they inter-Arab, Arab-Israeli, Arab-Western or even East-West conflicts affecting the area—have invariably drawn energies and resources away from domestic development. They dominated the Arab scene after turning points in relations with the West (e.g., the Soviet-Egyptian arms deal of 1955), the big crises (e.g., the 1956 Sinai-Suez war) and major revolutions (e.g., the 1963 Ba'th revolutions in Iraq and Syria).

The two moderate leaders of the Maghreb underscored differing aspects of this clash. King Hassan II of Morocco stated at the opening of the third Arab Summit Conference in Casablanca that the struggle against Israel was "primordial," but economic development was "no less important." [22] Tunisia's President, Habib Bourguiba, referred to a more basic aspect during a visit to Morocco: "If certain African leaders busied themselves more with their countries, instead of with imperialism or neo-colonialism, and if they rid themselves of their revolutionary or leftist complexes, I think their countries would gain by it." [23] He added that by devoting more energy to development, nations would assure stability and obtain much-needed aid.

In his 1965-66 foreign aid message President Johnson stressed that long-term loans would be concentrated in countries which help themselves, eliminate waste and avoid expenditures on "un-

[22] The New York *Times,* September 14, 1965.
[23] The New York *Times,* October 24, 1965.

necessary armaments and foreign adventures." He singled out Tunisia and Turkey as the two Middle East countries meeting these standards. On the other hand, Washington frequently advised the Nasser Government that its foreign involvements were major stumbling blocks to continuing American aid. As the leading Arab country constantly attempting to maintain its revolutionary momentum, the UAR has been the focal point in most inter-Arab and some Afro-Asian disputes; for the same reason, it tended to emphasize prestige projects and military expenditures which were often linked to its external goals.

NATIONAL VERSUS REGIONAL DEVELOPMENT

The intractable Arab-Israeli and inter-Arab controversies also cost the nations of the area the gains they might have derived from regional integration. The Middle East lags behind all other developing areas in supranational economic cooperation. It is the only part of the world without a regional UN Economic Commission (because of the refusal of Arab countries as far back as 1948 to include Israel) [24] and the only one without a regionally-sponsored development bank. The economic costs of non-cooperation between the Arab states and Israel are staggering. Aside from the burdens of the arms race and the human and physical losses of two wars and hundreds of border clashes, they include the forfeiture of benefits from trade, tourism, communications and technical collaboration in such fields as desalinization and arid zone hydrology. But the most glaring example concerns the Jordan River waters. Not only are the separate Israeli and Arab water diversion projects much costlier than the unified scheme proposed by the United States-sponsored Johnston Plan, but ironically even constructive irrigation works have led to increased military spending to protect the opposing schemes.

Among themselves too, Arab states chose national over regional development, just as they elected particular nationalisms in preference to area unity. The list of Arab League-initiated paper schemes is long: a $56 million Arab Development Bank first proposed in 1951, an Arab Construction Company, Arab Petroleum Company, Arab Aviation Company, and an Arab Navigation Company. Be-

[24] Kurt Grunwald and Joachim O. Ronall, *Industrialization in the Middle East,* New York, 1960, p. 7.

cause these and many other schemes have failed, the national prestige projects seem all the more conspicuous and wasteful. An airline or steel mill, which may not be economically rational for a single country, might well have been more feasible for a group of countries.

An Arab Common Market, proposed in 1957, was implemented in January 1965. However, only five of the thirteen Arab League members joined—Iraq, Jordan, Kuwait, Syria and the UAR. In July 1965 the Kuwait National Assembly voted to withdraw. Both a special parliamentary commission and the local press argued that the Common Market would only hurt the country's free economic system. The President of the Assembly explained that with import duties as low as 4 percent, Kuwait was already a common market for all Arab countries. Algeria, Libya, Morocco and Tunisia began preparing their own Maghreb Economic Community in November 1964, under the sponsorship of the UN Economic Commission for Africa, thus partly reasserting their earlier detachment from the problems of the Machreq (Arab East). A number of bilateral economic pacts between like-minded countries (UAR and Iraq, Saudi Arabia and Jordan) also have shown few concrete results.

The only regional project which has proved an immediate success was the Kuwait Fund for Arab Economic Development, unilaterally established in December 1961 by the Kuwait government with advice from the World Bank. Capitalized at $280 million, the Fund made $106 million in loan commitments for specific projects in five Arab countries as of June 30, 1965.[25] During 1961-65 the small sheikhdom also gave more than $400 million in budget-support loans from state reserves, with little expectation of repayment; half of this sum went to Egypt and most of the rest to Iraq, Algeria and Jordan.

CAPITALISM VERSUS SOCIALISM

The foregoing issues of economic development have taken place within the framework of three other broad sets of conflicts which are the most fundamental. The first concerns the choice of economic system (private versus public enterprise, or mixed capitalism versus mixed socialism), the second, the choice of ideology (revo-

[25] Kuwait Fund for Arab Economic Development, *Third Annual Report 1964-1965.*

lutionary or traditional), and the last, the choice of relationship with the great powers (the West or the Communist bloc).

In terms of economic systems, no area offers as much diversity as the Arab world. Lebanon is perhaps the last true bastion of *laissez faire* capitalism, a mecca of free enterprise. Egypt's economy is the most socialized in the non-Communist world. The socialism of the secular Ba'th Party in Syria sharply contrasts with Saudi Arabia's liberal economic system, which, according to King Faisal,[26] is fully compatible with Islamic law. Yet these extremes do not indicate the spectral variety of systems in the area, nor do they convey underlying trends of change.

The 1960-64 period was marked by nationalization and socialization in those Arab countries which chose the revolutionary-radical path to modernization. The process began on a systematic basis in Egypt during 1960-61. By 1963, the government controlled the country's entire foreign trade and a large share of internal trade, over 90 percent of industry, all banks and public utilities. The trend gained momentum with the seizure of thousands of French-owned farms and factories by Algeria in 1962-63 following independence. In Syria the seeds of socialism were sown during its union with Egypt. But it was not until the Ba'th came to power in 1963 that socialization began on a large scale, reaching its peak in January 1965 with the seizure of 115 industrial concerns. In March 1965 three foreign and six Syrian-owned oil distribution companies were also seized. The Syrian government had previously nationalized all banks and insurance companies and 80 percent of foreign trade. In July 1964 Iraq nationalized the banks and insurance companies and 32 large enterprises, organizing them on the Egyptian model in terms of administration, compensation, profit sharing and employee participation in management.

In Egypt and Algeria the seizures were directed first against the extensive foreign investments and later against large domestic enterprises. In Iraq and Syria, where foreign investment was negligible outside the oil sector, mainly domestic enterprises were affected.

By 1965, the UAR, Algeria and Iraq began to reassess their sweeping socializations (which left few enterprises worthy of nationalization) and to reconsider their attitudes toward private

[26] *Saudi Arabia Today,* October 1965.

enterprise and foreign investment. This reappraisal may have had something to do with the climate of economic reform introduced into the Soviet economic system by the post-Khrushchev leadership. Basically, these reassessments reflected a new mood of ideological pragmatism in the Arab world, in contrast to the more doctrinaire views which prevailed in the early 1960's. The new thinking can be traced to the collapse of the 1963 unity talks involving the three revolutionary countries of the Arab East (Egypt, Syria and Iraq) and to the more harmonious inter-Arab relations brought about by three summit conferences held in 1964 and 1965. The pause in the movement to unify the Arab world allowed the attentions of government to shift to economic development and other urgent domestic problems for the first time in several years. The liberalizing trend took a firm hold with the installation of new governments in the three countries in the last half of 1965. Finally, the reluctance of foreign companies to invest in countries which did not compensate expropriated investors, the loss of entrepreneurial talent, the flight of private funds to Lebanese and Swiss banks and the increase of domestic hoarding contributed to the growing realization that economic growth can be accomplished best by relying on both the private and public sectors.

Iraq—the most recent country to initiate revolutionary socialism —began the trend back to pragmatic socialism, in fact, to an empirical mixed economy. The Government of Premier Abdel Rahman Bazzaz, which took office in September 1965, not only reaffirmed the declaration of earlier cabinets as to the importance of both the private and public sectors, but also took the decisive step of liquidating the state Economic Organization which had been formed to run nationalized enterprises. The Government also announced that it planned to "correct mistakes resulting from the application of socialism" and to return the textile, cement and canning firms to private hands. The Premier defined the Iraqi version of socialism as the "social aspect of Arab nationalism that seeks to raise the standards of low income people." He stated on November 16, 1965, "We do not believe nationalization provides the only solution to our problems . . . we do not find it useful in Iraq." In another move, the Industrial Bank of Iraq offered foreign firms participations up to 40 percent in industrial ventures.

In 1965 Ba'thist Syria, which remained isolated in the Arab

world and largely outside the liberalizing trend, denationalized 26 small industrial concerns and returned a number of pharmacies to private owners. These actions were taken after the regime discovered that the seizures affected the middle class rather than big capitalists. Algeria's second President, Houari Boumedienne, who ousted Ahmed Ben Bella on June 19, 1965, declared that the country's industrialization plan would be based on local private capital and savings in collaboration with state and foreign investments. He stressed the need for a "climate of confidence" to encourage private investors.

Most significantly, the UAR began to revamp its socialist economy. The Government of Premier Zakaria Mohieddin, which was appointed in October 1965, did not denationalize any enterprises. However, in a major statement of economic policy, it announced that newly defined responsibilities of managers would allow more flexible decision-making and that material incentives would be provided for workers. The profit rate would serve as a yardstick for judging the efficiency of state enterprises.[27] At the same time, a government-sponsored National Production Conference issued a manifesto welcoming Western private investment. Egypt had previously exempted from nationalization only a select group of Western private concerns, mainly pharmaceutical firms and jointly-owned oil companies. The rationale for these exceptions was spelled out in the 1962 National Charter which accepted foreign investment as a last priority and only in indispensable operations "requiring new experience, difficult to find in the national domain." [28] The 1965 manifesto opened wider the door to foreign investment in a practical effort to utilize a deliberately-neglected source of outside capital and technology.

This new trend in the Arab world did not represent a change in basic outlook as much as it did tactical shifts of emphasis. The pendulum may swing back and forth, depending on the outcome of the new *coups* and relations with the outside powers. But the tendency toward economic realism was unmistakable in the dealings between Arab governments and Western oil companies. The resolution of several long-standing disputes in 1964-65 ushered in

[27] *International Financial News Survey*, XVII, November 19, 1965, p. 424.
[28] United Arab Republic, Information Department, *The Charter* [1962], pp. 61-62.

an unparalleled era of compromise and cooperation. A major royalty dispute between the companies and the Organization of Petroleum Exporting Countries was settled in December 1964. In July 1965—after nearly two years of negotiations—Algeria and France agreed to form a cooperative association for future gas and oil exploitation of the Sahara; existing Western oil companies were allowed to continue operations, despite earlier demands for nationalization. Also in 1965, the Iraqi government came to terms with the Iraq Petroleum Company on a variety of differences and announced a law would be issued to protect oil companies (and other concerns with special status) from seizure. Egypt began negotiations with several American oil companies for jointly-owned operations. Only Syria decreed that the state alone would own the country's still-unexploited oil wealth; however, late in 1965 a contract was awarded to a British group for construction of a pipeline from the Karatchuk field to the Mediterranean port of Tartus (after the Soviet Union indicated it could not supply the necessary pipe).

Demands for outright nationalization—voiced in some of the earlier Arab Petroleum Congresses—have been muted, as the oil-producing countries found several practical alternatives. These countries established national oil companies to operate in all phases of the oil industry, including petrochemicals. They also signed joint agreements with new companies (e.g., Japanese, German and Spanish) to reduce their dependence on the "majors." They negotiated successfully on *specific* demands for higher royalties, Arabization of staffs and surrender by the companies of part of the concession areas. The feeling of utter dependence on the oil industry—one of the main reasons for hostility to it—is also undergoing change as each country has begun to diversify its economy with the use of oil revenues. (Oil income has provided 60-90 percent of government budgets and even larger shares of foreign exchange receipts.)

These new departures in thinking manifested themselves as oil revenues of Arab governments mounted to $2 billion annually in the mid-1960's and as the list of major producing countries continued to grow. (Egypt, the chief "have not" country, expects to be a large exporter by 1970.[29]) The substantial indirect benefits from the oil industry also have become more widely recognized.

[29] National Bank of Egypt, *Economic Bulletin*, XVIII, Nos. 1 and 2, 1965, p. 6.

Almost entirely self-contained in the early 1950's, the petroleum industry is now more closely integrated in the national economies. The oil companies expended increasing sums on local wages and salaries and on purchases of local goods and services. They have encouraged local entrepreneurship and trained labor in new industrial skills.

## TRADITIONAL VERSUS REVOLUTIONARY

The most comprehensive conflict in the Arab world is between the revolutionary and traditional ideologies or approaches to modernization. This dichotomy has been stressed by a whole school of thought as the most useful framework for analyzing the contemporary Middle East; it has been the dominant thesis in the literature for nearly a decade. Indeed, the clashing ideologies embrace the entire gamut of issues facing the Arab nations: monarchy or republicanism, particular or pan-Arab nationalism, alignment or nonalignment, fundamentalist or reformed Islam. In terms of economic development also, the traditional and revolutionary camps show several notable differences. The revolutionary regimes have socialized large segments of their economies and relied heavily on Communist bloc aid. The non-revolutionary countries have maintained mixed capitalist systems and depended almost entirely on Western aid and oil revenues.

More importantly, entirely different elites are directing the development process and receiving its benefits. In the traditional camp, the ruling elites, holding both political power and wealth, include royal households, entrepreneurs, landlords, tribal chiefs and religious leaders. In the revolutionary camp, the new salaried middle class of army officers, technocrats and professionals is presiding over the disintegration of traditional society and the liquidation of the old elites and, at the same time, it is supervising modernization.

Yet the clash between the two groups is not nearly as sharp in the 1960's as it was in the second half of the 1950's when the "anachronistic, status quo, feudal oligarchies" of Nuri Sa'id in Iraq and Imam Ahmad in Yemen were pitted against the "progressive, liberated and reformist" Government of President Nasser. The salaried middle class and industrial workers also have gained steadily in the non-revolutionary countries. On the other hand, landless peasants and unskilled workers, who form the bulk of the population, have failed to share many of the benefits of social and economic reform in the revolutionary countries; their lot may have even worsened because of falling demand for unskilled labor caused by the break-up of large estates and automated industrial development. The age-old clash between mass and elite cuts across the traditional-revolutionary lines. The income and wealth gap between the new middle class and the masses is not as large as the gap between the oligarchy of the past and the masses, but as one observer stated, the gap in power and in education is actually greater.[30]

The main outlines of the development plans in both types of countries do not show striking variations. Both aim to double national income in ten years and both typically devote one-sixth of national income to investment. Even in such traditional countries as Morocco and Jordan, the share of government investment in the total is as high as 50 percent.[31] The differences in outside sources of financing are also narrowing, as Egypt and Algeria have turned to the West for new aid; some non-revolutionary countries (Kuwait and Jordan) have cautiously moved to establish economic ties with the Communist bloc. Above all, the results of development planning and social reform are too inconclusive to suggest that one or the other approach to the modernizing process is inherently superior.

Recent trends in the Arab world have shown greater signs of convergence than polarization. For as the revolutionary countries moved toward pragmatism, the traditional states put greater stress on accelerated development and moderate social reform. Indications of this tendency are evident in almost every country: vastly increased development spending in Saudi Arabia, large-scale low and middle income housing projects in Libya and Kuwait, tax and administrative reforms in Jordan, new labor and social security legislation in Lebanon. Thus an oversimplified convergence thesis,

[30] Albert Hourani, "Near Eastern Nationalism Yesterday and Today," *Foreign Affairs*, XLII, October 1963, p. 135.

[31] United Nations, *Development Plans: Appraisal of Targets and Progress in Developing Countries—World Economic Survey, 1964—Part I*, 1965, p. 33.

superimposed on an oversimplified dichotomy thesis, may provide new insights into the changing Arab scene.

## EAST VERSUS WEST

A final issue of vital importance is whether development will be undertaken in cooperation with the West or the Communist world. This choice has become available to the nations of the area only since the mid-1950's when the Soviet Union launched its aid and trade offensive. Between 1955 and 1965, the Communist bloc provided $2.3 billion in loan commitments to Arab countries. About $1.5 billion of the total went to Egypt (including $800 million promised for its second plan) and most of the rest to Algeria, Iraq, Syria and Yemen. This bloc also supplied several thousand technicians, 2,000 for the Aswan Dam alone. The chief advantages of Soviet aid have been its favorable credit terms (repayment in agricultural commodities with interest of 2.5 percent in 12 years) and its very existence as an alternative to Western aid.

Yet the Soviet drive has met with only limited success during its first ten years. In Syria and Iraq, there has been open disenchantment with the results of Soviet aid and large portions have remained unutilized even though the agreements were originally concluded in 1957 and 1959. Government changes in the two countries as well as in Algeria resulted in setbacks to Soviet influence, making the disenchantment reciprocal. Since 1963 Moscow began placing less emphasis on the revolutionary Arab countries (other than Egypt) and concentrated instead on strengthening ties with non-Arab Iran and Turkey. Separate agreements were signed with Iran and Turkey for joint dam projects. Trade was expanded with both countries. And in November 1965, the Soviet Union agreed to extend $200 million in credits to Turkey.

The chief reason for the limited gains is that the Communist economies simply do not have the capacity to underwrite economic development in the Arab world, buy its oil, meet its food deficits and satisfy the growing demand for consumer goods. Moscow's approach of concentrating on key countries (e.g., Egypt) also limited its ability to aid other Arab countries, particularly in view of commitments to less developed Communist nations and to Africa.

By contrast, much of the Arab world's postwar economic progress was linked directly or indirectly to Western activities. During World War II, Western armies left many public improvements and large amounts of money. Egypt, Palestine, Syria and Lebanon emerged in 1945 with sizable foreign reserves to initiate development; Egypt had accumulated $1.2 billion. Since the war, large-scale aid has come from the United States, Britain, France, West Germany and other Western nations. The U.S. alone provided $3 billion in aid between 1946 and 1964, the bulk of it in food surpluses purchasable in local currencies and in grants requiring no repayment. The World Bank and International Development Association (largely Western-supported) extended more than $200 million in long-term loans.

From 1946 to 1964 Arab countries received $14 billion in direct oil revenues paid by Western companies; wages and local purchases added another $2.5 billion. Most other sources of foreign exchange such as tourist income and emigrant remittances were also mainly Western (or were related to oil operations). Technical assistance came from private foundations as well as Western governments. The bulk of foreign trade, particularly imports, was conducted with the West. Lebanon turned to the European Common Market for a trade agreement in 1964; Tunisia and Morocco began discussions in 1965 for an association.

As one observer summed up the wide-ranging linkage of the countries of the area with the West: "The really massive source of gifts and loans was the West; their young men and women went West for education in a rising tide . . . ; those with funds to invest abroad bought shares in Wall Street, Zurich or London; and their economic advisers and technical assistance personnel came overwhelmingly from the West." [32] This same writer concludes that at no time has any nation or area, except perhaps nineteenth century England, been so dependent on overseas developments and commitments, and he forecasts that this dependence will continue to grow (in absolute though not in relative terms).

Yet it is this very dependence that spurred the drive of Arab nations for economic independence, creating clashes with the West

[32] Meyer, *op. cit.*, p. 74.

TABLE 2. *Oil Income and Long-Term External Aid* (in million dollars)

| | Oil Income[a] 1946-64 | United States July 1, 1945-June 30, 1964 | Soviet bloc[b] 1954-June 30, 1965 | World Bank and IDA as of June 30, 1965 | Kuwait[c] as of June 30, 1965 |
|---|---|---|---|---|---|
| *Arab countries* | | | | | |
| Algeria | 190 | 149.3 | 230 | 20.0 | 49.0 |
| Iraq | 3040 | 46.3 | 207 | — | 84.0 |
| Jordan | 35 | 431.6 | — | 8.5 | 37.6 |
| Kuwait | 4615 | — | — | — | — |
| Lebanon | 73 | 78.9 | — | 23.0 | 14.0 |
| Libya | 230 | 205.3 | — | — | — |
| Morocco | — | 451.0 | 12 | 32.1 | — |
| Saudi Arabia | 4842 | 46.6 | — | — | — |
| Sudan | — | 81.4 | 25 | 78.6 | 19.6 |
| Syria | 215 | 81.9 | 245 | 8.5 | — |
| Tunisia | — | 397.0 | 48 | 11.6 | 16.8 |
| UAR | — | 943.1 | 1441 | 45.2 | 209.4 |
| Yemen | — | 34.6 | 114 | — | — |
| Total | 13240 | 2947.0 | 2322 | 227.5 | 430.4 |
| *Non-Arab countries* | | | | | |
| Iran | 3020 | 798.4 | 6 | 157.0 | — |
| Israel | — | 996.8 | — | 70.1 | — |
| Turkey | — | 1933.5 | — | 98.6 | — |
| Total | 3020 | 3728.7 | 6 | 325.7 | — |
| Grand total | 16260 | 6675.7 | 2328 | 553.2 | 430.4 |

*Source:* All data compiled from United Nations and official government publications, supplemented by press sources.

[a] Includes only direct payments by companies to governments from the start of production through the end of 1964. Figures for Jordan, Lebanon and Syria refer to oil transit dues. Bahrain and Qatar received $167 million and $569 million in revenues between 1946 and 1964.

[b] Includes China. Data through 1962 are complete as summarized in United Nations, *International Flow of Long-Term Capital and Official Donations, 1960-1962*, E/3917, June 16, 1964. Figures since the end of 1962 include only loan commitments of $228 million for Algeria, $741 million for UAR and $72 million for Yemen.

[c] Loans by the Kuwait Fund for Arab Economic Development as well as from state reserves.

over foreign investment, trade and particularly aid.[33] Again, Egypt epitomizes this clash to its full extent. In 1964 and 1965, at a

[33] The clash has been sharpest between the nonaligned, revolutionary Arab nations and the West, fairly mild with the traditional Arab countries and negligible with Turkey and Iran. Developments in the two non-Arab countries have taken an entirely different direction. Both are linked with Western military alliances as well as the European Economic Community. Within the framework of their mixed economies, both have actively encouraged foreign investments and attempted to turn over state enterprises to private ownership.

crucial period for its economy, the government was locked in dispute with three major donors of Western aid. West Germany suspended aid (which totaled $400 million in various forms) over Cairo's implied recognition of Communist East Germany in retaliation for Bonn's recognition of Israel. The World Bank announced in September 1964 that no loans would be granted to the UAR and other members that expropriated foreign investments without fair compensation. (France agreed to lend $30 million in October 1965, only after Egypt released sequestrated French property.)

The long list of disputes with Washington includes the supplying of arms to the Congolese rebels, the involvement of some 75,000 Egyptian troops in the Yemen war, and the burning of the United States Information Agency Library in Cairo, not to mention Nasser's "jump in the lake" comment about American aid. In addition, Egypt violated the 1962-65 surplus food agreement by shipping rice to Communist countries in excess of agreed quotas. That agreement provided $432 million in American foodstuffs and during 1964 supplied over 83 percent of all wheat and wheat flour consumed by Egyptians. After expiration of the agreement in June 1965, Egypt requested $500 million in food over an additional three-year period. Even though many of the specific irritants were eliminated or moderated, Congress voted a provision in the 1965-66 foreign aid law limiting any new food agreement with Egypt to one year and requiring prior presidential determination that such aid was essential to United States national interests.

Regardless of motivation, Cairo's actions and words clearly clashed with the goal of seeking urgently needed aid. Similarly, the view expressed in the National Charter that aid was "a form of a tax that must be paid by the states with a colonialist past to compensate those they exploited for so long" [34] was hardly one which would have induced Western nations to offer amends for their alleged evils through indiscriminate outpouring of aid.

Indeed, many of the conflicts between the Arab world and the West go back to the colonial period. The colonial powers left behind a heavy psychological legacy and various distorting and retarding social and economic influences. In terms of mid-twentieth

[34] *The Charter,* p. 62. This view was reiterated by President Nasser in his opening speech to the Cairo conference of nonaligned nations in October 1964.

century values of welfare and development, they undoubtedly could have contributed more to the well-being of the peoples concerned. But the departing colonial powers also left behind an extensive infrastructure, a legal and administrative basis for development and a foundation for social services. They helped expand agricultural cash crops (cotton and sugar) and established mineral industries for export (oil and phosphates).

These "external economies" of colonialism are highlighted by comparing such extensively colonized Arab countries as Egypt and Algeria with Yemen, the only Arab country never touched by the Western powers in any form. Although a fertile country, Yemen has little to sell to the outside world. The republican leaders of the 1962 revolution openly admitted they had to start from scratch: the country had few roads, no railways, virtually no health centers and only a few dozen nationals with training of any sort. An American public administration expert, invited by the revolutionary government, observed in 1963: "If Yemen were an underdeveloped country, we might be able to help them here with technical advisers. But they haven't reached that stage yet. There's just nothing here to work with."

Despite this two-sided record of colonialism and the substantial role of the West in the postwar economic growth of the Arab world, national charters, press articles and independence day speeches have been quick to accuse past imperialism and present neo-colonialism for the area's economic backwardness. Plunder, exploitation, and more recently, the unfavorable terms of trade "imposed" on countries exporting primary commodities have been cited as the chief culprits. That this is not precisely the historical truth is of greater academic than practical importance. What is important is that the emphasis on the past or external causes of underdevelopment has distracted attention from the far more significant present and internal factors. The decisive factors slowing down economic development and canceling possible advances in living standards in the Arab world are those working from within: rapid population growth, unresolved power struggles, costly prestige projects, heavy military spending and—lofty though some of them may be—conflicting national goals.

# VII. The Politics of Rapid Population Growth in the Middle East[1]

## by J. C. Hurewitz

INCREASING ATTENTION HAS FOCUSED SINCE THE END OF WORLD War II on the rapid population growth that is taking place throughout the world, particularly in Latin America, Asia and Africa. For the most part the social scientists who have investigated the phenomenon have pointed to the serious economic and social dislocations to which it has given rise. But the political dislocations are no less serious. This is probably nowhere more evident than in the Middle East. The growth itself, in other words, is more than a matter of mounting numbers. It produces many changes in the distribution of population, while it intensifies and accelerates others. Interlocking political and economic factors also contribute to these shifts. It thus becomes necessary to probe into the entire process of

[1] The latest country statistics were taken from the United Nations, *Statistical Yearbook 1963*, New York, 1964, while the urban statistics for the most part were furnished by the statistical division of the Department of Economic and Social Affairs in the United Nations Secretariat. Reference was also made to Suzanne R. Angelucci and others, *The World's Metropolitan Areas*, Berkeley and Los Angeles, 1959, especially the tables on pp. 37-52.

A warning on Middle East statistics must be sounded. Census-taking machinery, introduced into one state after another, could commonly be described as little more than elementary. Iraq did not conduct its first nationwide census until 1947, while so large and long-independent a state as Iran waited nearly a decade longer. By 1964 only Libya, Saudi Arabia and Yemen (republican and royalist) have not yet tried officially to ascertain the exact size of their respective populations.

Though dependable at their best, Middle East demographic statistics are almost valueless at their worst. Anyone employing these figures must bear in mind that the margin of error varies from country to country. For it rests on the relative development of the state and on local conditions. The peasants, who basically mistrust the central government, are inclined to resist

population change before any balanced analysis of the political results can be made.

Rapid population growth in the Middle East as in the rest of Asia and Africa is a relatively recent trend, dating back essentially to the end of World War II. The region's population, it is true, had been rising steadily since the start of the nineteenth century. After 1945 it suddenly began to soar. The annual rate of natural increase in most Middle East lands in the years 1960-62 probably averaged 2.5 per cent, somewhat higher than the estimated world average in 1962 of about 2.1. No one may speak with certainty about Middle East demographic statistics. But on the basis of informed indications, at least 50 per cent more people lived in the area in 1962 than had seventeen years earlier.

It is generally conceded that the sharp postwar population rise in the Middle East may be attributed mainly to the concerted application of Western techniques of disease control. The process actually began in World War II, when Britain and her allies introduced into the region the large-scale use of modern drugs and insecticides to protect the health of their soldiers stationed in Middle East countries. The measures were stepped up after 1945 under the technical aid programs of the United Nations, the United States and other countries of the West and East. Efforts were made to eradicate malaria with DDT and tuberculosis with antibiotics. The enriching of diet built up the resistance of pregnant women and infants to debilitating or fatal maladies.

---

head-counting because of religious superstition no less than fear of conscription and taxation. Some governments omit altogether from their calculations the beduin. And in Lebanon, where in every respect the tabulation of vital statistics and the recording of occupations ought to be highly trustworthy, the census itself was so constructed as to avoid revealing the slightest modification of the numerical balance among the several religious communities on which local politics hangs.

Each country, moreover, fixes its own rules and categories, which makes it treacherous to use Middle East statistics for comparative purposes. Whereas in Egypt villages may range from a few hundred to well over 10,000 inhabitants, the Turkish government classifies as urban every administrative center whether it has 500,000 or only 500. Israel for its part breaks down the nonrural figures into municipalities, small towns, suburban districts and urban villages. The urban statistics of some countries include only the data for the cities as administratively defined; the urban statistics of others add the data for urban agglomerations. Despite manifest limitations, the available information can, if judiciously used, suggest the major outlines of the altering demographic patterns.

The accomplishments, though dramatic, could only be limited, because the low levels of sanitation and hygiene were just starting a leisurely and uncertain ascent. Still, the abrupt decline of infant mortality rates in many lands was impressive, as was the more gradual lengthening of life spans. Unaffected, of course, were the high birth rates. Overall improvement in health conditions would have to await the training of sufficient doctors, nurses and dependent technicians, the opening of hospitals, clinics and social welfare stations, and the dispersal of the medical and social benefits throughout each land. The only exception was Israel, whose levels of public health, personal hygiene and medical and social services compared favorably with those in the United States and the most advanced countries of Europe.

The Western methods for combating disease, it should be stressed, were adopted on the invitation of, and in cooperation with, the Middle East governments. The public employment of Western medical knowledge formed part of a comprehensive, irresistible and irreversible process variously labeled Westernization or modernization. Scholars studying the diffusion of Western technology through Asia, Africa and Latin America are prone to suggest that the process is a comparatively new one and that its impact on traditional societies almost everywhere has already been devastating.

Both premises in relation to most Middle East countries are overstated. Westernization as a concept for government action in the Middle East may be traced back to the Ottoman Empire in the eighteenth century. Yet admittedly, as a region-wide movement, it is a mid-twentieth century phenomenon. In the second postwar decade all Middle East governments—whether tradition-bound Yemen, Saudi Arabia and Libya or forward-looking Israel, Turkey and the United Arab Republic (Egypt)—were committed in principle, and most of them in fact, to programs that sought in varying combinations to develop economies, strengthen military establishments and raise social and cultural standards. Traditional society was manifestly being undermined throughout the region. But the results were uneven. The most dramatic changes were transforming the towns, while most Middle Easterners lived in villages, invariably the last places reached by modernization.

The startling growth of population in the postwar Middle East has contributed to the marked redistribution of population. The differences in the rate and quality of demographic change from zone to zone, and even from country to country, complicate the study, and where the pace is swift, almost defy durable analysis, since when pinned down and investigated in a static way, these postwar changes bear no more resemblance to the dynamic realities than does the pathologist's slide to the living organism. Yet, if the developments are examined closely, a pattern emerges.

The Middle East, which is here defined as stretching from the western frontier of Libya to the eastern frontier of Iran with an area of more than four million square miles, exceeds in size the United States and its possessions. Far more than half of the Middle East is desert, and indeed in some countries less than 5 per cent of the land is cultivated. Along the Mediterranean and in other zones where rain occurs, it tends, except on the Black Sea coast of Turkey and the Caspian coast of Iran, to be seasonal and the annual average low. Agriculture relies on rainfall, on the region's scattered river systems and to a small but growing extent on underground water resources. The region's population in 1962 was thrusting toward 125 million, or two-thirds that of the continental United States. More than four-fifths of the people of the Middle East live in countries possessing less than half the total land area; in fact, two-thirds of the total are bunched in the UAR, Turkey and Iran, which together encompass less than one-third of the land. Thus density estimates for Middle East countries can hardly be taken at face value. The density in Egypt, for example, is roughly seventy per square mile. But the density for the cultivated area along the banks of the Nile surpasses 1,800 per square mile, one of the most thickly settled agrarian districts in the world. The corresponding figures for Jordan are less than fifty per square mile for the country but probably close to 1,000 for the tilled acreage, primarily along the Yarmuk-Jordan river system.

Most affected by the population expansion have been the peasants, who account for some 70 to 75 per cent of the region's populace. Traditionally the peasantry sustained itself at the subsistence level, each village or cluster of villages living in virtually self-sufficient isolation. This was particularly true in countries or districts where the terrain was rugged and there were no rivers or seacoasts to offer natural means of transportation. In such places one of the first effects of large-scale road building, so conspicuously demonstrated in Turkey in the 1950's, was the progressive integration into the national economy of those villages situated along or near the new roadways.

From the regional norm, Egypt's experience differed visibly. The Nile furnishes a cheap means of transportation and delivers abundant water and fresh Ethiopian soil each year. This together with the warm climate makes Egyptian agriculture one of the most luxuriant in the world. Indeed, Egypt is the only country in the region whose traditional primitive rural economy is a market economy, as it was in ancient times when it produced grains and other foods for export. Egypt's population underwent a minor explosion in the early nineteenth century under the new regime created by Mehmed 'Ali Pasha, the founder of the late dynasty. The growth, in part aided by immigration, was due chiefly to economic, not medical, factors and, once set going, continued unchecked.

Under Mehmed 'Ali's management the cultivation of long-staple cotton was introduced, for which England became the best customer. The erection of irrigation canals and dams made it possible to bring a third more land under tillage and to augment the yields per acre. This policy, furthered by Mehmed 'Ali's grandson Isma'il, was continued after 1882 by the British, who at the opening of the twentieth century launched a system of perennial irrigation. Shortly before World War I the rate of natural increase started to outstrip the economic expansion and the desert tracts that could be reclaimed without ambitious development schemes. The ratio steadily worsened in the later decades. From a generously estimated three million in 1800 the number of people in Egypt multiplied ninefold by 1962, in contrast with a sixfold population growth in Europe in the two centuries between 1750 and 1950.

Elsewhere in the Middle East the improvement of farming did not get under way until after 1918. Almost all Middle East governments had to pay attention to rural economic development. But in many cases this depended, not on reclamation of unused arable land, but on the extension of the planted area and its more intensive use by harnessing rivers and discovering underground water resources. Such schemes required long-term planning, capital outlay, concerted effort, technical skills and, above all, time. After 1945, therefore, rural economic development began to lag behind the multiplying peasantry. More and more villages, in fact, were bursting at their demographic seams. The temporary imbalance between the number of fallahin and the capacity of established villages to support them could be seen even in Iraq, where the agricultural potential was greater than in any other Middle East state, thanks to the bounteous Tigris and Euphrates rivers. Land reclamation there had to await the construction of dams for flood control and water storage and the building of irrigation and drainage canals.

At the close of World War II there was still much idle, rain-fed land in Syria. In the northeast Jazirah district, watered by the upper Khabur River and its branches, the French mandatory administration had encouraged settlement in the 1920's. The Anglo-American Middle East Supply Center fostered the further cultivation of the area in wartime and handed out mechanized equipment to farmers. Nor did the movement of fallahin to the Jazirah fall off in the postwar years. In the quarter century ending in 1955 some 2,000 villages sprang up. By then the district, having become the nation's breadbasket, supported some 160,000 persons, of whom more than 30 per cent arrived in the years 1949 to 1953 alone. Most of these peasants had migrated from villages in less obliging districts where economic development, if it was occurring at all, was doing so at a snail's pace. In Iraq and Turkey, as in Syria, the rural population pressure was segmental. In Egypt, Jordan and Lebanon it was general.

More and more peasants were therefore leaving the villages to look for employment in the towns and contributing to the hastening rate of urbanization in the Middle East. Ten of the region's cities would be considered large by any standards. These are located in seven of the independent countries, and six are capitals. The population of Cairo, according to the official estimate, passed 3.4 million in 1961, making it the largest city in the Middle East and Africa and the eighth largest in the world. Tehran, the region's runner-up, was at that time approaching 1.7 million. Two other cities, Istanbul and Alexandria, could claim roughly 1.5 million apiece, while Ankara was moving toward three-quarters of a million. Aleppo, Baghdad, Bayrut and Damascus were estimated to have about a half million each, and Telaviv-Jaffa, 400,000. Typical of these countries was the crowding of the urban settlement in one or at the most two places. In Iran the second largest city,

Tabriz, had a population less than one-fifth that of Tehran, while Egypt's third largest city, Port Said, was probably no more than a sixth the size of Alexandria.

The surging urbanization, it should be pointed out, could not be attributed entirely to peasant pressure, for the larger cities held many allurements. In the capitals, jobs abounded in the swelling bureaucracies of the centralized Middle East governments and in the industrial, commercial, financial and public institutional ventures agglomerating at the source of political power. Ankara, the capital of Turkey, has trebled in size since the end of World War II. And the population of Riyad, the Saudi Arab capital, in the decade after King 'Abd al-'Aziz's death in 1953, reportedly spurted from about 80,000 to more than twice that figure.

A powerful urbanizing force since 1945 has been the oil industry. This irresistible magnet, like the Suez Canal in Egypt in the late nineteenth century, could transform fishing hamlets and beduin campsites into bustling cities with satellite towns. The effects were first seen in Iran, where the Middle East petroleum industry is oldest. When chosen on the eve of World War I as the location for the Anglo-Persian Oil Company refinery and port of crude oil export, Abadan Island had but a few mud huts; by 1956 it was almost as large as Oklahoma City. In the three years (1951-54) during which the barren principality of Kuwayt moved into first place in Middle East crude oil production, it underwent a doubling of residents, largely through immigration. As before, most of them gathered in the capital. In Saudi Arabia, instead of a mass of people in one large city, many small townships emerged in the oilfield, pipeline- and pumping-station and port areas, at times in places previously uninhabited.

Cities could also unfold in spurts for political reasons, as Cairo and Alexandria in World War II when Egypt served as headquarters for the British war effort in the Middle East. The striking postwar expansion of Tehran by an estimated half million or more in the first postwar decade could be explained in part by an infusion of Azarbayjanis who, remembering the wartime occupation by the Russians and fearing a renewal of Soviet aggression, sought refuge in the capital. Jordan's Amman could never have multiplied by more than 800 per cent in thirteen years (1948-1961), were it not for the trebling of the country's inhabitants by the accretion of the interior of central Palestine after the Arab-Israel War of 1948-49 and the influx of refugees. Sometimes urban populations could be transplanted whole. Of the more than 100,000 Iraqi immigrants into Israel in 1950-51, mostly originating in Baghdad, the vast majority settled in the cities, chiefly Telaviv-Jaffa.

The region's urban population, meanwhile, was changing as it was growing. In the twentieth century all Middle East towns have called forth an indigenous middle class comprising businessmen and bankers, contractors and engineers, lawyers and doctors, teachers and journalists, as well as white-collar workers. The native middle class at first competed with its alien counterparts and then gradually supplanted them altogether, sometimes forcibly, as in the case of the Greeks in Turkey in the 1920's, the Jews in Baghdad in 1950-51, or the British and French in Egypt in 1956-57. The towns were also spawning a class of urban workers, who congested the enlarging slum areas.

While the urban and rural sectors of the populace were growing apace, the nomads and semi-nomads who formed no more than 10 per cent, and probably much less, of the Middle East population were shrinking in numbers. From the mid-nineteenth century on, the beduin in the Arab provinces of the Ottoman Empire were forced back into the desert from which they had spilled in the period of Turkish imperial decline. In the twentieth century the coming of the truck, the airplane and increasingly efficient weapons began to dislodge the nomads even from their role as masters of the desert. Some beduin became farmers; many moved easily into other pursuits. In Jordan the army was largely recruited from desert tribesmen. Some three to four thousand of the 18,000 Saudi Arabs employed by the Arabian-American Oil Company in 1957 were beduin. As in the nearby oil-producing countries, many of these individuals, after receiving training and experience, left the company to become entrepreneurs, technicians and laborers in the satellite enterprises that grew up around Aramco.

The infusion of large numbers of new residents into any society, whether undergoing slow or swift internal growth, is bound to influence its politics. Kuwayt is a case in point. The trebling of its population in the postwar years might initially have appeared an unmixed blessing. The ruler, after all, received greater revenue than he could possibly put to use in converting his desert patrimony into a welfare shaykhdom, and the attraction of skills and talents locally unavailable could only improve the quality of the development projects. In any event, the early appearance of an imported middle class produced pressures for modernizing the political system; and the employment predominantly of Egyptian (and Palestinian) teachers in the new model school system assured the indoctrination of Kuwayti children with the UAR's Arab Unity slogans. The Shaykh's benevolence thus hastened the day when his type of autocratic dependency became outmoded. After achieving independence from Britain in 1961, he promulgated a constitution that provided for an elective parliamentary system.

The overwhelming majority of the early immigrants into Israel were Europeans, who firmly implanted European political ideas, institutions and practices. Later, immigrants from Asia and Africa exceeded all others and, in any case, assured for themselves by their higher rates of natural increase a majority of the population. This transformation of Israel's society threatens to lower the levels of political maturity and sophistication, although it has not yet appreciably modified its Westernized democracy.

Jordan's formal absorption of central Palestine in April 1950 nearly trebled the population of the almost landlocked kingdom. Into the placid Hashimi patriarchy were thrust an articulate yet politically desperate people of much higher living standards and better education than the original majority of nomads and seminomads. Particularly after the rise of Abdul Nasser in Egypt, most Palestine Arabs by emotional preference tended to look to Cairo for the liberation of their former homeland. In these circumstances, the power of King Husayn was drained away in the early years of his reign. He acquiesced in the demands of his subjects for eliminating the British military presence and for transforming himself into a truly constitutional monarch. By early 1957 he had gone so far that he appeared on the verge of losing his crown, if not his head. At that juncture, in April 1957, he cleansed his army of elements disloyal to Hashimi rule and, relying on enlarged and modernized forces, established a new role as authoritarian monarch. In the years that followed, the survival of the nonviable kingdom was further assured, economically by American aid and politically by the inability of its neighbors to agree on the division of its territory.

Jordan alone among the Arab states that had inherited from the Palestine War of 1948-49 substantial numbers of refugees (Jordan's share surpassed half the total) accorded them full citizenship. Lebanon found compelling domestic reasons for withholding such privileges in its determination to preserve the "numerical balance" among its multiple religious communities—all of them minorities. Syria and Egypt, on the other hand, based their refusal to absorb the refugees on the desire to keep alive the Palestine Arab political claims against Israel. The Arabs uprooted by the Palestine War remain for the most part in refugee camps in Syria, Lebanon, the Egyptian-administered Gaza Strip and even Jordan. In the camps the former peasants, who far outnumber all others, have become quasi-urbanized, thanks to the educational, health and welfare services provided by the international community. Despite their economic idleness in crowded camps, the displaced Arabs continued to multiply at roughly the same rate as that prevailing in the host countries. Nor did the annual drain off of a few thousand individuals by employment and emigration hold the refugee numbers in check, so that by June 1964 they reached nearly 1.25 million, an increase of more than 285,000 in fourteen years.

The initial impact of economic and social development in the Middle East was segmental. The construction of dams and hydroelectric works affected only those living along or near the harnessed rivers. The distribution of plots to the peasantry under land reform programs had necessarily to be selective, for almost everywhere, especially in Iran and Egypt, the candidates far exceeded the available acreage. But even in Iraq and Syria, where arable soil remained potentially plentiful, resettling the fallahin dictated careful planning and took time. Thus a fraction of the total enjoyed the benefits long in advance of others. At the same time, the modernizing of communications and transportation was tearing down the walls of rural isolation. As the villagers lost their parochialism, they became articulate and insistent. If their neighbors had more water and fewer mosquitoes, more education and less hunger, they wanted the same advantages. To mounting numbers were added mounting demands.

The flow of villagers to towns was motivated in no small degree by an urge to satisfy their new wants; and the thronging to the capitals of domestic peasantry and foreign immigrants alike was based on the obvious realization that the fruits of modernization were most plentiful in the metropolis where the programs were being framed and administered. Almost all the metropolitan centers comprised large numbers of illiterate, semi-urbanized ex-peasants and, in some lands, ex-nomads, crowded into characteristic slums; underemployed quasi-intellectuals, products of an educational system biased against manual labor and in favor of white-collar pursuits or the legal profession; and just plain students, for a rapidly growing society is also a young one, and the largest and best secondary schools and universities are located in the capitals. Taken together, these groups, collecting at the very source of national power, form an unstabilizing political force in many Middle East lands, as in Asia and Africa generally. They are the stuff of which street politics are made.

Street politics in a metropolis can at times be used to make or break a government or a regime and shape the course of national policy. King Faruq of Egypt unleashed the rout that ran amok in Cairo on so-called Black Saturday, January 26, 1952, and then used their violent deeds to proclaim martial law and dismiss the elected government. Prime Minister Muhammad Mosaddeq of Iran resigned on July 17, 1952, because he had been refused control of the War Ministry. Three days of tumultuous demonstrations in the heart of Tehran (organized by Mosaddeq's colleagues as well as religious fundamentalists and communist-front groups) sufficed to have the fallen premier reinstated. As an illustration of the possibilities of manipulating street politics in Arab lands by remote control, the Voice of the Arabs radio station at Cairo in December 1955 could claim primary responsibility for inciting the mobs that took over Amman, Jordan, discouraging King Husayn from adherence to the Baghdad Pact, and bringing down the cabinet that was prepared to sign the instrument.

For a half-dozen years after its second victory at the polls in 1954, the Menderes Government progressively suppressed civil liberties in Turkey. The efforts of opposition parties and the press to keep democracy alive merely elicited further repressions. Nor was it accidental that in the spring of 1960 student demonstrations in Istanbul and Ankara as well as public indignation at the Government's handling of them sparked the overthrow of the Menderes regime. The military regime that succeeded it prevented street demonstrations in the major cities through the imposition of martial law. The reimposition of martial law under the Second Republic enabled the civilian government to curb Turkish student demonstrations over Cyprus in the spring of 1964. Similarly, the relative political calm in Iran after August 1953 and in Jordan after April 1957 was traceable to bans on public demonstrations, enforced by armies loyal to the crown. On the other hand, the mob did not necessarily disappear under military regimes. In Egypt or Iraq, for example, it was assembled in public squares whenever the leaders sought an audience for major pronouncements. The substantial civilianization of the Sudanese government in the fall of 1964, moreover, could be ascribed to the inability of the six-year-old military regime to bring under control in Khartum persistent student demonstrations, promoted by the outlawed political parties.

Another consequence of burgeoning capitals is swollen civil services. To the tendency for bureaucracies to expand as governmental functions multiply, the Middle East states are prone to add a consideration of their own, converting the civil service into a sort of WPA to siphon off from the ever widening pool of unemployed some of the excess white-collar workers and unskilled ex-peasants. Visitors to government offices in most Middle East capitals are struck by the numbers of doormen, orderlies and other semiliterate functionaries jamming the hallways. The conduct of business itself demands filling out mountains of forms, collecting multiple signatures and licking as many stamps. The records then accumulate as dead weight or are so poorly filed that in either case they can be recovered only with the greatest difficulty.

Thus just when efficient bureaucracies are most needed to handle mounting public services, the administrative machinery of many Middle East governments is becoming more inefficient. This condition is symptomatic of the lag of economic and social advancement behind the numerical growth of the people. It is baffling enough to mobilize resources, skills and leadership for the general uplift of a slowly expanding society. But the difficulties of planned development are compounded by the multiplying mouths to feed, children to educate and people to employ. Economists estimate that for every 1 per cent of growth of population at least 3 per cent of the national income must be invested in development merely to maintain existing standards. A yearly investment of 9 to 12 per cent would thus be required to lift the per capita income in most Middle East lands.

This has been happening in the oil-saturated countries, where revenues from the petroleum industry soared from $55 million in 1946 to a sum approaching $2.0 billion seventeen years later. But per capita income in this context is meaningless as an index of economic development. The Middle East oil resources are concentrated in states (Iran apart) of low population and (Iran and Iraq apart) of low development potential. Moreover, countries such as Saudi Arabia, Libya and the Persian Gulf shaykhdoms are also the most backward lands, where the natural population increase is doubtless slower than elsewhere in the Middle East.

Over 70 per cent of the region's people today live in oil-poor countries, which include the two with the largest populations, namely Egypt and Turkey. To achieve the requisite rate of capital formation in these lands, therefore, it was necessary to acquire substantial outside aid and the services of able and imaginative administrators and technicians. Extra-regional agencies initially supplied the technicians, who were supposed to train local personnel. But these efforts were almost always hampered, sometimes even nullified, by unenlightened government.

In the first postwar decade the political elite in most Middle East countries was still typically recruited from the landed gentry. The European powers had confirmed their monopoly of domestic rule in the Ottoman successor states of the Fertile Crescent as well as in Egypt, Sudan and Libya. The nationalist leadership in these lands came from the same ranks in the struggle for independence and in the early years of full self-government. Wherever the landed oligarchy governed sovereign lands, they failed to modify their political habits or widen their political horizons. They paid no more than lip service to modernization and favored only the species that might enhance their own positions. This was illustrated in the extravagances of the late monarchy in Egypt, the royal family in Saudi Arabia and the ruling oligarchy in Iran.

In the second postwar decade, however, all Middle East governments, even the most unenlightened, had been forced because of the expansion of population and increasing urbanization to commit themselves to welfare services: to providing employment, raising health and education standards and promising the people

an abundant life. But although most of the political systems had
been patterned on parliamentary democracy, the imported institutions never really struck root. Elements of traditional autocracy
survived and were often reinforced under the centralizing impact
of Western technology—the introduction of instantaneous communication systems, the development of up-to-date transportation
facilities, the modernization of the armed forces and the governmental planning and execution of development programs. Often the
resentment of the public against their leaders for failing to realize
the aspirations of welfare statehood came also to focus on "democracy" and on the West from which it derived.

The rash of military *coups d'état* in the postwar Middle East
was greeted with popular enthusiasm, for the army officers were
widely believed to be the sole repositories of efficiency, honesty
and selfless devotion to national interests. The officers were the
best disciplined members of their societies, having been taught how
to take and issue orders and to manage complicated operations.
No other organized group in any Middle East land could boast
comparable size, the same abundance of talent and rival means of
enforcing its will. Since the army officers, by and large, were not
identified with the traditional politicians or traditional politics,
they became, on seizing power, the embodiment in the public mind
of the one great hope of forging the effective machinery and furnishing the requisite leadership to achieve welfare statehood for an
expanding society.

Because of their lack of political experience the new leaders
were inclined to assume that they would be able with ease to
eradicate corruption, institute essential reforms and carry out
modernization programs. The military elites, however, have learned
that it is much easier to seize political power than to use it intel-
ligently. Abd al-Karim Qasim's regime in Iraq (1958-63) dismissed many administrators and technicians of the Development
Board, not for incompetence but because, having originally been
employed under the monarchy, they were politically tainted. What
is more, Qasim in 1961 precipitated a disastrous and expensive
civil war with the country's large Kurdish minority. Thus ironically, the one Middle East country that seemed to possess all the
essential ingredients for development—reclaimable land, plentiful
water and assured revenues, including ample hard currency—

faced a marked slowdown of its development efforts under a regime that proclaimed itself the inspired author of a social revolution. The multiple military regimes of Syria succeeded one another so swiftly as to prevent the implementation of any consistent government-sponsored modernization program. The exceptional military regime in the Middle East was that of Egypt which gradually and pragmatically, after 1957, framed and carried into effect an economic and social revolution.

The relentless growth of population and of the demands for development that helped bring into power the new military regimes and increasingly threatened the region's surviving civilian governments constitutes a problem that none of them has yet proved able to tackle forthrightly. The Middle East predicament, moreover, has become an American predicament. In almost all Middle East countries, the United States foreign aid program was sponsoring public health projects and distributing or selling agricultural surplus, both designed to keep more people alive. At the same time the program was avowedly seeking to give the economies of the recipient states the necessary thrust to become self-generating. On this issue the United States found itself immobilized in the late 1950's because of the public controversy over the desirability of the government's encouragement of birth control measures overseas. Nor did this position markedly alter in the early 1960's. It is therefore little wonder that the feeling prevails among those concerned with foreign aid that the unchecked population expansion is basically frustrating the attempts to achieve economic and social advancement in many Middle East lands.

# VIII.   The Economics and Politics of Oil in the Middle East

## by Stephen H. Longrigg

THE AREA TO BE COVERED DOES NOT PRECISELY CONFORM TO THAT
of the Middle East, for it cannot reasonably omit the Arabic speaking oil-bearing territories of North Africa, and cannot completely
be identified with the Arab world, since it must include the highly
productive territory of Iran and the as yet unproductive territories
of Turkey and Israel, geographically Middle Eastern but non-
Arab. A great deal of what can validly be said of the political and
economic aftermath of oil discovery applies, with varying degrees
of incidence, to all western-Arab, eastern-Arab and non-Arab
states alike, from Morocco to Iran.

Discoveries of oil in this region are of recent date; a bare half-
century has elapsed since the first strike in Iran. Thirty years ago
that country, Iraq, Bahrain and Egypt had a combined output of
less than 9 million tons a year, of which 7.5 million tons were
from Iran. By the end of the Second World War, production from
Iran had doubled to 14 million tons, Saudi Arabia had begun with
an output of 2.5 million tons, and Egypt and Bahrain maintained
their smaller contributions. During the last twenty years, the
original major producers have vastly increased their output and
have been joined by Kuwait, Qatar and Abu Dhabi on the Arabian
Peninsula, and by Libya and Algeria in North Africa. The hinter-
land of remote Oman has held strong hopes of future production
since mid-1964. No oil capable of making any appreciable impact
has yet been discovered in Yemen, South Arabia, Sudan, Jordan,
Lebanon, Israel, Tunisia or Cyprus. Deposits so far located in

Syria, Turkey and Morocco are, at the time of writing, practically negligible.

Among Arab countries in Africa, in 1963 Algeria with 24 million tons and Libya with 22 million easily led the way. Egypt, with 5.5 million tons, and Morocco with .15 million tons, followed. In Asia in 1963, the productive giants were tiny Kuwait with 97 million, vast desertic Saudi Arabia with 81 million, Iran with 73 million, Iraq with 56 million, and the jointly-owned Kuwait-Saudi Neutral Zone with 19 million tons. Qatar produced 9 million; Abu Dhabi, a newcomer, 2.5 million; Bahrain, a veteran, 2.5 million; Turkey, .75 million; and Israel, .15 million tons. Thus the total output of our designated region was some 390 million tons. It may be noted, for comparison, that North American production in the same year was 409 million tons, that of the Caribbean, 185 million, and that of Western Europe, 18 million. This summary of current production is subject to the proviso that the 1963 figures will certainly be exceeded by important percentages in 1964 and in subsequent years.[1] This is especially true of countries only recently in production in North Africa and Abu Dhabi. The rate of increase in annual production in our designated area has hitherto easily exceeded that recorded in any other part of the world, and this should continue to be the case.

This production derives from a multiplicity of fields in most countries. Only in Bahrain and Qatar is a single field responsible for all output, while in the major producing countries from four to twenty fields are in current production. These fields include a number of the largest in the world, and are characterized by extraordinary productivity, the need for relatively few wells, varied but highly marketable crudes produced under pressure, the advantages of single control over vast structures, the successful solution of technical and administrative problems and company management in the hands of experts with great experience. The relatively low cost of labour and the intelligence and adaptability of the popula-

[1] Production figures for January to June 1964, with the percentage by which these exceed the same period in 1963, are: Kuwait, 53.7 million (12.5 per cent); Iran, 41 million (11.4 per cent); Saudi Arabia, 40.7 million (1.8 per cent); Iraq, 30 million (11.2 per cent); Neutral Zone, 10 million (22 per cent); Qatar, 4.4 million (−0.8 per cent); Abu Dhabi, 3.7 million (311 per cent); Egypt, 3.3 million (17.5 per cent); Libya, 18 million (108 per cent); and Algeria, 13 million (10.5 per cent).

tion go far to compensate for often harsh desert conditions, lack of communications to operational sites, absence of any existing industrial infrastructure and remoteness from the world's main consuming markets. The oil should remain, in production cost, relatively cheap and certainly competitive, as long as producer-government relationships permit.

Production alone, however, does not exhaust the activities of the industry. There is, almost everywhere, continuous activity in exploration for new fields: constant oil field expansion, construction and maintenance; networks of connected installations, pipelines and wharfs; domestic and institutional housing; and services on a formidable scale. There are, moreover, in all but a few territories, one or more refineries, ranging from small topping-plants to full-scale export refineries. In certain cases—Bahrain, Aden, Syria, Lebanon—crude oil derived from another territory is treated. Some of the territories possess, as their main stake in the industry, transit corridors equipped with trunk pipelines. Thus Iraqi oil is piped across Syria and Lebanon, Saudi Arabian oil crosses these countries and Jordan and Persian Gulf oil heading for Europe passes through Egypt's Suez Canal. To summarise, a few of these countries are major producers of crude oil and are also important refiners—Kuwait, Saudi Arabia and Iran—while others are major producers with smaller-scale refining—Iraq, the Neutral Zone, Libya and Algeria. Some are medium-scale producers with only local refining—Qatar and Egypt—others have small or no production, but important refining—Bahrain, Turkey, Israel and Aden. Still others are without production but have transit interest as well as small refineries—Lebanon, Syria, Jordan and Tunisia—or have refining without such transit or production—Sudan and Morocco. These different categories, and all that follows from them, obviously affect the impact of the oil industry in each country.

A clear majority of Middle Eastern and North African countries, then, are either without oil or with humble resources, while the internationally important deposits are confined to two areas: the Persian Gulf and, on a smaller scale, central North Africa.

The present oil-output of the rich Middle Eastern area, amounting to only a quarter of current global production, is still but a feeble indication of its potential. The proved reserves of the region, on the other hand, add up to some 60 to 65 per cent of those of the entire world,[2] from which it follows that the deposits of some of these territories will certainly, in terms of recoverable liquid petroleum, outlast by decades those of all other regions, including North America. Meanwhile the area, by far the most important oil-exporting region in the world, is called upon to supply the needs of Western Europe, of much of Asia, Africa and Australia, and of the United States, to whatever extent American governmental regulations permit.

With the exception of this oil, the region is unusually deficient in natural sources of wealth. Desert, steppe and barren mountains fill the greater part of its land-surface. Rainfall is scanty; fertile soil, confined; exportable produce, limited; mineral wealth, humble; stock-breeding, forests and fisheries of little international significance; and industry as yet ill-developed. The area has suffered, as the first of its ills and main cause of its economic and social backwardness, from sheer indigence. Low living standards, limited ideas and initiatives and only rare accumulations of local capital have been the recognizable phenomena. With a few pockets of some affluence, the picture has been one of age-long, pervasive poverty.

The achievement of political independence by the countries of the Middle East and North Africa was roughly, but significantly, contemporary with the general spread of conceptions of government and society which demand a fairly high standard of national wealth. The new states have therefore attempted from the outset to maintain fully developed administrations, social services, armies and communications of twentieth-century size and quality. For all of this, the revenues of the treasury, as well as the purses of the citizenry, must be considerably larger than what would suffice for the relatively simple, bare-subsistence standards of the Turkish provinces or the Arabian patriarchal communities of yesterday.

In particular, one might cite Iran, Iraq and Bahrain as states which had been, before the discovery of oil, satisfied with a low standard of living and government. Countries scarcely viable without new wealth, but today abundantly blessed with it, are Saudi Arabia, Kuwait, Qatar, Abu Dhabi, Libya and Algeria. Oman may

[2] Proved reserves, in millions of barrels, were assessed in 1962 approximately as follows: North America, 45,000; South America, 23,000; Europe, 1,800; Africa, 12,000; Far East, 12,000; Middle East, 209,000; Soviet Bloc, 35,000 (though they claim vastly more). (Convert barrels to tons by dividing by a factor varying between 7.6 and 6.8—or, very roughly, by 7.)

soon join this list. Lesser recipients of the new revenue, but more or less viable without it, are Egypt, Syria, Jordan and Lebanon. The contribution of oil-derived revenues to these states varies from around 90 per cent in Saudi Arabia, Kuwait, Qatar and Abu Dhabi, to lower but still important percentages in the Fertile Crescent, Iran and the Lower Nile.

The process of compensating the local governments is carried out primarily by whatever concern has been, after bargaining, entrusted by the state with the exploitation of its oil, a resource which is considered state property throughout the region. This concern is, in most countries, the "blanket" or large-area concessionaire. Such is the case in all the leading producing countries. The sole exception is Iran, where complicated arrangements have superseded the original concession since 1954, but with similar financial results. The Iranian government has also lately entered into partnerships with foreign companies for the development of hopeful areas. In the North African countries arrangements with the foreign concerns are for limited rectilinear blocks of territory, for generally shorter periods and subject to a national petroleum law defining obligations and rights. Egypt alone has nationalized her oil production, processing and trading. In all cases, with the exception of Egypt, concessions have been modified from time to time, sometimes fundamentally, and always in the interest of the host country. Petroleum laws, where these exist, have similarly increased in severity. The principle whereby the government receives half the net profits made locally by the operating concern—that is, half the difference between the cost of producing the oil and conveying it to the point of export, and its value at that point—has prevailed everywhere since about 1950.

There are three channels through which the producing operators make their payments. First is the crediting to government of the royalty-cum-taxation dues on the tonnage produced. These are the massive block payments which have, more than anything, transformed the finances of the half-dozen most fortunate recipients. The total thus paid over by foreign companies in the region was nearly $2 billion or almost £700 million in 1963.[3] Secondly,

[3] Some figures for 1963 (millions) are: Kuwait, $560 (£200); Saudi Arabia, $475 (£170); Iran, $380 (£135); Iraq, $308 (£110); Qatar, $59 (£21); Algeria, $45 (£16); Libya, $92 (£33); very roughly one may assume that $6.30 (£2.25) are payable per ton of oil.

various local or departmental bodies in the host country have their claims, for urban taxes, customs and port duties, railway and air charges, and postal and telegraph dues, which must be met. In the transit countries there are important way-leave payments by the pipeline owning companies to the governments, as well as canal dues in Egypt. Tonnage dues on refinery throughput of foreign oil, as at Bahrain and in Lebanon, can be considerable. Thirdly come the numerous items, partly invisible, whereby the companies and their employees directly aid economic development. Examples of these are the distribution of wages[4] and salaries, the profit on greatly varied local purchases, the hire of lands, buildings and transport, and the often important profits accruing to local contractors for buildings, engineering, supply and transport.

Of the second category of those classified above, little need be said. Governmental claims in some places represent a considerable subsidy;[5] in other places, merely a useful increase in current departmental receipts. Of the third category, the significance is clear: it involves the infusion of substantial sums directly into circulation among employees of the various companies in oil field, refinery and terminal areas, together with the payments made to non-employees for goods supplied and services rendered. This leads to an immediate rise in the local standard of living, and the gradual diffusion of this into other parts of the country. It can also lead, often with specific company assistance, to the launching of local enterprises. Such small-scale industrialisation has flourished in Saudi Arabia, Kuwait, Iraq and Iran, and is often a fact of much social significance. The many industrial skills acquired from the companies—their workshops, installations and high-grade technical schools—are diffused throughout the land.

To return to our first category: the receipt by government of its

[4] Figures for many of these disbursements are not available, but total oil-company employees in Iraq are about 11,000; in Iran over 20,000 (including refinery employees); in Saudi Arabia about 13,000. In Iran the Consortium companies in 1963 brought £30 million ($84 million) into the country for wages, salaries, local purchases and contracts, and customs dues. Other major producing companies probably reached similar totals.

[5] Examples are pipeline way-leave payments by the Iraq Petroleum Company in 1963; to Syria £9.8 million ($27.5 million); to Lebanon £1.8 million ($5 million). Similar Aramco payments to Lebanon in 1962 approximated £1.88 million ($5.28 million); to Syria £1.4 million ($3.16 million); to Jordan £1.32 million ($3.66 million).

royalty and taxation income, it might well be asked how this money is used by those states, already named, for whom oil-revenues have represented a sudden flood of wealth. Here a distinction must be made: the record of spending in Saudi Arabia, because of its primitive political conceptions, has been markedly different from that of other countries. Its too-numerous ruling family and their entourage have squandered millions of dollars on palaces, luxury travel and a variety of other non-social purposes. Only recently, with a change of control at the seat of power, has there been wiser and more enlightened spending.

Elsewhere, a first result of the new wealth has been striking relief from problems of foreign exchange, and a new confidence in all foreign dealings. In some cases, notably that of Kuwait, this has included the placing of considerable investments in Europe and the United States, thereby securing an assured income independent of domestic vicissitudes and providing a reserve against the future decline of oil revenues.[6] The recent financing of an inter-Arab Bank of Development, mainly by Kuwait, has already brought benefit to a number of Arab states, as well as such semi-political steps as a generous low-interest loan by Kuwait to Iraq. For the first time, Arab money is moving productively from country to country.

At home, the oil-rich countries have found channels in plenty through which to direct their wealth. Of mainly administrative but also of economic interest are the many steps taken to improve the conditions of service, pay rates, housing, equipment and status of public officials: a "new look," for example, in the law courts and security forces, overhaul of the financial departments including those of revenue-collection and state enterprises, the improvement of government-owned properties, and increases, considerable and at times lavish, in expenditure on the armed forces.

More socially important is the sincere and largely effective effort being made, in all Middle Eastern states but outstandingly in the recently enriched, towards greatly improved social services. In this field scores of new village schools, urban schools and colleges at every level, and technological and specialized institutions and universities are open to women as well as men. These new institu-

[6] The same motive has inspired some public-service enterprises at home (e.g., revenue-producing ports and airports) and much of the encouragement given to industry.

tions, housed ln well-equipped buildings, are staffed by both indigenous and imported teachers. To this picture, in which private
and religious-community schools usually maintain their place, must
be added many scholarships to foreign universities. Of the field of
public health much the same may be said; rural and tribal dis-
pensaries, village clinics, central big-city hospitals, both general
and specialised, epidemiological services, attention to sanitation,
food and water control, medical education and research—all these
form part of the new services placed within the reach of all and
may appreciably raise the hitherto depressed standards of health,
nutriment and well-being. They are accompanied by extensive
slum-clearance, town planning, low-rental housing and the provision in towns and villages of improved water-supplies, electricity,
drainage and sewage services, public parks and the like. Such
measures, together with much new building by private enterprise,
have transformed the appearance of scores of Middle Eastern cities,
in which also new museums, art galleries, libraries, broadcasting
and television studios are to be seen.

Large-scale spending on the improvement of communications
include the building of main and branch roads and bridges, improved telephone, telegraph and wireless systems, provision for
river and harbour dredging and adaptation for river craft, as well
as ferries and port facilities—the latter a task in which the operating
oil companies take a leading part. To these improvements may be
added railway extension and modernization, public transport
services, and the provision of airports together with, in most cases,
the creation of a prestige-building national air line. These activities
serve not only economic, social and political ends, but also those
of national *amour propre;* with them appears the promise of an
augmented tourist industry, aided further by development of the
hotel industry and that of summer and winter holiday resorts, and
easy access to historic sites. The development of banking and insurance enterprises, both indigenous and foreign-based, is a concomitant of such modernization.

Since in these territories industry on a factory scale is reckoned
a sign of modernity and a sure provider of wealth, enriched governments are everywhere encouraging such industrial development
where local materials or other advantages render it possible. In
places, the government itself is the owner and entrepreneur; in

others, private initiative is made possible by state financial assistance or by other forms of indulgence. The region is today the scene of scores of new industrial enterprises designed to profit from some local resource, to employ labour and to enhance prestige. Few of such industries are of the "heavy" type, though mining, iron and steel works (in Turkey and Egypt), cement, brick- and tile-making, and car or truck assembly, are not unknown. More numerous plants deal with the making and processing of cotton, woolen or silk textiles, food and drink processing, the treatment of hides and skins, the manufacture of carpets and mats, tiles and plate-glass, and domestic utensils. There is also some capacity in electrical equipment, furniture, clothing, footwear and leather goods, soap, fertilisers and insecticides, chemical and plastic products, paper and matches. The industrial effort, partly but not wholly based on oil-wealth, is thus considerable and widespread; many such enterprises prosper, but a number, unwisely conceived or sited, must fail. Technically trained manpower is limited, the research or the patience of the entrepreneur (including government) is often inadequate, political or personal pressures can be embarassing, local buying power is restricted and foreign competition severe. But the social and even political effects of the total effort involved are considerable and growing.

These countries, however, where they are not totally arid, are above all agricultural, and their main potential, with the exception of oil, is clearly in that field. Oil-derived wealth is consequently being spent here, mainly by governments but also by individuals, on a conspicuous scale; and if a more prosperous and stable rural population is realisable, this expenditure will greatly enhance general well-being. Specialised staffs, providing research and tuition, and also pilot-schemes and assisted enterprises, are improving stock breeding, fisheries and forests. Major works, including barrages, flood-protection, new canals, drainage and full (or sometimes, unfortunately, insufficiently full) reticulation, have been a leading feature in Iraq, and to a lesser degree elsewhere. Such works, based upon one of the great rivers, are costly and protracted, but produce the most substantial benefits. A number have been successfully completed. Agriculture and horticulture, varying greatly in method, form and product from country to country, can with well applied scientific knowledge, keen apprehension of local conditions and the injection of fresh capital, be thus immensely aided and developed. Such progressive steps might include an overhaul—or the creation—of exact cadastral records, an improved land-tenure system based thereon, the formation of agricultural co-operatives (as already started in a number of territories), the provision of agricultural loans or credits by governmental agencies, instruction in canal upkeep and drainage and new techniques (including those of harvesting, transport, storage, grading, cleaning, marketing), and the distribution under close supervision of improved seed and fertilisers. Such measures, selected and integrated, can transform the face of agriculture in the Middle East, with immense benefit to the people. The new infusion of oil income makes such a revolution for the first time possible, and in some places already in part a reality.

This whole picture of comprehensive development and improvement, in the oil-rich countries is calculated to please, even to inspire; but, on closer inspection, can it also disappoint? There are, indeed, serious adverse factors. One is, that all this wealth handed to governments in no way represents, as elsewhere it would, the taxation share of a solidly earned national income from country-wide agriculture or industry: it represents money-bags from a single source, handed free of charge or effort to the national government, to be diffused by it *tant bien que mal* to the population. The difference is both economic and psychological, and renders much more difficult the integration of the new wealth among all classes and in all parts of the nation. It also does little to enhance a true popular comprehension of economic facts. A second adverse factor is that of dubious effectiveness in some (or much) of the eager, large-scale spending above described: dubious by reason of the imperfection of economic and political vision, the scarcity of really competent planners, some reluctance to act on expert advice (especially if offered by foreigners), and a tendency to hastiness and inadequate study of projects. There is also sometimes a susceptibility to distorting political influences, an ill-developed social conscience in the dominant classes and (as against agricultural innovation, for instance) a deadening conservatism in the masses.

Thirdly, the whole "Golden Age" itself may end! Apart from the certainty that even vast oil deposits must one day be exhausted —and provision against that day, though not absent, is not yet adequate in current planning—the chance exists that major oil sources elsewhere may be discovered, robbing the Middle East of its primacy in foreign markets. It is also not inconceivable that other energy-sources may be perfected or cheapened and may, if not entirely, at least largely, displace oil from its present indispensability. A still more likely interruption to the stream of oil-wealth lies in some breach in company-government relations, such as occurred in Iran in 1933 and 1951, capable of halting production operations: of killing or maiming, in fact, the golden-egged goose. The attitude of governments and publics to the (as they feel) too-rich, too-successful, too-pervasive foreign operating companies, upon whom in fact everything depends,[7] is often suspicious or hostile, as popular press and broadcast comment indicates. There are applauded and never-ceasing attempts to augment the host government's share of the profits, to extend that share to all "downstream" and worldwide operations of the industry, to press for production of ever greater tonnages of oil (perhaps regardless of market possibilities, and certainly of other countries' claims), to re-negotiate concession terms,[8] and to achieve cost-free or privileged governmental participation in shareholding. Apart from directly financial objectives, an increase of the host government's representation on the company's board, the increased employment of local citizens (qualified or otherwise) ever higher in the company's hierarchy, and the surrender of wide areas of concession-held territory are all political objectives from time to time. Seeking such aims, and now joined together with apparent unity in the

[7] Oil development in these countries by national agencies, theoretically far preferable, was and is still in practice precluded by lack of local capital, of capacity in vast-scale industrial operations or of entry to the indispensable foreign markets throughout the world. Existing concessions may nevertheless—as they have, formally, in Iran—change much of their present appearance and orientation. And the national oil companies, such as most of the states have now founded to seek entry into the otherwise foreign-dominated industry, will certainly play an increasing part, especially in refining, distribution, tanker-transport and, perhaps less, in production itself.

[8] For example, by basing "profits" on unreal posted prices at the point of export, without heed to true prices as realised; and by demanding the "expensing" of the royalty element in the government's share, before calculating the 50 per cent due to the government.

O.P.E.C. organization,[9] oil-producing nations can bring many and diverse pressures to bear on companies' policies and operations, often such as seriously to impede them. Herein lies a major current problem. Palliative elements, however, are the present world over-supply of oil, the possible precariousness of unity within O.P.E.C., the deadliness of the blow at national aspirations involved by any serious oil-stoppage, and the looming appearance of the U.S.S.R. as a direct, intrusive oil-marketing rival from its own resources. But the true identity of interest between all these governments and their concession-holding companies is too real and obvious, one would hope, to be safely ignored.

Oil production in these countries, however, does provide the drive behind the forces making for modernity and Westernization in patterns and standards of living, for emancipation and for anti-traditionalism in society and in politics. Whatever the loss (as some may feel) in authentic tradition, local pride and dignity, in continuity of and respect for family or community life, and possibly also in inherited moral standards, the new fashions of life, thus reinforced, will never revert to the old. This must involve a gradually or even rapidly emerging new type of electorate, with anti-feudal, egalitarian, largely socialist—and even Marxist—ideas. These conceptions in no way preclude a chauvinist nationalism and a high self-confidence, but they are clearly inimical to the permanence of the "old regimes" of government, based on an Islamic culture of seemingly decreasing vitality. Such feelings thrive visibly among a new class in these territories, the industrial proletariat, which today contains thousands of rootless, restless and ambitious expatriates from other countries.[10]

Scarcely less in the constitutionally more developed states than in those of authoritarian regime, the advent and diffusion of wealth, abolishing much of the poverty that led to instability, restlessness and violence, has disappointingly failed to perform the expected miracles; there is indeed as yet little sign, in the Iraq or Iran of the oil-age, of greater stability, authority or continuity in the political field. The reasons for this must here be briefly summarised: the glittering prizes of political success are greater, the

[9] Organisation of Petroleum Exporting Countries: present members are Iran, Iraq, Saudi Arabia, Kuwait, Venezuela, Indonesia, Libya, Qatar; not unlikely future members are Nigeria, Algeria, Trinidad, Colombia.
[10] In Kuwait or Saudi Arabia they include, notably, ex-Palestinians.

contest ever more strenuous. The educated and under-employed, impatient and aspiring middle class is more numerous, but no more contented. Emotional broadcasts, and the influence of the press, do little to produce maturity of thinking, or patient action. Mobs, tribesmen and students can still be mobilised for demonstrations with the greatest ease. Stronger armies may be used—but with no greater restraint—for faction-fighting or for enthroning or unseating successive dictators. These are all sadly familiar phenomena not created by national oil wealth but, it appears, rather accentuated than cured by it.

The international position of these states has been notably enhanced by the attention attracted to their new wealth and confidence, and their score of votes in the United Nations. The whole region, always of strategic importance and traditionally coveted, becomes more than ever a scene of Soviet penetrative and subversive activity, while the West is not less anxious to consolidate a position based on a measure of national goodwill—as difficult as this seems to achieve. The relations of the oil-processing and oil-transiting states to the Western countries to which the great operating companies belong are drawn notably closer by shared activity, interest and resulting contacts, but are frequently embarrassed by frictions arising at company-government level on the spot, and these can too easily lead to intergovernment clashes.[11] In interstate relations in the Middle East itself, oil can, in the same way, be anything but a lubricant; one recalls Iraqi-Kuwait troubles five years ago, the aggression of Saudi Arabia against the Buraimi oasis, the squabbles on Algerian frontiers with jealous neighbours, the recurrent broadcast polemics and financial covetousness; nor is it axiomatic that transit countries will never quarrel with, or fail to use their powerful hold over, the neighbours whose oil is, while in transit, at their mercy. In this area, as in others in which giant oil deposits have their place, one must study the aspirations and weaknesses of haves and have-nots in unequal juxtaposition—and hope for the best.

[11] For example, as between Iran and Great Britain in 1951-1954.

# IX. Saudi Arabia: The Islamic Island

## by George Rentz

I

THE GREAT LAND-MASS OF THE ARABIAN PENINSULA PROVIDES A striking contrast to the arc of the Fertile Crescent which it sub-tends. While the life of Iraq, Syria, Lebanon, Jordan and Israel is nourished by a relatively copious water supply, in the Peninsula water is in a sense more precious than gold or oil because it is so difficult to find. Lebanon apart, the countries of the Crescent have stretches of desert on the edges nearest Arabia, but for them the desert is an annex rather than the atrium.

Since early times the people of Arabia have called their land the Island of the Arabs, confined as it is by the sea on three sides and the desert on the fourth. Its isolation, however, has never been complete. The sea has served as a highway for the Arabs, whose staunch, small sailing craft go as far as the southern ports of the East African coast. The desert belt in the north can be crossed by raiders, ranging nomads or merchants in caravan.

The expansion of Islam beyond Arabia, though bringing the Peninsula into closer association with some parts of the world, has tended to cut it off from others. All Moslems hold the Prophet's home sacred, and it is their duty to try to make the pilgrimage to Mecca at least once before dying, but with a few exceptions they focus their gaze on the Hijaz and ignore the rest of Arabia. Jealous of the sanctity of the land, the inhabitants shut fast the doors of the holiest shrines to unbelievers, and the forbidding nature of other parts has kept them for centuries unknown to the world out-side.

Occupying roughly three-fourths of the Peninsula's total area of a million square miles, the Kingdom of Saudi Arabia has a much smaller share (perhaps a third)[1] of the Peninsula's people. Only one corner of the Kingdom, Asir in the southwest, receives enough rain from the Indian Ocean monsoons to support a population comparable in density to that of Yemen. While the unifying and isolating forces of Islam have both been strong in the Hijaz, the latter long prevailed in Najd, the central region of Arabia. For the past two centuries Najd has been the fortress of the doctrine called Wahhabism by Westerners and Moslems unsympathetic towards it.[2] This doctrine adheres to an extremely conservative interpretation of Islam. For five generations and well into a sixth, the House of Saud ruled and preserved the Wahhabite state as an Islamic island, marked by the religious fervor of its sovereigns and subjects, and by its imperviousness to extraneous influences.

## II

Among the developing societies of the twentieth century, Saudi Arabia presents a unique case. Most of these societies are handicapped by insufficient means. The possession of certain natural resources has, however, enabled some to secure substantial, if not always adequate, income and foreign exchange. Three of the five states leading the world in the production of oil are developing countries: Venezuela, Kuwait and Saudi Arabia. Venezuela, with its Latin American environment and history, bears little resemblance to the Arab states. Kuwait, on the other hand, is a sort of Saudi Arabia in miniature. Saudi Arabia has an area about a hundred times larger and a population perhaps ten times more numerous, but Kuwait's income from oil is greater.[3] Dependence before the discovery of oil on trading, shipping and pearling made Kuwait less insular than its massive neighbor used to be.

Among the Arab states outside the Peninsula, the closest parallel to Saudi Arabia is provided by Libya, which also has a vast expanse of desert, a sparse population and a sizable production of oil. With a population about a third as large as Saudi Arabia's, Libya in 1964 produced nearly half as much oil. Another conser-

---

[1] The scarcity of accurate statistics makes hazardous the use of population figures for Arabia.

[2] The followers of the doctrine call themselves Unitarians, stressing their belief in the unimpaired unity of Allah.

[3] In 1964 Kuwait produced 106,714,000 metric tons, and Saudi Arabia 85,700,000.

vative version of Islam, Sanusism, has its home in Libya, where its political strength is centered in the royal family and its numerical strength in the western region of Cyrenaica. Sanusism, however, is less xenophobic than Wahhabism, and Libya's closeness to Europe and the concentration of its settled areas along the coast have also left the country open wider than Saudi Arabia to the penetration and influence of unbelievers.

Besides a source of steady income, Saudi Arabia also enjoys a number of inherited advantages. Thanks to the long rule of the House of Saud, the fundamental institutions of the state are of indigenous growth, not imposed by alien authority.[4] The people of Saudi Arabia are bound together by ties of common descent (some, it is true, are not of Arab blood, but even they have become thoroughly Arab in their ways), a common language and a common religion. To appreciate what this means, one should regard the heterogeneity of the scene in India or the Congo.

Arabian society is also relatively homogeneous in not having an elaborate system of strongly pronounced class divisions. Early Islam with its doctrine that all the faithful are brothers did not favor a hierarchy of classes, and in this respect it has continued to exert its influence in Arabia. There have always been the rich and the poor, but until recently they were not far apart. The ruler built his modest mansion out of the same sun-dried brick his subjects used for their huts, he wore much the same garb as they did, and he and they spoke with each other on a first-name basis. Other members of the aristocracy—notables in the towns and tribal chiefs—were just as close to the common people. The ulema as guardians of public morality were dedicated to spreading Wahhabite beliefs and maintaining Wahhabite control over the commonwealth. More than the members of other professions, the wealthier merchants had interests reaching beyond Arabia. The great commercial families of Najd, for example, had branches in Cairo, Bombay and other centers in the nineteenth century. Agriculture not being practiced on a large scale in Arabia, most of the farmers were small landholders or laborers. Slaves might have

[4] Traces of former Ottoman rule in the Hijaz have virtually disappeared. In 1960 the Saudi Arabian Government, for example, abolished the peculiar division, inherited from the Turks, of the riyal into 11 or 22 qirsh. The terms riyal and qirsh illustrate foreign influences, the first being of Spanish origin and the second of German, Groschen.

been considered a separate class, but the duties and rewards of many slaves were hardly distinguishable from those of free men doing the same sort of work.

The homogeneity of Arabian society was not perfect; tribal, sectional and factional differences existed. In Arabia a distinction has always been made between the nomads and the settled folk, with hostility rather than amity characterizing their relations. Tribalism was stronger in the desert, but its workings penetrated into the oases as well. Tribal loyalties and rivalries were so intense that even closely related tribes or clans were often at odds or at war over grazing rights, access to water or blood feuds. Islam in the beginning had sought to substitute the higher loyalty of brotherhood in the faith for tribal ties, but in Arabia it fell short of success. In the eighteenth century Muhammad ibn Abd al-Wahhab, the preacher of Wahhabism, and the House of Saud undertook to make Islam function as it was supposed to, harnessing tribal energies to build a true Islamic state. Ruling from 1902 to 1953, Abd al-Aziz (popularly known as Ibn Saud) acquired his reputation as the greatest figure in Arabia in modern times largely through his genius in managing the tribes, relying on them as long as they served his purposes and breaking their power when they challenged his authority.

The system of communications inside Arabia was grossly inadequate, with the journey from one end of the land to the other taking arduous weeks. Isolated from one another, people thought of themselves as citizens of the Hijaz or of Najd rather than of a larger entity. The more cosmopolitan residents of the Hijaz looked down upon the men of Najd as eastern barbarians, while in the view of Najders life in the Holy Cities was effete and tainted by foreign manners. Wahhabism made many converts, but among those who steadfastly resisted its appeal were the Shiite oasis dwellers on and near the Persian Gulf. For Wahhabites and ordinary Sunnites these Shiite devotees of the Prophet's son-in-law Ali were beyond the pale.

## III

From the seventh century to the early twentieth, life went on in Arabia with hardly any changes in the basic fabric. The remoteness of the Peninsula during this span of 1,300 years is indicated by the fact that firearms and coffee were almost the only important commodities introduced from abroad.[5] At last, during the reign of Abd al-Aziz, the people of the Islamic island began to become more fully aware of what was happening in the world outside, particularly in the technological field, and to take steps to catch up. Development in this sense began before the discovery of oil, showing the native capacity of the Arabian people for fitting themselves into the scientific environment of the twentieth century. When a concession was granted to the Standard Oil Company of California in 1933,[6] Saudi Arabia already had automobiles, airplanes and a wireless network. A revolution in communications was needed before broad development in other fields could be achieved, and Abd al-Aziz began the revolution before the oil companies went to work. Even if oil had not been found, it is likely that Saudi Arabia would have followed much the same course it did in fact follow, though at a considerably slower pace.

What impelled Saudi Arabia to turn in this direction? Islam is a total way of life, and the old Islamic society of Arabia was sufficient unto itself, but in the end it became apparent that the faithful were not getting enough of the good things of life. This was perhaps more the fault of the harsh circumstances of the Arabian scene than of Islam itself, but a basic shortcoming of Wahhabism was its emphasis on looking backward. Every effort, in the view of the ulema, should be bent to emulate the Prophet and the pious generations immediately succeeding him. What they had not known was not worth knowing. The twentieth century showed that even the best protected of Islamic islands could not go on living mainly in the past. The good things people began to want were not only material articles; ideas and techniques strange to the closed society also exercised an appeal. The first newspaper in the domains of the House of Saud appeared in Mecca in 1924,[7] to be followed by regular radio broadcasts and since 1958 by television. Lively dis-

---

[5] Tea was also probably first imported during this period, but unlike coffee it has not been a favorite subject for Arab historians.

[6] An oil concession had been granted to the Eastern and General Syndicate of London in 1923, but funds could not be found for exploitation and the concession lapsed.

[7] Bearing the name *Umm al-Qura* (The Mother of Towns), one of the sobriquets of Mecca, it is still published as the official gazette of Saudi Arabia.

cussions of public issues before audiences multiplying in size have contributed to the emergence of a public opinion of a type not known before in Arabia.

## IV

Although oil was discovered in 1938, the great impact of the oil industry did not begin to be felt in Saudi Arabia until the years just after World War II, when production and the government's income both started soaring. These were the last years of Abd al-Aziz's long reign and, after his death in 1953, the first years of the reign of his son Saud. Neither father nor son had the financial wisdom or experience necessary for the proper management and spending of tremendous sums in the public interest, and both were inclined to be overindulgent towards relatives and intimates. The outpouring of funds which ensued was bound to produce a measure of development, but it was largely haphazard and ill planned. In 1958 unbridled extravagance brought Saudi Arabia to the verge of bankruptcy. At this point it should be emphasized that the reckless spending of the House of Saud and the country as a whole lasted only twelve years, and that the unflattering reputation Saudi Arabia acquired during that time, which still persists in some quarters, has been substantially reversed by subsequent events. In March 1958, Prince Faisal, King Saud's brother, took over full powers for the direction of government affairs and inaugurated a program of fiscal responsibility. This was the turning point. From this time on the revenue of the state was to be used primarily to promote the interests of the nation as a whole. Strict budgetary controls were introduced and income and expenditures subjected to the discretion of the Saudi Arabian Monetary Agency, whose functioning was supervised by competent experts from Pakistan and Egypt. Faisal, as Prime Minister, and his Council of Ministers adhered to regulations governing the business of the Council. The government's planning organization was assigned the task of plotting the course of development. Recourse was also had to the technical advice of the United Nations, which appointed a resident representative for Riyad, the capital. Even so, liberal elements in the country felt that Faisal and his colleagues were not doing as much as they should to foster economic and social development. When King Saud returned to power in December 1960, his

Council of Ministers and circle of advisers contained young men with bold ideas for remaking Saudi Arabia. The King and the young men, however, did not play as good a game in office as they had talked out of office. In October 1962 Faisal was again granted full powers to enable him to deal with the problems created by Saudi Arabia's involvement in the civil war in Yemen, following the September revolution which established the Yemen Arab Republic. This time Faisal began his administration by publishing in November a reform program in which he stressed the government's determination to move ahead with economic and social development. The dethroning of Saud and Faisal's accession in November 1964 have made it possible for the government to concentrate more effectively on implementing the program.

V

During the past two decades Saudi Arabia has developed in such a way that it can no longer be properly described as an island. Its external communications now reach out in every direction, providing avenues for the inpouring of ideas and technical devices from the United States, Britain, West Germany, France and Japan, as well as from the spheres of Arabdom and Islam. Many inhabitants of the Kingdom go abroad for study, business or pleasure; on returning they contribute to the stimulation of the evolving life of their homeland. By setting examples and providing technical aid, the oil companies and other foreign concerns operating in Saudi Arabia are lending a very helpful hand. Membership in the Arab League and the United Nations and attendance at numerous international conferences have meant a broadening of horizons, especially for statesmen and diplomats. Petroleum experts have experienced a similar broadening as a result of the leading role played by Saudi Arabia in the Organization of Petroleum Exporting Countries, the other members of which are Kuwait, Iraq, Qatar, Libya, Iran, Venezuela and Indonesia. Internal development in Saudi Arabia has also had much to do with bringing the country out of its isolation. In agriculture Saudi Arabia has collaborated with the Food and Agriculture Organization; and in public health, with the World Health Organization. In education Saudi Arabia has relied extensively on other Arab states.

Although the isolation is gone, Saudi Arabia remains a thor-

oughly Islamic society in spite of a recent trend towards secularization both in the government and in some segments of the population, particularly in the larger towns with their easier access to the
extra-peninsular world. This secularizing movement is not fundamentally anti-religious; its aim is rather to diminish the degree of
religious control over mundane affairs. During the time of Abd
al-Aziz, the ruler's old religious title of Imam was exchanged for
that of King. In Islam the King is expected to serve the Lord, but
he is not the Lord's anointed. At the same time, the original basis
of the state has not been forgotten: a compact between the founder
of the dynasty and the preacher of Wahhabism to work together
in defending and propagating the Unitarian doctrine of Islam. As
a direct descendant of the two who made the compact, King
Faisal [8] is a living demonstration of its durability, and he regards
himself as bound to do all that he can to further the cause of Islam.

The trend towards secularization is accelerated by the rise of
new elements to positions of influence. The government, which
for two centuries functioned with a very simple structure, has
grown tremendously, acquiring in the process a bureaucracy more
Western than Islamic in its organization and methods. A regular
army, a small air force, and an embryonic navy—all drilled in the
Western style and outfitted with Western uniforms—have taken
their place beside the tribal levies, whose *forte* was the raiding
tactics of ancient Arabian warfare. Both at home and in schools
abroad a new generation of youth, studying sciences and the
Western humanities, is delving into subjects remote from the
Islamic curriculum. A new class of industrial workers is learning
that progress depends on technical skills, and the more skilled are
moving up towards the managerial ranks. The readiness of the
government to alter drastically the web of society is indicated by
the seriousness with which it is investigating schemes to settle large
numbers of Bedouins on the land.

The process of secularization is energetically resisted by the
conservative elements. When the progressives publicly assert that
the country needs a constitution, the conservatives retort that the
Koran has always been its constitution and that no man-made
document can compare with this God-given book. Both Ahmad
Ben Bella in Algeria and Gamal Abdul Nasser in Yemen found

[8] His mother was of the house of Muhammad ibn Abd al-Wahhab.

the conservative believers in Islam stronger than they apparently calculated. The strength of the conservatives in Saudi Arabia, though still great, seems to be slowly but inexorably on the ebb. The conservative position is weakened by changes occurring in the older elements of society. The royal family has relaxed its virtual monopoly of the highest lay offices, assigning a number of them to commoners. The spreading apparatus of the central government has greatly curtailed the independence of action once enjoyed by provincial governors and tribal shaikhs. Merchants and businessmen, as a result of their increasing connections with Western firms, are adopting Western ways of handling their affairs. On many sides opposition has appeared to the interference of the ulema in the daily lives of men through the prescribing of standards for almost every facet of community or individual activity. The ulema were inclined to defend slavery as an institution sanctioned by the Koran and the Prophet's practice, but in 1962 Faisal emancipated all the slaves in the Kingdom, and the government has undertaken to give help to those who need it in finding a new place in life.

Conservative resistance to secularization has not been the only brake on social and economic development. Saudi Arabia shares the fate of many other developing countries in not having nearly enough men or women[9] trained in the new disciplines or nearly enough native teachers for the training programs now instituted. Although private enterprise is allowed ample scope, the main burden of fostering national development still rests on the government, and its machinery in many instances is new and creaky. Some of the wealthier citizens devote a large share of their investment capital to Lebanese real estate or similar ventures rather than to productive undertakings at home. In the past Saudi Arabia has been handicapped by a paucity of natural resources other than oil and gas. Recent geological surveys indicate that this situation may improve, with deposits of iron, copper and silver having been discovered, and with the prospect of finding other minerals being at least fairly favorable.

Progress has also been made towards composing the old tribal, sectional and factional differences. Tribalism as a political force

[9] Women are just beginning to take up a few select callings, such as teaching and journalism.

has been subdued. Inter-tribal warfare has been brought to an end; occasional brawls between tribes still take place, but in general the tribesmen now pasture their herds and flocks and traffic with each other in peace. Men of the Hijaz and men of Najd are coming to think of themselves first as Saudi Arabs rather than as citizens of their respective regions. The Shiites, whose communities lie in the area of the oil fields, have on the whole fared well in working for the oil industry or in local businesses catering to its needs. In various ways the government is mitigating its once contemptuous attitude towards these heterodox subjects.

Some of the youth with a Western education, some of the officers and other idealists or innovators, including even members of the royal family, find the pace of development too slow. They become disenchanted when Faisal announces in his reform program of November 6, 1962 that "the time has come for the promulgation of a fundamental law for the country" and three years later the law is still under study. For these impatient ones Arab Socialism is apt to have a powerful appeal, and Gamal Abdul Nasser to be a hero as the Arab leader who gets things done, though the glow of his image has been at least slightly dimmed by the events of 1965. Since 1962 they have found fault with the House of Saud for aiding the royalist cause in Yemen, in opposition to the new republic with Abdul Nasser on its side. Some believe that if the United States had not openly demonstrated support for the House of Saud,[10] it would have fallen like the House of Hamid al-Din in Yemen. No organized revolutionary movement inside Saudi Arabia has been identified and the dissidents living abroad are men of little consequence, but the danger exists that the advocates of a faster pace may, out of exasperation with Faisal's gradualness, provoke civil strife. The government's awareness of the discontent is perhaps the main reason why the tribal levies have been reorganized as a National Guard with

[10] United States policy, primarily concerned with insuring the free flow of oil from the Persian Gulf, may be justified on the grounds that the House of Saud has a long history as a stabilizing force, that Faisal has demonstrated the sincerity of his intentions in carrying out a reform program and that no acceptable alternative to the House of Saud is in sight. The shakiness of the Yemen Arab Republic and its complete dependence on Egypt since its inception suggest that republicanism and Arab Socialism may not be the immediate answer in the Arabian Peninsula.

modern arms and equipment, to serve as a counterpoise to the regular armed forces.

Islam as a system for governing the realm is now on trial in the land of its birth. If its liberal and conservative followers succeed in harmonizing their efforts, development in Saudi Arabia should proceed in a fashion more satisfying to the advocates of urgency. The latest promised solution of the Yemen question, announced in August 1965 after meetings in Jiddah between Faisal and Abdul Nasser, should, if achieved, encourage men of good will in Saudi Arabia to find common ground on which to stand and work for the welfare of the whole nation and thus to ensure the stability of this Islamic state.

# X.  Kuwait: A Super-Affluent Society*

## by Fakhri Shehab

STRETCHING OVER SOME 6,000 SQUARE MILES OF THE HARD, GRAV-
elly and waterless northeast corner of the Persian Gulf, Kuwait
has been thrust from oblivion into sudden prominence by her
hidden wealth and the creative genius of Western enterprise and
technology. In less than two decades, since the first shipment of
oil left her shores, material riches have changed the face of her
barren territory, and Kuwait is now experiencing a host of complex social, political and economic problems which are shaking
her essentially tribal and primitive structure. The purpose of this
essay is to discuss the nature of the challenge presented by this
transitional phase and to examine Kuwait's response to it. But in
order to appreciate the magnitude of the task that confronts this
city-state, the reader must first know something of the static society that used to exist and of the main events that have so radically
transformed it into what it is now.

Present-day Kuwait was reportedly founded in the early eighteenth century by tribesmen driven from their home in inner Arabia
by warring kinsmen. The tiny fishing village they founded offered
few and meagre resources; but its very austerity was perhaps its
main asset. For the rigorous physical environment rendered the individual tough, imaginative, enterprising and excellent in team-
work. These qualities have, for over two centuries, distinguished
the Kuwaitis as the Gulf's most successful businessmen, sailors and
sea-farers.

Broadly speaking, Kuwait was comprised of three main groups:

* Reprinted by special permission from *Foreign Affairs,* April 1964. Copyright by the Council on Foreign Relations, Inc., New York, New York.

a ruling family, an oligarchy of merchants and a working class—mostly fishermen, pearl-divers and shipbuilders. Of these groups, the second has been by far the most powerful and dynamic social force. It was the merchants' enterprising spirit that provided the ruling family with their meagre income in the shape of customs duties and provided employment for the rest of the community. A triple social structure still exists in Kuwait, although, as we shall see, new circumstances are altering it.

This small community needed peace first and foremost to enable it to eke out a living, and, in the two and a half centuries since they settled on the Gulf, the Kuwaitis have had no more than two internal crises involving serious violence, and only a few skirmishes with neighboring tribes. Crimes of violence are almost unknown and even litigation is a rare indulgence. As with individuals, so with the state: the desire for peace eminently characterizes Kuwait's relations with her neighbors—a monumental diplomatic feat considering the struggle for power that divides the Arab states.

Of governmental organization Kuwait possessed little more than the traditional tribal type in which power was vested in an autocratic ruler, who, in conformity with tradition, was chosen from among members of the Subah family for his superior personal qualities. The choice of a new ruler was usually regarded as a family affair; and while clearly it was no democracy, this primitive political system allowed the Kuwaiti wide freedoms of action and expression. Regard for tradition made public opinion an important political force. Hence, it was the general practice for the ruler to consult the elders of the community on matters involving serious decisions. Law and order were maintained in a simple and unceremonious way in accordance with Islamic law as modified by tribal usage and local custom. Internal security was preserved by a small bodyguard, and in times of emergency external security was the responsibility of all able-bodied men (and sometimes women). Education was confined to a few primitive and privately run semi-religious institutions and not until 1912 did the town notables organize the first elementary school. As for health services, Kuwait's first hospital was not opened until well after her oil had begun to flow, in 1949.

This tribal structure held sway until 1937 when popular endeavors to modernize it finally led to the election of the short-lived Legislative Assembly whose only legacy was the creation of certain government departments with broadly defined functions. These departments formed Kuwait's basic administrative framework until 1962, when constitutional government was introduced.

Import duties, varying between 4 and 6 percent, constituted the main source of public revenue. The scope of the government operations may be seen from the fact that in 1938-39 public revenue totaled some £60,000 (approximately $290,000), of which nearly two-thirds came from import duties and the rest from miscellaneous dues and fees, plus a small royalty paid by the Kuwait Oil Company following the discovery, though not the actual extraction, of oil. This primitive financial system drew no distinction between public domain or revenue, on the one hand, and the ruler's personal estate and income on the other. At this stage, the city-state had hardly emerged as an independent and recognizable entity and the ruler, still resembling a tribal chieftain, combined with his basic responsibilities of maintaining law and order the traditional and costly functions of tribal hospitality.

As for the private sector, pearling and seafaring together absorbed the majority of Kuwait's labor force (estimated at some 8,000 to 10,000 men). It is said that average earnings in pearling hardly exceeded 100 rupees (just over $35 at the prewar rate) for a season of three to four months. This was often supplemented by seafaring, which brought in an additional 150 or 200 rupees for an expedition of some six months. Exceptionally, an enterprising man could add to these two sources of income by trading, and might make a profit of some 100 or 200 rupees. Thus, at best, average family earnings from various sources barely touched 500 rupees (rather less than $180) a year. Assuming an average family of five, these calculations would suggest an average personal annual income of some 100 rupees (roughly about $35). As for an unskilled laborer, he barely managed to reach subsistence level. His daily wage was not more than a half rupee, and employment was rarely available throughout the year. These conditions were far worse than those then obtaining in the agrarian communities of Iran or Iraq.

## II

Today such conditions exist only in memory, for Kuwait now is a land of superlatives. It is the largest oil producer in the Middle East and the fourth largest in the world; it boasts the world's largest oil port where the world's largest tankers are loaded in record time; at 62 billion barrels, its proved oil reserves are the largest in the world; and the magnitude of its oil receipts in relation to the size of the native population is such that even if all other sources of income in both the private and public sectors are disregarded, the annual revenue per citizen amounts to K.D. 1,200 (Kuwait Dinar = U.S. $2.8).

In sharp and dramatic contrast with the austerity of former times, Kuwait's current foreign trade statistics list an extraordinarily wide range of luxury goods transported by sea, land and air from some 60-odd countries, at an annual expenditure averaging in recent years nearly $300,000,000, or about $825 per inhabitant. More impressive still is the present-day expenditure on fresh water distillation and power supply which costs the state not less than $140 per inhabitant, while every tree and shrub that decorates her thoroughfares and public squares costs an average of some $250 a year. As for social services, a welfare state of unsurpassed munificence has suddenly emerged. Expenditure on health and education and other benefits (mostly in pecuniary forms) has placed this tiny state on a higher level than some of the most sophisticated societies in the world; for in the fiscal year 1961-62 it reached some $240 per inhabitant as compared with $210 in the U.K. and slightly less in Sweden.[1]

What has been the impact of the sudden explosion of wealth upon this primitive society? In less than two decades the whole face of Kuwait has changed beyond recognition. But behind the spectacular physical change lie fundamental problems which have rarely, if ever, been faced by an affluent community before.

One basic question has always been asked: how long is it going to last? The Kuwaitis are quite alive to the precariousness of their riches. Anxiety over the future dominates their thoughts and many

[1] Both the British and the Swedish figures include payments by the private sector in the form of employers' and employees' contributions.

of their actions. It is evident in the attempt to build up their social capital, to set up an organized public service and to foster rapid industrial development; it is evident in the determined effort to accumulate foreign reserves; and, above all, it is evident in the desire to achieve all this in a desperately short time. Haste is, indeed, the order of the day.

But growth is a function of time and the hurried transformation of Kuwait from the poor, obscure and stagnant society it used to be into one of uncommon complexity and sophistication has proved challenging and, at times, even dangerous.

Oil receipts began to accrue in 1946. In the early stages no more than rudimentary physical planning of the town was needed. The sharp increase in revenue in 1951 made clear that planning required expert advice, and foreign consultants were engaged for this purpose. Subsequently, a group of five engineering firms was engaged to carry out the work on a cost-plus basis. It was soon discovered, however, that this procedure pushed up costs unduly and left much room for abuse, and it was abandoned. It was realized that the task of building could not be simply farmed out to foreign contractors. Responsibility for planning and executing a development program was then entrusted to the Public Works Department. This was a tribute to the courage of the government, considering Kuwait's small population and the acute shortage of trained personnel.

Paucity of population is not necessarily associated with economic backwardness; the shortage of trained people is. The presence of both in a setting of extreme wealth makes the story of Kuwait unique. The earliest population figures available for those years are from the first census of 1957. They give Kuwait's total indigenous labor force as being 23,977, all between 15 and 60 years of age. By far the largest group (over 19,000) was composed of those with either no training at all or with only minimal professional qualifications. Another group, designated "professionals and technologists" and totaling some 4,000, includes only one chemist, one geologist, two physicians, two author-journalists, eight accountants and 156 clergymen.

The government's difficulties thus can hardly be exaggerated. To ensure control of its own affairs, it gave preference to its own citizens; and if suitable Kuwaitis were not available preference went to other Arab citizens and only in the last resort to non-Arabs. With abundant financial resources and in the absence of a strong civil service tradition, there soon evolved an administrative machine which was vast, complicated, cumbersome and not always guided by the highest ethical standards.

This created more problems for the state than it solved. Since all top administrative and executive jobs were reserved for citizens, the responsibility for final decisions invariably lay with them; the presence of the foreign technician or adviser did not help much. The Kuwaiti policy-maker was still called upon daily to evaluate highly technical, and not infrequently conflicting, proposals which ranged from the choice of some complex electronic equipment for an ultra-modern telephone system to the assessment of the chemical components of local soils as factors affecting the choice of road-construction techniques. As the great majority of Kuwaiti executives came to their new responsibilities unprepared, vital decisions were often deferred, and when they were made, showed the pressure of vested interests.

There was also the problem of the mere volume of the new business. At the start, far too many projects were undertaken and as time went on the number increased. The demands on the limited time of the Kuwaiti executives and policy-makers grew correspondingly, resulting in insufficient guidance from the top. This shortage of leadership in Kuwait was alarming, since it involved the one thing that could not be imported from abroad.

Meanwhile, business was offering unlimited scope for success and, to the qualified few, its attraction was too powerful to be resisted. Some sort of a compromise had therefore to be devised to eliminate this competition, and it was found by permitting civil servants to run their own businesses side-by-side with their public offices. This concession caused immense harm. It overtaxed the limited time and energy of those in key positions, strained their allegiance to the state, exposed them to grave temptations and meant that the public service ceased to be considered a career. Senior appointments were generally accepted for prestige reasons, mostly by those who lacked distinction; and employment in the lower echelons was regarded more or less as a sinecure, or as a means of channeling a certain amount of the wealth to the average citizen.

These factors have led to such overcrowding in the public service that salaries and wages now create a very serious drain on the treasury. The city-state at present has on its payroll no less than 53,000 men and women, both indigenous and aliens, excluding those in the armed forces, at an annual cost of nearly $168,000,-000. This means that every three citizens are being served by one public servant at an average cost of about $1,120 per citizen.

This, then, was one of the results of the second phase of the experiment. It raised public expenditures for administration to an incredible level. It placed in positions of great responsibility either men of an older generation, whose views and standards were hopelessly outdated, or very young persons, who lacked the required experience; and it put a heavy strain on their loyalties. Further, it eliminated competitive selection for the public service and thus encouraged complacency in the new generation and a tendency to judge performance by local standards alone.

### III

It was only natural that the new wealth should create a demand for services hitherto unknown in the country. The resulting problem was made especially acute by the ambitious projects planned by the government, and its determination to carry them out all at once. Inevitably, a uniquely attractive market for labor was created and a flood of skilled and unskilled workers flocked from the four corners of the globe, but mostly from neighboring countries. This influx created new problems. The ethnic and political composition of this immigrant labor was heterogeneous, though the largest proportion (about 70 percent) were Arabs. Their social habits, cultures, creeds and, above all, political leanings were numerous and widely divergent.

Moreover, by far the largest group of these aliens (73 percent) were males mostly between 15 and 50 years of age, which meant that they were transient immigrants.[2] It is this transient population that provides the bulk of Kuwait's skilled labor and 78 percent of her unskilled workers. It is they who supply the city-state with her teachers, doctors, architects, engineers and administrative

[2] This fact is reflected in the number of air travelers, which in recent years has reached some 230,000 annually, or more than 70 percent of the total population.

and managerial personnel. They are the makers of her laws, the builders of her industry and the founders of her financial institutions. So pervasive has been their influence that there is hardly an aspect of national life which does not bear their mark. It affects the Kuwaitis choice of fashion, architecture and interior decoration; their cultural and artistic interest; their entertainments and dietetic habits; and even their colloquial Arabic, which has considerably changed under the influence of the newcomers.

Yet this all-powerful community of aliens has no permanent ties with the host country. Their services will apparently continue to be in demand indefinitely; yet the individuals themselves are constantly changing and are regarded by their hosts as changeable. This situation has inevitably led to a lack of continuity in planning and performance as well as to a sense of instability among the resident aliens, discernible in their behavior and their attitudes to the state.

The ephemeral status of the members of this community is especially marked among manual and menial workers. Grim unemployment in neighboring countries has driven tens of thousands of these men to search for a living in this rich oasis. But in turn the unlimited supply of labor has inevitably depressed wages to the point where the now derelict and nearly forgotten "iron law" may be seen in full swing. At present an unskilled laborer in Kuwait makes between nine and twelve shillings a day (about $1.25 to $1.65). This is generally higher than average earnings in the region; but the advantage is lost in a country where most goods are imported, where major imports are controlled by oligopolies and where rents and utilities are inordinately high. The result is that families are often left at home, and the wage-earner's remittances to his dependents reduce him to hardly more than subsistence. Thus the fate of thousands of aliens is to live in squalid hovels, indefinitely separated from their homes and families, desperate for employment; they have exchanged the best of their working years for wages that can just keep them and their dependents alive. Against the background of superabundance and prodigality existing in Kuwait, the wide gulf between the two segments of the population is not only indefensible but is bound to engender social resentment and instability.

Nor is this all. The remittances of the resident aliens are a permanent drain on the national income. The extent of it cannot be ascertained, but is conservatively estimated at some $120,000,000 a year. If this labor force could be persuaded to strike roots in Kuwait, this drain on national wealth would be minimized and the base of the economy would be broadened. This viewpoint is gaining recognition, but not fast enough.

Finally, the growing size of this foreign labor force has suddenly awakened the Kuwaitis to the fact that they are about to become a minority in their own country. According to the 1961 population census, they barely exceed half the total. This would be serious enough in any country, let alone in one so small, underpopulated and rich, and where the indigenous community lacks all the vital technical skills.

IV

The discovery that it was being swamped by aliens alarmed Kuwait and prompted defensive measures. Foremost among these was the naturalization decree of 1959 and its amendment in 1960. This legislation, a landmark in Kuwait's history, confined Kuwaiti citizenship to residents in Kuwait prior to 1920, to their descendants in the male line and to foreign women upon marriage to Kuwaitis. For Arabs, naturalization is now possible only after 10 years of residence, and for non-Arabs after 15 years, commencing, in both cases, from the date of the amending decree. Moreover, only 50 persons are to be granted citizenship in any one year. Exceptions to this general rule are that Arabs in residence before 1945, and foreigners before 1930, as well as other Arab nationals who have performed outstanding services to the state, may be granted citizenship without waiting.

The legislation also confined certain basic rights and privileges to the citizen class. All imports and retail trades and all contractual business are either limited to Kuwaiti nationals or have to be transacted through Kuwaiti agents. In the civil service, pension rights, permanent tenure and certain key executive positions are the exclusive privileges of citizens. The entry of aliens into some professions such as medicine and law, where not many citizens could compete for a long time to come, is restricted to a stringent licensing system.

A unique feature of this transformation is the ingenious device evolved to diffuse the new wealth among the citizen class through public expenditure. As we have seen earlier, the distinction between public income and property and the ruler's income or property was unknown in Kuwait. Gradually, as budgetary practices and controls were introduced, all public receipts were paid into the Exchequer.[3] Since the process was confined at first to annual disbursements and receipts of money, control of the public land was overlooked; and so long as realty was not of great economic significance the oversight was not serious. But then real estate prices rocketed. Meanwhile, large tracts of worthless desert had been seized and fenced in by those who had either the foresight or foreknowledge to anticipate the coming public projects; and they subsequently were compensated handsomely by the state. With a rapid turnover of land and in the absence of legislation covering the acquisition of land for public uses, the cost to the Treasury was fantastic.

The process within the city itself differed somewhat from that outside the old city wall. Land was purchased in excess of what was actually required for public projects, and the surplus was later sold back to the public, often at a fraction (estimated at 4 percent) of its cost to the Treasury. Enormous private fortunes were amassed by both selling to, and buying from, the state. It has been estimated that between 1957 and 1962 close to $840,-000,000 of public money was spent on land.

This huge expenditure would have been justified on the grounds that it engendered economic activity and diffused a large portion of the new wealth, were it not that in fact only a limited amount was piped into the local economy. By far the larger part was remitted abroad either directly, or indirectly through the banking system. Further, the wealth was not spread evenly, the greater part going to those at the top of the social pyramid, even though, because of the small size of the indigenous community, a fair amount did go also to the masses. It now is argued that unless the process is continued, large-scale bankruptcies will wreck the economy, since substantial bank advances have been made to merchants who are said to have invested them in land. It is difficult

[3] However, this new practice does not include Kuwait's substantial reserves which still remain with the Bank of England in the name of His Highness the Emir.

to ascertain whether this is true; but banking statistics show that advances to Kuwaiti residents (about $110,600,000 toward the end of 1963) represent just over 40 percent of total visible imports —a fact that hardly bears out the argument. Yet the practice continues unabated despite serious warning by government advisers and the recommendation of the World Bank.

The process of diffusing the new wealth was not confined, however, to land purchases. Social security benefits and state aid in most generous and varied forms, free medical treatment and scholarships for training abroad, the granting of free building sites and loans at very low interest—all were made available to the citizen as his birthright.

v

The effects of these measures on Kuwait must be evaluated from two standpoints: the response they evoked from the aliens and the impact they had on the citizen class.

That they have been effective in achieving their aim is obvious enough. They have introduced a sharp distinction between the two classes of society; and they have reserved to the citizens all the fruits of the windfall of riches (with the lion's share going to a relatively small group within this class). Little else can be said in favor of these measures. They have permanently estranged and embittered the most efficient and indispensable element in the community—the resident alien. Uprooted, often separated from his family, insecure and unsettled, he has now become envious and resentful. With little or no hope of being permanently integrated into the community, he is left without any sense of allegiance to Kuwait.

Let us look now at the impact of these protective and restrictive measures on the citizens for whom they were devised. An immediate consequence was the reversal of the old order that made the state and members of the ruling family dependent on the merchants, for now it was the latter who sought favors from the state. They wanted not only compensation for land but also the preservation of their commercial interests. While the state has been strengthened by its financial independence and has become less susceptible to pressures from this group, the change was not an unmixed blessing, considering that the government is not dependent upon popular consent for its annual income.

Further, the ease with which wealth has been acquired has impaired the enterprise of the mercantile class and made them dependent on the state. Hardly any worthwhile financial or industrial venture which deviates from the established pattern is ever attempted by Kuwaiti entrepreneurs (of whom there are, in any case, very few) unless it is assured of state financing, protection or guarantee. Conversely, private capital can be forthcoming to excess when an expatriate entrepreneur, acting with state cooperation, comes forward with new ideas for investment.

Developments are disturbing, too, at the other end of the social scale. Here the state's compensatory payments were naturally less extensive, since the property involved was mainly private dwelling houses. The money received was promptly spent, usually on prestige items or travel abroad. When this spurt was over, the common citizen was assured a modest income from a minor government sinecure, and various state benefits, plus a small private income from, say, a taxi or a tiny retail store—the whole accepted in much the same spirit as that of a pensioner receiving his dole.

Originally intended to preserve the identity of the old community, reserve the bulk of the new wealth for its citizens and protect them against the intruding aliens, these measures have inadvertently forced competition out of national life and made Kuwait an insular society. The elimination of competition now probably presents the most serious social danger facing Kuwait. Young people have lost their perspective, their urge to acquire knowledge, their acceptance of discipline. As a result, the drive, diligence and risk-taking that characterized the old Kuwaiti are no more. At both ends of the social scale the new citizen is content to enjoy a life of leisure and inertia, and is unwilling that this happy state of affairs should be disturbed. Protected, pampered, lavishly provided for and accountable to no one, he lives in a world of make-believe.

Another serious threat is posed to Kuwaiti society by the social vacuum which these measures have created. By relegating the traditionally dynamic classes to a position of only titular authority at the apex of the social pyramid or else to one of passive contentment, they have placed a premium on inertia and prevented the rise of an indigenous and dynamic middle class. The vacuum thus created is naturally filled by watchful and enterprising aliens.

The people attracted to Kuwait by its new wealth were of varied backgrounds, experiences and standards of conduct. The avarice and intrigues of many of them have brought bitter disillusionment to the Kuwaiti. Consequently, traditional Kuwaiti behavior is changing and men for whom the spoken word used to have the sanctity of a written contract have become instinctively suspicious of strangers and new ideas.

Further, the magnitude of the new wealth has given money and material possessions an importance and their owners a sense of power hitherto unknown. Naturally this has resulted in false perspectives. Ostentatious consumption, prodigal expenditure, idleness and pleasure-seeking are common; frugality, moderation and enterprise have become the antiquated virtues of a bygone age.

Finally, and most important of all, the new wealth has assumed such proportions that it is beginning to threaten the very concept of the state. This is because the lavish welfare benefits and privileges have entailed no effort or sacrifice on the part of the public, which sees no need to contribute to a state whose chief problem is what to do with its income. A fundamental principle in the relationship between state and citizen has therefore been jeopardized—namely, that in exchange for protection and benefits, the citizen has a duty to serve it and to make necessary sacrifices for it. The idea of the state as a communal institution demanding service, sacrifice and devotion, and as an embodiment of political and social ideas, exists today in the minds and hearts of very few and exceptional Kuwaitis.

### VI

This tiny city-state: prodigal, complacent, short of technical skills, unperturbed by the acquisitiveness of its upper classes, the torpor of its common citizens and the savage rivalry among its resident aliens—what chance has it of survival in a poor, covetous and unstable region?

First it must be noted that most major events in the Middle East are influenced by external and regional forces; the survival of political régimes does not solely depend on their own economic or social merits. However, the record of Kuwait's achievements is such that (barring the unexpected) one may suppose that disruptive forces from outside will encounter there an exceptional degree of viability and resilience.

Kuwait entered the modern era of welfare and technology with very few handicaps from her past. Unfettered by rigid traditions or conventions, she was free to experiment and adopt institutions and practices best suited to her own circumstances. Naturally anyone willing to follow the rough path of trial and error must be prepared to pay the price; Kuwait was willing and has done so. This willingness to experiment with new ideas gives the state both dynamism and flexibility not often found in old societies. Kuwait is not stagnant, nor has her social fabric as yet assumed final form. Her social and economic legislation is constantly revised and improved; her public services are being reorganized and streamlined; her city planning is being reviewed.

There is, further, a feeling on the part of the indigenous community that its present privileged position can be preserved only by total and unqualified domestic solidarity. Solidarity among the Kuwaitis is a time-honored tradition, and the recent waves of immigration have so strengthened the need for it that any deviation is now simply inconceivable. This was plainly demonstrated in 1961 when the entire community rallied around the Emir in the face of Kassem's threats; all past rancor was forgotten as autocratic rule was wisely replaced by constitutional government.

Despite the shortcomings and dangers attending the rapid transformation of a primitive society into one of great sophistication, certain fundamental traits in the character of the individual Kuwaiti remain unimpaired. He still remains tolerant, placid, and, above all, devoted to and proud of his freedom. These qualities explain why differences of opinion continue to be settled by debate and not violence; why the fundamental freedoms of speech and the press are respected; why censorship and the secret police —two monumental features in every Arab state—do not figure in Kuwait's political life, and have no impact on the thoughts or actions of her people. It is fortunate that the drafting of the constitution should have been completed during this period of Kuwait's history when these qualities are still a salient feature of the Kuwaiti personality.

There remains one more item on this balance sheet which calls for special mention, namely Kuwait's attitude toward the massive, woeful and demoralizing poverty outside her boundaries.

Here again, Kuwait's perspicacity and high-mindedness have been extraordinary. Transcending all the animosities and feuds of contemporary Arab politics, she has single-handedly set up the most enduring and constructive institution ever attempted by a small state. This is the Kuwait Fund for the Economic Development of the Arab Countries, with capital resources totaling altogether K.D. 300,000,000 ($840,000,000). This institution has been established to make loans to other Arab states to enable them to carry out projects directly useful in developing their economies. It is a permanent, well-administered organization with clearly defined objectives and intelligent criteria for evaluating projects. It stands out as a monument to Kuwait's foresight and generosity. It also marks a turning point in her development as a state, for it demonstrates that she recognizes her responsibilities and is willing and able to live up to them. Within less than two years of its inception, the Fund . . . lent $19,600,000 to the Sudan for the modernization of its railways; $21,000,000 to Jordan for agricultural and industrial projects; and $18,200,000 to Tunisia; besides substantial sums pledged to Algeria, the Yemen and the UAR.

Naturally, Kuwait is very proud of her achievements; but in determining her fate her own assessment of her performance is far less important than the opinion of her neighbors. Whether or not her extravagance will be excused because of her generosity, only time will tell. What is certain is that she can justify her survival as a political entity in this age of regional internationalism only by serving effectively and impartially as a distributor of substantial economic aid to her neighbors. Herein lies Kuwait's present *raison d'être*. In order to maintain her independent identity she will have to pursue her plans for economic aid with a zeal induced by the knowledge that it is an essential part of her struggle for survival.

# XI. Social Structure and Ideology in Iraq, Lebanon, Syria and the UAR

## by Charles Issawi

THE FOUR MOST DEVELOPED EASTERN ARAB COUNTRIES—LEBA-
non, Syria, Iraq and the UAR—show a wide spectrum of economic
and political ideologies and systems. Lebanon is a genuine parliamentary democracy and a firm believer in private enterprise.
The same was largely true of Syria until quite recently, but at
present it is hovering undecidedly between an army dictatorship
and a multi-party system and between a free enterprise and a
socialist economy. Iraq, after violent oscillations, expressing themselves in successive army *coups,* seems, with the nationalization
laws of July 1964, to be following the path blazed by the UAR.
The latter has, since the nationalizations of 1960 and 1961, been
advancing steadily along the road of "Arab Socialism." This means
in politics the dictatorship of the army, which is trying to establish
a basis of civilian support in the Arab Socialist Union; and in
economics state ownership of practically all means of production
except agriculture, and state control over all economic activity of
any significance.

These differences are quite recent. Fifteen years ago all four
countries were ruled by more or less oligarchic cabinets and parliaments, elected more or less freely, and in all, government participation in economic life was quite small. It is true that the governments exercised some control over economic activity, through
such measures as exchange control, import licensing, agricultural
price supports or acreage control and the provision of agricultural
or industrial credit to enterprises which were not served by the
commercial banking system. But in none of these countries did

government ownership extend beyond such fields as irrigation works, railways and airlines. And in none did the government expenditure amount to more than at most 20 per cent of gross national product, a figure below those prevailing in the United States, Britain and France at that time.

Since then all four countries have moved in the direction of extension of government ownership and a relative as well as absolute increase in government expenditure. But both the pace and purpose of this movement have been very different.

The explanation of this divergence is to be sought in many fields. The great homogeneity of the UAR, compared to the geographical, anthropological and religious diversity of Lebanon and Syria, made it much easier for its government to carry out a drastic revolution in its economic system.[1] Again the existence in Egypt of an old, large and relatively effective bureaucracy may be contrasted with the weakness of those of Lebanon and Syria; here Iraq occupies an intermediate position. The far higher levels of income and education in Lebanon, and the distinctly higher levels in Syria (at any rate until the last five or six years) probably increased the attachment of these countries to constitutional government and free enterprise. And, perhaps even more important, whereas Lebanon and Syria obtained their full independence, including the complete evacuation of foreign troops, in 1943-46, in both Egypt and Iraq the presence of foreign troops and the continuation of unpopular alliances with the West were constant sources of irritation, which led to demonstrations, riots and the eventual overthrow of the regimes and undermining of the social structure.

All these factors are very significant. But, in this writer's opinion, there are two other basic ones which have been at work for a long time but which have received very little attention: the difference between a rain-fed agriculture and one based on river-irrigation; and the varying degree of development of the native bourgeoisie. For these two factors have to a large extent determined the nature, wealth and power of two classes whose support

[1] It is true that, religiously and ethnically, Iraq is still more heterogeneous than Syria and Lebanon, and that it has an even larger proportion of beduin. But it is yet to be seen how easily, and how far, the government can carry the people along the road chosen by it. The still unsettled Kurdish revolt is an indication of the obstacles faced by any Iraqi government and the limits to its freedom of action.

of free enterprise and parliamentary democracy has in many countries been crucial, the farmers and the middle class. This article is therefore devoted to an analysis of the interplay of these two factors in the four countries under consideration.[2]

Agriculture has always been the mainstay of the economy of the Arab world and is still the leading sector, employing at least two-thirds of the total population. It is therefore natural that differences in agrarian patterns and structures should have deep effects, both direct and indirect, on the rest of the society. In Egypt, "the gift of the Nile" in Herodotus' often quoted phrase, the determining factor has been the nature of that river. In the first place the Nile provides a superb means of communication throughout the whole country—particularly because the current flows northward while the prevailing winds blow from north to south, enabling boats to sail upstream and float downstream. Secondly, to quote the great irrigation engineer Sir William Willcocks, "of all the rivers in the world, the Nile is the most gentlemanly." It is free of salt, carries little sediment, and rises and falls in a regular way and at the right times for the sowing and harvesting of winter crops. This has meant that Egypt always had a thriving agriculture, the basis of its wealth and power. But it also meant that the country had to be unified and tightly controlled by a government which ensured the necessary labor and cooperation on irrigation works, a task considerably facilitated by Egypt's compactness.[3] This in turn meant the development of a large bureaucracy of irrigation engineers, land surveyors, registrars and tax collectors, who have always played a major part in economic and social life.

Under Muhammad Ali a new element, cotton, was introduced. This provided a large source of income and made it possible for Egypt's population to multiply tenfold between 1800 and 1960.

[2] The North African countries also show a wide gamut, ranging from socialist Algeria to conservative Libya, with Tunisia and Morocco occupying intermediate positions; here the main factors at work have been the intensity of the struggle against foreign domination after the Second World War and the extent of previous foreign control over the economy. The other Arab countries—Jordan, Saudi Arabia, etc.—are only just reaching the stage where the struggle of economic and social ideologies begins to be meaningful.

[3] See the illuminating book by Karl Wittfogel, *Oriental Despotism,* New Haven, 1957, p. 166, where it is rightly pointed out that Egypt is the most compact of the major "hydraulic societies" in world history.

But cotton, being a summer crop, could be grown only under perennial irrigation, which demanded a much more elaborate network of dikes and canals than the "basin" or "flood" irrigation hitherto used. This in turn required a great tightening of government control, and Muhammad Ali responded by taking over the ownership of all agricultural land, dictating land use and the choice of crops, advancing seeds and working capital to the peasants and buying back their crops at (very low) fixed prices. For good measure, he also took over the other main sectors of the economy, including transport and a large part of foreign trade; moreover, he founded a sizable modern industry. But this early attempt at state socialism ran counter to the prevailing world trends and foreign pressure forced Muhammad Ali to dismantle his system of state controls and monopolies. Under his successors private property prevailed in agriculture and Egypt soon had hundreds of thousands, and later millions, of small peasant proprietors. But—given the sharp limits to the extension of the cultivated area and the absence of industrialization—the rapid population growth created a large surplus of labor in the countryside. The result was the growth of a landless peasantry, a sharp rise in rents, the fragmentation of land into dwarf farms, and the impoverishment of both tenants and small proprietors. In other words, in spite of the relative diffusion of property, Egypt did not acquire a class of prosperous, conservative peasants who in so many countries have constituted one of the main pillars of democratic capitalism.

In Iraq the situation was much worse. The Tigris and Euphrates provide much less favorable bases for agriculture than the Nile. For one thing, they are only partly navigable. More important, their high salt and silt content, their great irregularity and unpredictability and the fact that they have their annual flood in April and May—too late for winter and too early for summer crops—have meant that they could be harnessed only through a system of perennial irrigation. This implied a vast network of irrigation and drainage canals, as well as dikes for flood protection, and the elaborate and fragile structure so built required constant upkeep. Any weakening in the government resulted in a sharp contraction in cultivation, a phenomenon that has repeatedly recurred in the long history of Mesopotamia. The last such decline began with the weakening of the Abbasid state and was precipitated by the Mongol invasion, which ruined many irrigation works. During the next six centuries Iraq never had a government strong enough to restore its irrigation system, hence large tracts of land were spoiled by salination and the nomads took possession of the countryside, imposing on it their form of tribal ownership. When, starting in the second half of the nineteenth century, Iraq began to revive and land acquired an ever greater market value, the successive Ottoman, Mandatory and Iraqi governments tried to settle land titles, with the result that both tribal and government-owned land were appropriated by the former tribal leaders. By the 1950's, some 85 per cent of the arable land was owned by only 33,000 persons and the bulk of the rural population was landless. Such an agrarian structure was hardly conducive to the growth of either free enterprise forms of production or democratic political institutions.

Unlike that of Egypt and Iraq, the agriculture of Syria and Lebanon is rain-fed, irrigation having been negligible until the last ten or fifteen years. This prevented these countries from achieving a large agricultural production and explains their constant subordination to either Iraq or, more often, Egypt. But it also meant that they never experienced such breakdowns as Iraq, since even the Mongols could not destroy the rain! It meant too that the role of the government in agriculture was negligible.

But a further important difference should be noted between the coastal zones in Lebanon and parts of Syria where rain is abundant and fairly regular, and the interior where it is both scarce and erratic. This promoted in two ways the diffusion of property in the coastal areas and its concentration in the interior. First, regularity of rainfall enables the small peasant proprietor to raise, year in year out, enough produce on his land to assure his subsistence, whereas the possibility of two or three successive droughts can ruin him; hence in the interior only large landowners can survive.[4] Secondly, the abundance of rain makes it possible to raise tree

[4] It is not accidental that the great agricultural expansion in Syria in 1942-58 was the work of neither the government—as in the irrigated areas of Iraq and Egypt—nor of small owners but of large landlords and merchant entrepreneurs.

crops and other valuable products which demand the constant attention and labor which an owner, not a tenant, can best provide.[5] It is not fortuitous that the only Middle Eastern country in which *mulk,* or freehold, land tenure has been prevalent is Lebanon; in all others it is restricted to areas within towns or villages. If we add to this the effects of the Lebanese agrarian revolts of 1840-1860—the only ones in the Middle East—the diffusion of education through Christian missionary schools and the impact of emigration to the Americas and the subsequent inflow of capital and ideas, it will be realized why Lebanon is the only country in the region with a self-reliant, moderately prosperous, peasantry. And this peasantry could both adopt progressive capitalist forms of agriculture, in the shape of fruit and vegetable growing for export, and play a positive part in the political process.

Passing to the second factor, the composition and strength of the bourgeoisie, a general consideration which applies to all four countries should be borne in mind. In Western Europe a large part of the bourgeoisie was recruited from the ranks of the handicraftsmen, and the growth of factory industry later greatly broadened and strengthened the middle class. But in the Middle East the handicrafts were ruined by the competition of European machine-made goods, and hardly any industrialists emerged from their ranks. However, it is worth pointing out that the handicrafts were first shaken in Egypt—by Muhammad Ali's policy and the inflow of foreign goods facilitated by Egypt's early accessibility and good transport system—and then in Iraq, and that they lingered longest in Syria and Lebanon, playing a significant part in Aleppo and Damascus until the 1930's.[6] And, for a variety of reasons, a modern factory industry began to develop only in the 1930's in Egypt, and the 1940's or 50's in the other countries, too late to strengthen the bourgeoisie significantly before it was assailed by hostile forces.

As for the other sectors which could sustain the bourgeoisie—trade, finance and transport—the most striking feature in the Middle East has been their domination by foreigners or, to a far smaller extent, minority groups. Except where they were built and operated

---

[5] See Jacques Weulersse, *Paysans de Syrie et du Proche Orient,* Paris, 1946.
[6] For details on this and other changes in the nineteenth century, see Charles Issawi, *The Economic History of the Middle East, 1800-1914* (in Press).

by the state, as in Egypt and Iraq, railways were owned by foreign interests, as were street cars, river transport, the major bus lines and other public utilities. Until the 1920's all the large banks—and except in Lebanon and Syria most of the small ones as well—were foreign-owned, and the same was true of insurance companies. As for foreign trade, it came under European domination at an early date and except in Lebanon, and to a lesser extent Syria, remained so until the last few years. Thus in Iraq on the eve of the First World War, a list of the thirteen important firms engaged in foreign trade shows only one Muslim name; five were Jewish and the others foreign, and the situation did not change fundamentally until the Second World War.[7] In Egypt, until the Second World War, there were only three Egyptian cotton exporting firms; the others, and practically all large importing firms, were owned by foreigners or members of minority groups. Perhaps the best over-all indices are the two following figures. In 1929 the President of the British Chamber of Commerce in Egypt estimated that 90 per cent of Egyptian securities were owned by foreigners.[8] And as late as 1951, after thirty years of independence during which the government had made great efforts to Egyptianize business and while the Misr group had started a wide range of enterprises, only 31 per cent of company directors were Muslims and 6 per cent Copts.[9] In other words in Egypt the "productive middle class," as distinct from the "salaried middle class," consisted until quite recently almost wholly of foreigners or members of minority groups and could therefore put up very little resistance against the indigenous radical forces—Muslim Brotherhood and nationalist socialism—that emerged in the last twenty years. The growth of the Muslim bourgeoisie came too late to counter this trend.

[7] A. Lanzoni, "La Mesopotamia economica," *Bolletino della Società Geografica Italiana*, XLVII, Rome, 1910. Similarly the capital of the government-owned banks was distinctly greater than that of the private banks.

[8] L. A. Fridman, *Kapitalisticheskoe razvitie Yegipta*, Moscow, 1963, p. 241. A more accurate study showed that in 1934 half the share and bond capital of Egyptian companies was held abroad, to which should be added the bulk of Suez Canal shares. See A. E. Crouchley, *The Investment of Foreign Capital in Egyptian Companies and Public Debt*, Cairo, 1936. Of the balance, a substantial proportion was held by resident foreigners or members of minority groups.

[9] By 1960 the figures were 66 and 4 per cent respectively; see Charles Issawi, *Egypt in Revolution*, London, 1963, p. 89.

In Iraq the exodus of the Jews (who played a very important part in trade and finance) after the Arab-Israeli War greatly reinforced the small native bourgeoisie, which stepped into their place. Moreover the vast inflow of oil revenues after 1950 also strengthened the Iraqi middle class, both directly by providing opportunities for builders, contractors and others and indirectly by being channelled to local industries by the government-owned Industrial Bank and other agencies. But the oil revenues accruing to the government strengthened to a much greater degree the army and the bureaucracy.[10] This factor, added to the deeply unhealthy agrarian structure which obviously called for radical changes, left the "productive" bourgeoisie very vulnerable, particularly after the overthrow of the monarchy in 1958. The struggle between the "salaried middle class" and the "productive middle class" is still going on, but the former seems the likely winner.

In Lebanon, on the other hand, and to a lesser degree in Syria, the native bourgeoisie showed much more vigor at a far earlier date. Already in 1827 a French consular despatch from Beirut stated that of 34 commercial firms dealing with Europe, 15 belonged to local Christians and 6 to Muslims and, in 1839, 34 out of 67 firms were Lebanese. As for the silk reeling industry, the leading one in Lebanon, in 1862, out of a total of 44 firms, 33 belonged to natives, who controlled 1,350 out of the 2,200 pans in use.[11] Later, the Lebanese established many small banks, and, more recently, they founded almost all the industries operating in the country. They have also acquired a large, and sometimes predominant, share in many enterprises founded in Lebanon by foreign capital, while other such enterprises were bought back by the Lebanese government. Similarly, the Syrians have played a significant part in banking and an almost exclusive one in trade and industry. In other words, in Lebanon, and to a lesser degree in Syria, a native bourgeoisie developed early, came to control a significant portion of the economy and struck deep roots in society.

[10] Thus, on the eve of the Revolution in 1958, private investment in industry amounted to only 13,220,000 dinars, while government investment totalled 34,517,000.

United Nations, *Economic Developments in the Middle East, 1958-59,* New York, 1960, p. 18.

[11] Charles Issawi, "Economic Development and Liberalism in Lebanon," *Middle East Journal,* Summer, 1964, Washington, D. C.

It was therefore far better placed to withstand the onslaught of hostile forces. In effect, the smallness of the foreign-owned sector in Lebanon and Syria made capitalism in both these countries much less vulnerable to socialist onslaughts than in Egypt, or in Iraq with its huge foreign-owned oil industry presenting an almost irresistible temptation.

It only remains to evaluate, in conclusion, the overall balance of forces. Throughout history the two foci of what is now the Arab Middle East have been the Nile and the Tigris-Euphrates valleys. Syria and Lebanon have always gravitated towards one or other of these centers, generally Egypt. The above discussion has shown that both Syria and, to a greater degree, Lebanon have certain internal resistances to the forces making for state ownership and control, a fact which accounts for many of their actions in recent years, particularly Syria's secession from the UAR in 1961. But it is also clear that if Iraq should follow the UAR further along the path of "Arab Socialism" the pressure on Syria and Lebanon will be immensely increased and the pull of the river valleys may once more prove to be irresistible.

# XII.   Palestine: The Broken Triangle

## by Erskine B. Childers

*A small State, precariously perched on a coastal shelf, with its back to the sea and defiantly facing on three sides a hostile Arab world.*
—Count Bernadotte, 1948[1]

THE ARAB-ISRAELI CONFLICT REMAINS ONE OF TOTAL DEADLOCK. In face of this, the prevailing Western tendency, both at government and non-government levels, is to reiterate the following formula: the existence of Israel is a fact that must be accepted; we do not wish to take sides in this conflict; we seek close and friendly relations with the Arab world; we stand ready to use our good offices for mediation whenever an opportunity occurs; but until then, the *status quo* must be maintained, aggression from any source must be halted, and an arms equilibrium must be ensured.

Behind this formula, there appears to be a general thesis about the likely future of the Arab-Israeli conflict, provided the West ensures the arms equilibrium and the *status quo*. I will call this the thesis of attrition by Arab social reform. Like most other notions and assumptions about Palestine, its origins may be traced far back before the establishment of the State of Israel. From 1918 onwards, it was a persistent theme of Zionist publicity in the West that Arab hostility to Zionism was artificial. The "ordinary Arab" was not really interested in politics, but was being whipped up and deliberately made uneasy by "a handful of agitators" using Zionism as a diversion for their own feudal interests and rival ambitions.[2]

[1] In his UN Mediator report to the Security Council, July 12, 1948.
[2] *Viz.* the Israeli State propaganda booklet, *Facts About Israel*, p. 15 annually; Chaim Weizmann, *Trial and Error* for the whole Mandate period; Weizmann's, Samuel's, Meinertzhagen's letters, in *Documents on British Foreign Policy*, Series 1, Vols. IV & XIII for the theme in 1919-20.

This Zionist theme was very widely accepted in the West, and its effects were by no means only negative. It not only appeared to explain all reports of Arab unrest and violence; it had the quite positive implication that "firmness" by the British in fulfilling the pledges to Zionism would be morally justified and politically successful. Once Zionism was irrevocably entrenched, the Arabs would "accept Zionism's existence." [3] But at its most positive the theme became a moral argument for Zionism itself, for it was widely argued that the Zionists, bringing their dynamic "socialism" into Palestine, would themselves free the ordinary Arab from the clutches of the "agitating feudalist" leaders. Much of what concern there was among liberal Westerners for the Arabs was thus canalised into sympathy for them, not *vis-à-vis* Zionism, but *vis-à-vis* their own leaders.

Each of these adopted notions is now embodied in the present thesis of attrition. The Palestine Arab refugees are seen as being "caged like animals in suffering as a deliberate political weapon." [4] But in time, it is believed, the refugees will refuse to go on being "caged" and will demand resettlement—especially if they are made to see that the occupation of their former lands and homes by Israeli settlers is irrevocable. As to the wider Arab world, it is believed that the social revolution now accelerating will make it less and less possible for "self-seeking rival autocrats or dictators" to use Israel as a diversion. An ever-growing new Arab intelligentsia will see the reality of Israel, oppose the social cost of heavy armaments, and even, perhaps, see the justice of the Israeli case. Furthermore, the more newly independent Arab countries, remote from Palestine and the memory of 1948, will refuse to be drawn into the conflict and will press Egypt and the others to abandon it. This has been a widespread assumption about Morocco, Algeria and Tunisia.

These, it appears, are the prevailing assumptions about the likely future course of the conflict—assumptions held both in the West and in Israeli general opinion. They are undoubtedly the

[3] *Documents*, IV, *passim*; Zionist proposals for specialists in "firmness" from the Black and Tans to be transferred from Ireland, Meinertzhagen, *Middle East Diary*, pp. 112-6.

[4] Leon Uris, *Exodus*, as an instance of the theme reaching millions of Westerners.

most comforting available, and like the original theme begun in 1918, involve no searching questions for the West. But suppose this whole social-reform thesis of attrition proves to be wrong? The consequences will be very grave indeed. More years will have been lost without tackling any of the roots of the conflict itself. The arms confrontation will have become more lethal, even if in supposed equilibrium. Continued blanket Western support of the Israeli *status quo* will have jeopardised Western relations, not with a weak and unstable Arab world, but a dynamic new Arab society of one hundred million people, astride one of the great strategic and commercial axes of the world. And for the three million odd Israelis, inside their tiny beach-head, the future will contain no greater prospect of peace, to put it at the happiest estimate.

What, then, are the indications for the future of the dispute as of today? In this writer's judgment, the attrition thesis has no foundation in discernible fact or trend anywhere in the Arab world. Perhaps such trends may appear in the future; but there are very sound reasons for doubting it. The evidence that is currently available suggests the reverse. The Arab social revolution does not appear to be "softening" hostility towards Israel: it does appear to be adding a whole new dimension of strength and determination to that hostility.

No one who is familiar with either the leading, or the little-known, exponents of today's Arab social revolution can fail to be struck by the approach they take to the Palestine issue. It has a moral and emotional scope very considerably *larger* than was evident in the early years following Israel's establishment. In the era of the *ancien régime* generation of Arab politics, the primary grievances of that generation against Israel were diplomatic, political and military. An Arab people had been forcibly denied political self-determination by Britain with the approval of other Western powers, in order to introduce into their land an alien statist force. That statist force had succeeded in gaining recognition, and in occupying and emptying most of Palestine of most of its Arabs. The existence of the Israeli state was regarded by *ancien régime* Arab politicians primarily as a diplomatic affront, a political injustice and a military danger. But for the new, revolutionary generation there is an added dimension of grievance and revulsion—the social dimension.

This is evident in the speeches and writing, not only of the top revolutionary leaders like Nasser, but in the very currency of talk about Palestine among Arabs of the new generation. The fact that Nasser speaks of Zionism and Israel as a race-supremacist settler force, and not simply an enemy state, has been little noted in the West—and where noted, has been derisively dismissed as mere polemic addressed to the new African states. But it is not only Nasser and other eastern-Arab leaders of his outlook who are making such statements. Both the Ben Bella and the Boumedienne Governments of Algeria have repeatedly spoken in such terms about Palestine. In 1964 President Habib Bourguiba of Tunisia described Israel as "the policy of colonial settlement pushed to the degree of paroxysm . . . the problem of Palestine is the same as South Africa." [5]

President Bourguiba's statements about the subject in 1965 prompted a wave of speculation throughout the West to the effect that he had made serious "peace proposals" reflecting a significant new shift in Arab opinion. I can only record my own conclusion which is that the 1965 "Bourguiba Affair" reflected more than anything else the Western propensity for tragically facile wishful thinking on Palestine. A few observations will suffice to clarify this position.

President Bourguiba, while on a tour of the Middle East, was personally incensed by the overwhelming pre-eminence of President Nasser among the Arabs. He was already angry over expectations in Cairo and other capitals that all Arab governments would react with uniform severity to West Germany's secret arms deal with, and subsequent recognition of, Israel. President Bourguiba suddenly and unilaterally stated that he could envisage a time in the future when Israelis and Arabs, relieved of extremism on both sides, could co-exist. He then went on publicly to doubt that the outside world would ever allow the injustices done to the Palestine Arabs to be redeemed by military force. Finally, he outlined those terms which, in most Western newspapers, were so promptly described as "new peace proposals."

However, they were nothing of the kind. His speech had merely

[5] Interview with the correspondent of *Le Monde* in late July 1964: the correspondent expressed surprise over the vehemence with which Bourguiba spoke of Palestine.

reiterated the official Arab formula—enunciated by both the Palestine leaders and by Nasser for years—that negotiations could begin on the basis of the UN resolutions on Palestine, including partition and free choice of repatriation or compensation for the Arab refugees. As on every previous occasion, Israel promptly rejected these proposals. President Bourguiba himself then said publicly that he had fully expected that Israel would reject them, and that he had only tried to take an initiative that would expose Israel's real policies. He was vociferously attacked throughout the Middle East, not because he had repeated the official Arab formula, but because—without any evidence that Israel would this time respond—he had broached "peace" in a way which Arabs knew would be used against them. That they were correct in their angry fear can scarcely be a matter of conjecture. Israel's total rejection of the Bourguiba "peace proposals" was almost ignored in the West. However, the Israeli and Zionist use of his speeches to promote the traditional theme of an "artificial" Arab hostility (i.e., all the work of "Nasser") received excellent Western coverage.

But behind these new mists of unreality between the West and the Arab view of Israel, the massive additional sense of social injustice in Palestine to which I refer has continued. In every private discussion this writer has had with the little-known and unknown Arabs of the new generation, it has emerged as an integral part of their view of the Arab world. They see the recent history of their region as one of social injustice and exploitation, as well as of a more formally political nationalist-struggle against Western pressure. Allusion to the conduct of Zionist settlers and their social and economic impact upon, and eventual removal of, the mass of Palestine Arabs, has become part of one comprehensive retrospect that embraces landlord-domination in Egypt or Iraq and *colon*-domination in the Maghreb.

Behind this deeper and far more intensely angry perspective on Palestine there lies another of the influences which, in the Western attrition thesis, is supposed to produce moderation towards Israel, namely, education and the sheer tide of information about events in the rest of the world. And in taking note of this factor, the attitudes of Palestine-Arab refugees themselves must be included. The majority of the nearly three-quarters of a million refugees were peasants, without much education: their feeling for their fields and towns is built on the primaeval human emotion of longing to go back to everything that was familiar and loved. But a whole new generation of Palestinians has now grown up in exile—and they have received education. It has in no way made them "realistic."

For these new generation refugees, as for all young Arabs, the story of Palestine is one of moral contradiction on so great a scale as to make them burn with anger. To assume that this could be the product of sheer "hate-indoctrination," as alleged by Zionists, is undoubtedly convenient, but in no way helpful for us in the West or ultimately, I am convinced, for Israelis. The point is of such commanding importance that it must be elaborated all the way back to the beginning. For the contradiction that the new Palestine and other Arab generation now sees even more sharply than their parents involves the whole question of what I call the Palestine triangle.

The Palestine conflict is, and always has been, a triangular confrontation of the West, the Zionists and the Arabs; but one in which the only real, or "two-way" dialogue has been on the Western-Zionist side. It began, however, on a single axis entirely within the Western world—the axis of dialogue between Western Gentiles and Western Zionists.

A tiny group of Jews concluded from all the centuries of vicious Gentile persecution that all Gentiles, for all time and irremediably, were racially anti-Semitic. Chaim Weizmann frequently described it as a "bacillus" which every Gentile carried within him, whether he knew or admitted it, or not.[6] The corollary for this tiny group of Jews involved a categorical assumption "on behalf of" [7] all Jews, everywhere, that they were for all time a "people" or a "race" who could never be safe from the Gentile "bacillus" except in a return to a Jewish State. Setting out to obtain international recognition of this race-people doctrine, and of a millennial title to Palestine, Zionist leaders used highly selective arguments among Western statesmen and influential figures, according to their suscepti-

[6] Cf. R. H. S. Crossman, *A Nation Reborn*, 1960.

[7] Weizmann's classic admission at Czernowitz in 1927, that ever since 1917 he had "trembled lest the British Government would call me to ask, '. . . Where are they, your Zionists?' . . . The Jews, they knew, were against us; we stood alone on a little island, a tiny group;" P. Goodman (editor), *Chaim Weizmann*, Ch. XIV, 1945.

bilities.[8] But running through all these persuasions, and above all among Western liberals who later led the support of Zionism through to statehood, there was an appeal to the Western-Gentile conscience—the debt of shame over treatment of the Jews.

By definition, both this appeal and the ultimately massive response to it under the horror of Nazism had nothing at all to do with Palestine, save in one particularly hideous historical paradox. One of the first Western-Gentile burnings-alive of Jews did take place in Palestine—by the Crusaders[9] when they seized Jerusalem from the Arabs, under whom Jews had enjoyed freedom of worship and autonomy.[10] But the legacy of this Western anti-Semitism now devolved upon Arab Palestine: the axis of the Gentile-Jewish dialogue was shifted, and the Zionist end of it was pegged into that land, the site demanded for Western redemption of Western crimes. This transferred dialogue became one side of the triangle that is now inaccurately called a "local" or "regional" dispute in the Near East.

Palestine in 1917 had an over 90 per cent indigenous, rooted and homogeneously Arab population. In all Zionist drafts for the Balfour Declaration, these Arabs were not even mentioned. In the final document, they were politically evaporated into the phase, "existing non-Jewish communities" by a tactical British insertion which the Zionists thoroughly disliked.[11] The phrase was never intended to impair the substance of the British-Zionist compact.[12] This was that Britain, endorsed by the U.S.A. and other Western governments, would temporarily control Palestine "in trust for the Jews," [13] withhold majority self-rule from the Arabs[14] and suppress any rebellion by them, while allowing mass Zionist immigration to produce a Zionist state. The Arabs were not to be consulted about any of this; [15] it was the underlying intention actually

[8] Well summarised in Alan Taylor, *Prelude to Israel,* 1959.
[9] Cf. Runciman's documentary history, *The Crusades,* 1951.
[10] M. de Goeje, *Le Conquête de la Syrie,* 1900.
[11] Chaim Weizmann, *Trial and Error,* p. 260.
[12] L. S. Amery, who drafted it, *My Political Life,* Vol. II, p. 116.
[13] Weizmann to Cecil of the Foreign Office, April 25, 1917, cf. Leonard Stein, *The Balfour Declaration,* p. 422.
[14] David Lloyd George, *Peace Treaties,* Vol. II, p. 1138; Meinertzhagen, p. 104; Ben Halpern, *The Idea of the Jewish State,* pp. 295-309.
[15] Foreign Secretary Balfour's secret memo, August 11, 1919, *Documents.*

to remove them clear out of Palestine.[16] But they were to be assured, both by Britain and by the Zionists, that no Zionist state was envisaged, only partnership in a "joint autonomy"; and they were so assured.[17]

British control, and the general Western pledge to Zionism in Palestine, at once set up another side of today's triangle—that of a Western-Arab dialogue. But at no time, from the first fearful rumours of the Balfour Declaration in 1917, was this a viable or "two-way" dialogue. At no time was Arab opposition to Zionism artificial and agitator-induced.[18] The reasons why the Western-Arab side of the triangle was at all time sterile were two-fold. The Arabs simply did not believe the British-Zionist assurances; they saw the real intention behind the camouflage, both because of the experience they had already had of early militant-Zionist pioneers before 1917, and because of actual Zionist behaviour under British auspices after 1917. The facts about this really cannot be disputed: they are in Zionist documentary record and the Jewish testimony of writers like Ahad Ha'am.

Whatever the moral justifications held by Zionists, and pressed on Westerners by them, in terms of Palestine and its overwhelming indigenous Arab majority, Zionism was a race-supremacist settler movement. In his novel *Altneuland* for Western consumption, Theodor Herzl depicted happy Arabs, *in situ,* in a future Jewish State; in his secret diary, he had already set down a plan to "spirit the penniless population across the frontier by denying it employment." [19] By 1914, Zionists had already launched the complete strategy for Zionist supremacy, in a network of basic policies that were accelerated under the British Mandate through the Jewish Agency, the various Zionist funds and the "socialist" Histadruth.

All lands bought by the Jewish National Fund became legally, racially "Jewish" and could never be re-purchased by a non-Jew.[20]

[16] A Weizmann Archives acknowledgement, see *Jewish Observer,* March 6, 1964.
[17] Weizmann to Arabs in Jerusalem, 1918; 1921 Zionist Congress resolution; 1922 "Churchill" White Paper, *et cetera.*
[18] As reported by every responsible British official, *Documents,* and by the American King-Crane Commission, which was wholly ignored.
[19] Entry of June 12, 1895, *Complete Diaries,* Vol. I, 1960, p. 88.
[20] Jewish Agency Constitution Article 3 (d); see Hope-Simpson's description of the displacement effect on Arabs, HMG Cmd. 3686.

Arab tenant-farmers and labourers were evicted or driven away by the Zionist racial boycott of Arab labour which was extended to all possible Zionist enterprise, urban as well as rural.[21] If Arabs had to be employed under British directives, they received lower wages than Jews for the same work.[22] It was laid down as early as 1913 that the objective was "a closed Jewish economy." [23] To establish this, there also had to be a racial boycott of the produce of Arabs, if necessary imposed on urban Jews by force.[24] Mixed government schools were boycotted; Zionist schools taught Zionist exclusivism.[25] An underground Zionist army was formed; Arab arms were severely prohibited.

We have today voluminous evidence of the pattern of responses by other indigenous majorities to all other settler minority groups employing precisely these practices. The Arab response was identical. It is equally to be noted that all other settler groups have sought Western support through the same themes as are propagated by the Zionist movement. No one who has studied Algeria, Kenya, Rhodesia or South Africa can possibly ignore the parallels. The Zionist themes included: bringing "civilization" to the native; native neglect or non-use of land; discriminatory acts being only "temporary" until Zionism was really established, so that it could really begin "partnership"; the "ordinary" native not being interested in politics; all native unrest being purely artificially agitated; the native in any case having no innate rights in the territory; the "crude arithmetical" concept of democracy by majority being dangerous, and so on.[26]

---

[21] Jewish Agency 3 (e); JNF lease-form Article 23; Palestine Foundation Fund Article 7: "only Jewish labour . . . Jewish workmen only," *et cetera*.

[22] As late as 1946, Crossman noted this continued Zionist practice, *Palestine Mission,* p. 47; cf. also Nevill Barbour, *Nisi Dominus,* 1946, pp. 135-6; Hope-Simpson, *op. cit.*

[23] Zionist leader Arthur Ruppin to the 1913 Zionist Congress.

[24] Hoffien's 1953 address, Bank Leumi, in A. Rubner, *The Economy of Israel,* 1960, p. 99.

[25] Peel Commission *Report,* HMG Cmd. 5479 of 1937, p. 250.

[26] de Haas, the American Zionist, laid down the argument of no Arab political rights in Palestine; a similar thesis is advanced against the Africans by *apartheid* exponents in South Africa. The rejection of "crude arithmetical" democracy, interestingly enough in an argument against America assuming a Palestine mandate, was made in an official Zionist pamphlet in 1919, cf. Stein *op. cit.,* p. 612, because it was feared that the U.S. might give the Arabs majority self-government.

It should be emphasized that to cite these documented facts and to note these parallels should not be held to be "anti-Jewish." They concern the actions of only one particular group within world Jewry; and not within the Western cultural context of anti-Semitism, but in Palestine. So far as this writer can perceive, the sense of collective shame and guilt that he shares with every liberal non-Jewish Westerner for the crimes of his society against Jews in that society, cannot obscure these realities.

Indeed, to note this is to return to the Western-Arab side of the Palestine triangle. It was because of the concrete and increasingly grim facts of the actual Arab experience of Zionism that there never could be any meaningful Western-Arab dialogue. But it was also because there was no common basis of morality on which the West could discuss Zionism with the Arabs. The only morality available was the one in which the Arabs, by definition, could not be expected to share. The West was, in effect, asking this indigenous people to acquiesce in their own political extermination and physical eviction, in order to enable the West to pay for crimes of which the Arabs were innocent; crimes committed by the West, in the West, against Western Jews. No other indigenous people has even been asked to make such third-party payment by obliteration. It can scarcely be held surprising, or immoral, or "unrealistic," that the Arabs have been refusing to accept such a fate ever since.

And this in turn leads back to the even wider moral contradiction that has been an inevitable feature of the education of the new social-revolutionary Arab generation today. It is not simply that these millions of rising young Arabs, imbued with a dynamic sense of social justice, see the history of Zionism as that of a race-supremacist settler force. The contrast between the fate of Palestine's indigenous Arab population and that of all other indigenous populations in former colonial territories is now a hundred times sharper and more provocative than it could be for earlier Arabs. To the young educated Arab, it is a kind of giant nightmare—in which everything that the West and the United Nations has said and done everywhere else in the former colonial regions, must not be applied to his fellow Arabs of Palestine. He sees the issue of minority settler-supremacism already resolved in Kenya, Zambia, Malawi, Algeria and Tunisia—with overwhelming Western and

UN support for those indigenous peoples. And he sees the same
clear support fully committed in the remaining conflicts in southern
Africa. But not for Palestine.

To call such an outlook the product of "hate-indoctrination"
must surely have very sinister implications. It implies that the new
generation of Palestine Arab refugees and all other Arabs should
in some Orwellian fashion have been taught a separate morality,
and have been isolated morally and mentally from the whole outside world. To postulate that they ought not to have acquired this
view of the Palestine contradition is to suggest that they should
have had specially expurgated editions of the UN Charter, UN debates and resolutions, of world history textbooks without the Wil-
sonian precepts, the Atlantic Charter, the history of modern Afro-
Asia and the very history of their own fellow Arabs in Algeria.
I submit this, not in sarcasm but in plain logic, and it is of such
importance that it needs elaboration.

How else, for example, was any one of the young Palestinians
of this generation to be educated? It is a sobering and an instructive exercise to imagine the role of a teacher in an UNRWA
refugee school, under some hypothetical order to produce at grad-
uation a young man or woman meeting the requirement involved
in the attrition-thesis, and not open to the Zionist charge of "hate-
indoctrination." Consider what such a young graduate must be
educated to think of himself and the world around him.

His education must have omitted the history of Arab civilization, and of Palestine as an Arab-inhabited and Arab-cultured
country over more than a thousand years. His retrospect must be
as a human digit in an "existing non-Jewish community," in a
territory that had really always been "Jewish" because it had contained Hebrew kingdoms for very brief periods some two to three
thousand years ago. He must emerge from school believing that,
although the rooted people speaking his language and living in
his culture were an overwhelming majority in 1917 and still a
majority in 1947, they had no right to oppose the transformation
of Palestine into a Zionist state for alien settlers. His "non-Jewish
community" had no innate rights in Palestine at all.

Watching the Western world exerting increasing pressure on a
settler-supremacist minority in South Africa, this hypothetical
young Arab must see no contradiction. His teacher either censored

from his mind any suggestion that there had been race boycotts and evictions of his own people, and, finally, terrorisation and expulsion of them—or all of this was convincingly explained to him as necessary to redeem the distant West for its crimes against Jews in the West. He must have been instructed that when his own people and their kinfolk neighbours tried to resist settler-supremacy in 1948, they were wrong to do so and guilty of "aggression." But when Africans in South Africa, and their kinfolk neighbours in liberated states, resort to arms, this is right, and is supported by the liberal West. He has necessarily been taught that the 1949 Armistice lines around Palestine are sovereign, *de facto* frontiers of a peace-loving UN member-state; and that this state did not terrorise and drive out his own family and some 650,000 other people; their memories were all faulty; they left on "their own leaders' evacuation orders"; Israelis all wanted them to stay.

The "Bantustans" being created by the Verwoerd Government in South Africa would strike no parallels in this specially conditioned young Arab mind. He would expect that, when his own political leaders are asked by Africans and Westerners to vote at the UN to condemn South Africa *apartheid,* they will never suggest that the same code be applied to Palestine history—because it was quite different.

And so on . . . the range of mental and emotional conditioning required will perhaps be obvious from the above. That none of this has happened, but indeed the very reverse, ought not, surely, to be surprising. I am deeply aware that the above analysis will be offensive to very many liberal Westerners, non-Jewish and Jewish alike. But the problem that such reaction poses is not one of some vacuum of jurisprudence, political ethic and practical reality. It is *the* problem of the Israel-Arab conflict today, and of the broken triangle of dialogue that pins the West into that conflict in a manner that robs us of any chance of "mediation."

Let me try to summarise this problem as bluntly, but as realistically, as I can. The Israeli, or devoted Western pro-Israeli reader of this article may be outraged by it. Many Western readers not necessarily deeply committed to Israel may be surprised and even shocked by the facts and submissions in it. But unless those facts and submissions can be shown to be wrong both in themselves and in the view of the Arab world, none of this reaction will have the slightest bearing on the future of the Palestine conflict itself.

This is another way of defining the very essence of the broken triangle. It is natural that the Israeli government, and its Zionist predecessors all the way back to 1917, should have sought to produce a given Western view of the facts and ethics of the Palestine problem. Zionism and Israel were created in the West, and— to quote a perceptive comment by the traditionally Zionist *Guardian* newspaper—"Zionism was, in fact, the last successful surge of European colonialism into alien territory." [27] In turn, predominant Western policy and opinion may try to present, along the Western-Arab side of the triangle, the received Zionist and Israeli view of the facts and ethic of Palestine history. But it has not worked; it did not produce Arab acquiescence through all the years of trying up to 1947; and it has not produced an iota of yielding in all the years since. So far as this writer can see, the modern version of the post-1918 thesis of "artificial agitation," to be eliminated by "firmness" and social reform, is as hollow today as it was proven to be when it was first launched.

At the outset of this article, I quoted a warning prophecy by the late Count Bernadotte, the UN Mediator, about Israel's future. He was in essence describing a beach-head community. In the nature of such a situation, logistical support from the home base is vital: Zionist and Israeli existence in Palestine is based only upon such logistics—diplomatic, military and financial. Just as a commander on a beleaguered beach-head has often had very faulty intelligence about the morale of the forces surrounding him, so it has been a marked characteristic not only of the Israelis but other settler communities that they are dangerously ignorant of the thought and feelings of the surrounding native communities. As long ago as 1891, the great Jewish writer Ahad Ha'am observed this of Zionists in Palestine—and again in 1911, 1914 and 1920.[28]

---

[27] *Guardian* editorial, August 1, 1964.

[28] In 1891: "They treat the Arabs with hostility and cruelty and deprive them of their rights . . . think that the Arabs are all savages and do not understand what is happening around them. But this is a great mistake."

In 1911: ". . . the want of insight and understanding shown on our side to an extreme degree."

In 1914: "they [militant Zionists] wax angry towards those who remind them that there is still another people in Eretz Israel that has been living there and does not at all intend to leave."

In 1920: "we have regarded the Arabs as non-existent ever since the beginning of colonisation."

Other Jewish figures have noted it ever since,[29] and this writer has been struck by the self-insulated, dream-world of Israeli leaders over and over again in their analysis of Arab affairs.

The deeper the beach-head commanders feel their commitment, the more strenuously they are liable to send back faulty estimates of their situation to the home base. In turn, if they detect the least faltering in determination among those furnishing the logistical support, they are inexorably driven to counter-propaganda in the home base to prevent any re-thinking of the whole conflict. That all of these patterns have been marked in the Zionist-Western dialogue since the beginning is not a matter of polemic but of sober analysis. It has always had to be that way.

But it has not helped either ordinary Israelis, in the beach-head, or the West to help them. To cite one concrete and extremely pertinent example: from late 1949 onwards, Israel mounted a very strenuous global campaign to explain the Arab exodus of 1948 as being the result of "Arab evacuation orders." The campaign was brilliant, and very largely successful *in the West*. But far from making it more likely that the victims of the exodus would resignedly seek resettlement and the Arab states "realistically" undertake that (economically impossible) task, the actual consequence for the conflict has been an even greater sense of Arab outrage.

To demand that the victims make peace, while telling the rest of the world—in their hearing—that what was actually done to them simply never happened, is not normally recognized as sound peace-making. In a very real sense, Israel's "peace offers" are not, by their very nature, directed to the Arabs at all. They are addressed Westwards, to a kind of caricature of the Arabs and of their experience in Palestine; a caricature which Zionism first began developing in the West with the assertion that Arab hostility was "artificial."

In 1965 there was a fresh and unusually vivid example of this process, and it is perhaps worth citing here. As already mentioned, the general Western picture of the Palestine conflict had been confused all over again by wishful interpretation of President Bourguiba's so-called "peace proposals" on the one hand, and by almost total neglect of the fact that Israel rejected them in entirety.

[29] *Inter alia*, Reb Binyomin, Judah Magnes, Nathan Chofshi, T. R. Feiwel, Leon Roth.

The Western image of Arab hostility towards Israel had thus again been placed in caricature, as "artificial." On May 17 there was injected into this atmosphere a further image, by way of widespread Western headlines, to the effect that Israeli Premier Eshkol had just made an "appeal for peace to the Arabs." Yet a study of the actual text of his speech showed that he had not offered a single, remotely meaningful or negotiable proposal to the Arabs. Indeed, his speech had even repeated the standard Israeli myth that the indigenous Arab people of Palestine had fled in 1948 on a "planned policy of evacuation" ordered by their own leaders. In short, what to Westerners was an Israeli "peace appeal to the Arabs" was, to those Arabs themselves, another enraging Israeli rejection of any possibility of settlement. Two weeks later, Israel resumed the old policy of heavy, intimidatory "reprisal" attacks across the armistice lines.

This mechanism, which in my view is inherently self-defeating, also extends far outside the issues and realities of the Arab-Israeli conflict itself, and always has. At least as early as 1921, Zionist leaders began actively denigrating Arab nationalism in the West. Today, while declaring its readiness to "negotiate tomorrow with President Nasser," the Israeli government is engaged in a continuous campaign to portray the selfsame Nasser to the world as a second Hitler and a menace to international peace. And most significantly, this campaign is not limited to Nasser's hostility to Israel: it is extended to denigrating domestic reform in Egypt and to every other facet of Cairo's role in the Arab world, however far from Palestine. This is not a matter of judgment but of official Israeli record. Once again, this would not normally be recognised as peace-making.

In these conditions—the realities of the conflict itself as distinct from the caricature of it—any attempt at a blueprint for a settlement would be a mere paper exercise. I have attempted only to submit that the Western-Israeli thesis for the future, of some sort of attrition by reform on the Arab side, is on all available evidence as fantasy-founded as most past notions. We are beginning to see a new Arab world, dynamic and modernising, confident in its own slowly evolving new ideology and institutions, and conscious of its ancient heritage. It is going to be a world of one hundred million human beings, and its very size and location will make it less and less possible for Western governments to risk all basic interests there in order to maintain a beach-head *status quo* for perhaps three million Israelis. It is going to be a world in which the revolutionary leadership, far from "giving up" its defenses against Israel and for Palestinians, will feel more strongly and deeply than ever that if the United Nations will not act, the united Arab nations must do so alone.

These, I submit, are the indications. It may be tempting to believe this picture false; but I would urge that if this is believed, then in prudence it must be upon some new body of fact and assumption, because every such assumption applied by the West and the Zionists in the past to the future of Palestine has been proved false.

It might be pleasing to hope that the Arabs will one day see the fate of Palestine, as Israelis have to, and as Israelis want the West to. But to hold this hope seems to me to postulate that the Arabs are not human beings.

It is surely at least possible that the real and vital roots of this conflict lie deeper than the redeeming body of myth and emotion from which we in the West have proceeded, and from which we have created a conflict which we now try to suggest is one in which we "do not take sides."

# XIII.   Israel and the Arab Nations

## by Don Peretz

FOR A DECADE AND A HALF THE PALESTINE PROBLEM HAS BEEN
on the agenda of every session of the General Assembly. It has
been one of the most discussed items in the Security Council.
Numerous special United Nations organizations have been created
to cope with it. At present the special UN bodies directly involved
include the UN Conciliation Commission for Palestine, the UN
Relief and Work Agency for Palestine Refugees, the UN Truce
Supervision Organization and the UN Emergency Force. Few
international organizations or personalities of note have not become
involved. The field of international relations is strewn with sterile
proposals for resolving the bitter struggle. Formulas for settlement
range from direct compromise involving the Arab-Israel frontiers
and the Arab refugees to indirect schemes such as that of former
United Nations Secretary General Dag Hammarskjold for economic rehabilitation of the whole Middle East. Official and unofficial Israelis and Arabs as well as statesmen from all the great
and most of the minor powers have conceived innumerable plans
to bring peace to the Middle East ranging from liquidation of the
Jewish State on the one hand to Arab acceptance of Israel and
all its gains on the other. So varied are the proposals that it would
seem no effort has been spared to seek a working formula for peace
between Israel and its Arab neighbors. Why, then, is peace apparently as illusive as ever? Is the failure caused by fundamental
stubbornness or inherent ill will of Jews and Arabs? Or have those
who have been dealing with this problem overlooked some vital
phase of its tortuous complications?

The Palestine problem resembles an iceberg. Those parts which are visible attract the most attention, while the far more dangerous mass lurks beneath the surface, unseen and unknown to the passing observer. The surface may seem not overly complex to the average Westerner concerned with international affairs. It appears to be a matter of resolving a number of specific material issues through rational compromises: through redefining borders, through equitable treatment of the Arab refugees or through implementing United Nations resolutions.

Beneath the surface of political demands over borders and refugees there is a deep ideological conflict between two new nationalities, each with valid claims to a territory in which neither is willing to concede a major loss. The circumstances of contemporary history have brought Zionist and Arab nationalism into an inevitable clash over the territory of Palestine, which each regards no less vital to its national interests than does the other. Had these two movements flourished at different eras of history they might not have conflicted, but Palestine is a focal point in the national renaissance of both. To ardent Zionists there can be no Zion without the Holy Land. Arab nationalists' aspirations will remain incomplete until all Arab lands including Palestine are within Arab borders. The circumstances of history brought both national movements to a peak of territorial aspiration during the twentieth century. Both flourished in an era of many new nations, and external pressures created deep anxieties for both. Imperialism and the European conquests in Asia Minor during the century before World War II threatened Arab national fulfillment. The outburst of persecutions in Czarist Russia and the liquidation of a third of world Jewry during World War II made national hegemony an essential of Zionist dogma. These anxieties have been exacerbated by the pressures that Jews and Arabs have exerted on each other.

The victors in this struggle have so far been the Zionists, for they have prevailed over all Arab attempts since 1920 to thwart realization of their national goals. The Zionists have established their state in the Arab heartland. It has survived unlimited political onslaught and two military wars of no small consequence. But Zionist victory has not been attained through overwhelming defeat of the Arab national movement. On the contrary, Arab nationalism has fed upon its defeat and continues to grow. The more secure Israel seems in its remarkable attainments, the greater becomes

Arab resolution to remove it; the more ardent become Arab irredentist claims to Palestine.

Shortly after the first United Nations truce temporarily suspended fighting in Palestine during 1948, Dr. Constantine K.
Zurayk, the Syrian Vice President of the American University of
Beirut, wrote *The Meaning of the Disaster*. This short book was
the first introspective evaluation of the struggle with Zionism by
an Arab intellectual of note.

Others had written of the subject before. Indeed, at the beginning of the century, before either Zionism or Arab nationalism had
taken root in Palestine, another Syrian Christian Arab nationalist,
Neguib Aboury, wrote about his fears of Jewish aspirations. Zurayk's book was significant as the writing of a contemporary progressive nationalist who viewed the impact of Zionism, not only
on the Arabs of Palestine, but on the Arab world at large. Although Dr. Zurayk's book was written nearly a generation ago,
it is still significant, even if it no longer reflects the author's outlook, for it presents the viewpoint of contemporary radical Arab
nationalism regarding Palestine.

Until the 1950's Zionist sympathizers stigmatized Arab hostility
as the rantings of a "landed clique" opposed to Jewish progress in
Palestine because it endangered their feudal prerogatives. Once the
Jewish State were established, they argued, Arab nationalist hostility would disappear, and the downtrodden fellahin would see for
themselves the benefits to be gained from creative Zionist efforts.

Zurayk indicated that opposition to Zionism was not the exclusive view of the communists on the one hand, or of the "feudal
elite" on the other. He represented the thinking of the small but
growing group of Arabs who placed the major burden of responsibility for their failures on the weakness of Arab society itself. He
attacked that very feudal system which Zionists and many of their
Western supporters regarded as the chief enemy of progress in
Palestine. Without an insight into these views it is impossible to
comprehend the nature of the continuing struggle between Israel
and the Arab nations today, or to approach realistically the question of solutions.

On the single issue of Palestine there is a similarity of outlook
among Arab nationalists from the radical left to the last outposts
of the "feudal right." The amalgamation of these views, their

unanimous hostility to Israel, and the psychological reaction they create in Arab lands toward Zionism, toward Israel and toward world Jewry constitutes the greatest obstacle to Western rationalistic approaches to the Palestine problem.

Most significant is the total image of Israel and Zionism prevailing among modern Arab nationalists. They do not view Israel as it is generally seen with Western eyes—a tiny struggling nation of some 8,000 square miles and 2,500,000 inhabitants. They regard it as an international colossus with strong allies in the French Chamber of Deputies, in the British Parliament and in the United States Congress. It is believed to command the vast resources of Western communications media and major political influences.

Although the Palestine defeat is considered tragic, it is less a territorial loss than the threat of the "Zionist-imperialist" colossus that concerns Arab nationalists. The Arab masses and much of the educated class, warned Zurayk, "continue to be far from having a sufficient awareness of the great danger which Zionism represents for every country in the Arab world . . . they have not perceived the true extent of Zionism, its world-wide strength, its goal of conquest and annihilation, and its naked cruelty in realizing this goal." [1] It is important, he writes, to

> make clear to the Arab mind and the Arab soul that the Zionist danger is the greatest danger to the being of the Arabs. The other dangers either threaten some limited part of their being or else they include both the Arab world and the rest of the world. This danger threatens the very center of Arab being, its entirety, the foundation of its existence. All other [dangers] are simple in relation to it and may, for the sake of repelling this most serious and all-important danger and for the sake of preserving one's self from it, be endured, or at least have their solution postponed.[2]

After calling attention to the "danger of Jewish power in the United States," [3] the author warns that,

> The forces which the Zionists control in all parts of the world can, if they are permitted to take root in Palestine, threaten the independence of all the Arab lands and form a continuing and frightening danger to their life. The facilities that the Zionist forces have for growth and expansion will place the Arab world forever at their

[1] Constantine K. Zurayk, *The Meaning of the Disaster*, Beirut, 1956, p. 14.
[2] *Ibid.*, p. 16.
[3] *Ibid.*, p. 66.

mercy and will paralyze its vitality and deter its progress and evolution in the ladders of advancement and civilization—that is, if this
Arab world is permitted to exist at all.[4]

While the plight of the Palestine refugees and loss of a not insignificant area of the Arab heartland are disasters from the Arab
viewpoint, of even greater consequence is the psychological trauma
caused by the defeat: the fear of Israel's power and of its close
identity with the West. These fears are unlikely to be assuaged by
token or symbolic acts such as concessions on the refugee problem, border rectifications and the like.

"The defeat of the Arabs in Palestine is no simple setback or
light, passing evil," writes Zurayk. "It is a disaster in every sense
of the word and one of the harshest of the trials and tribulations
with which the Arabs have been afflicted throughout their long
history—a history marked by numerous trials and tribulations." [5]

In his *Philosophy of the Revolution* Egypt's President Nasser
comments in a similar vein on the danger of Israel. The Jewish
State "is nothing but one of the results of Imperialism. For if
Palestine had not fallen under the British Mandate, Zionism would
never have been able to get the support necessary for realization
of the idea of a national state in Palestine. The idea would have
remained a mad impossible dream." [6] In one of his most recent
comments indicating his intentions for the second Arab Summit
Conference held in Alexandria during September 1964, President
Nasser underscored that nationalist views of Israel have changed
little. Arab soil, he stated, must be "purged of imperialism and
its stooges;" Palestine must be

liberated from the clutches of Zionism and become an Arab country
again. This objective is no longer a mere hope cherished in our
hearts, or a slogan included in our aspirations; it has become a
bounden duty for which we must prepare ourselves. We must
make full use of our scientific potential, of planning, of our armed
strength and we must concentrate on winning public opinion. . . .
They say it is a matter of Arab dignity injured in the War of 1948,
that it is a racial dispute, a dispute over borders or compensation for
a number of homeless people. The true nature of the case has

[4] *Ibid.*, p. 69.
[5] *Ibid.*, p. 2.
[6] Gamal Abdel Nasser, *Philosophy of the Revolution*, Book I, Cairo,
n.d., p. 67.

emerged: it is a foreign, Zionist occupation of a part of the Arab land, from which a part of its population has been expelled . . .[7]

Zurayk, Nasser and most other Arab commentators who represent the progressive to radical nationalist outlook have concluded that the Palestine disaster resulted as much from Arab weakness as from any other cause. Their observations sparked the first critique of Arab society, leading to a chain reaction of political upheaval since 1948 in Egypt, Syria, Lebanon, Jordan, Arabia and Iraq. Determination to rid Arab society of those responsible for the disaster set off the 1952 Egyptian Revolution. The Revolution's impact on the Arab East has been much like the French Revolution and the Napoleonic era upon Western Europe.

The Palestine defeat did not topple all the Arab "old regimes," but it did vitalize new currents of nationalist thought strongly emphasizing Arab unity, social and economic reform, and a distinctive Arab foreign policy orientation free from great power maneuver. However beneficent such results may be to the Arab nations, they have been seriously vitiated by continued fear of Israel, resulting in ever expanding military budgets, dissipation of national resources and energies and increasing international tension in an area which could become a focal point of great power conflict.

The dilemma presented by this historical paradox is not simple. On the one hand the creation of Israel and Arab defeat in the Palestine War caused an Arab awakening which is galvanizing Arab society. On the other hand, Arab society has not, nor is it likely in the near future, to recover from the trauma of defeat or to overcome its fear of the force which sparked the Revolution.

The dilemma is compounded by Israel's inevitable counter-reaction. Arab hostility at its present pitch of intense fervor only strengthens those in Israel who argue against any change in the country's militant position *vis-à-vis* the Arabs; it underscores the need for strong allies as well as strong armed forces. Those responsible for the country's security can well support their defiance of pressures to make concessions to the Arabs on such vital issues as borders and return of refugees. There is little to indicate that Israeli concessions in areas affecting the country's security will not

[7] *Jewish Observer and Middle East Review,* XIII, No. 36, September 4, 1964, p. 7.

be regarded as signs of weakness rather than indications of good will, or that such concessions would not be turned against Israel by its avowed enemies.

The vicious circle of Arab fears, determination to be rid of their cause and Israeli determination to strengthen its political and military position to face these implacable fears, eliminates "rational" compromise. While responsible Arab leadership regards liquidation of Zionism and the State of Israel in its present form as the final solution of the Palestine problem, there is little to be gained by continued makeshift proposals to "solve" the dilemma through peripheral and secondary issues such as border changes, refugee compensation or repatriation. Arab discontent with Israel's borders, with the continued presence of refugees in their capitals and with the failure of the refugees to regain their homes, is only symptomatic of fundamental Arab fears of Israel and world Zionism. To remove the symptoms will not cure the organic disorder. Continued bartering over theoretical formulas for an illusory "solution" of the problem has only sharpened mutual antagonisms and intensified the resistance of both Israelis and Arabs to international pressure for a settlement. If, then, a final solution imposed from the outside, or one imposed by the force of either protagonists is not a realistic possibility in the near future, what alternatives are open to those interested in preventing renewal of dangerous strife in the region? Realistic possibilities are both long and short term.

It is neither likely nor possible that Israel will change its fundamental political orientation or policies that result from that orientation in the near future. The country is, and will remain, a Zionist and a Jewish State. It is unlikely to loosen its ties with the large and strong Jewish communities of the Western world. These ties are essential for economic, ideological, psychological and security reasons. If they were to be cut or weakened, Israel's economy and its security position *vis-à-vis* the Arabs would be jeopardized. To the degree that these ties are loosened, affiliations with the Western powers upon which Israel's security is grounded would be undermined. Ties among world Jewry were drawn tighter than ever in recent years during the Hitler regime. The trauma of Jewry's experiences during that era is deep and still unhealed. To many, Israel has become a beacon of emotional security to which they and their children still look. Their not inconsiderable influence in the Western world, against the background of Western guilt feelings about Hitler, creates potent ties with Israel.

There is little reason for Arab nationalists, embroiled with their own complex of problems, to appreciate or to understand the reason for, or nature of, Jewish ties with Israel or for Israel's ties with the West. On the contrary, it is exactly these ties which fortify determination to eliminate this "Western presence" from the Arab East. In an era when Arab and other radical national-isms are resolved to remove the last vestiges of former "colonial" or "imperialist" rule from their realms of influence, it is unlikely that they would develop the sophistication required to comprehend the problems, past and present, of world Jewry. The war in Yemen, Arab involvement in the Cyprus dispute and in the pan-African movement are indications of Arab nationalist determination to eliminate the last remnants of non-Arab influence from the Middle East. A Western oriented and committed Israel is, from their point of view, an anachronism, as intolerable in the Arab heart-land as was Goa to India or as is white dominated South Africa to the pan-Africanists.

The inevitable commitment of Israel to the West as against Arab determination to be free of Western influences makes the Middle East a logical battleground in the cold war. Soviet aid and political support for Arab nationalist causes during the past decade versus Western support for Israel has only strengthened the reluctance of the antagonists to seek compromise, although it is not the fundamental cause for tension. However, Soviet ex-ploitation of the tension has only made preventing outright conflict much more difficult.

While Israel's claims to existence as a Zionist and as a Jewish State are irreconcilable with Arab determination to liquidate such a nation, it is essential to prevent either side from using military force against the other. The Arab blockade and boycott of Israel, the continual propaganda war that each wages and the ever-mount-ing arms race are certainly threats to peace, but they are not in and of themselves *causi belli*. They too are symptoms of the un-resolved differences; symptoms of such magnitude that they can-not be removed except by the use of force or through the unlikely final resolution of the cold war. In these circumstances the best that can be hoped and planned for in the immediate future is to prevent incidents which are outright *causi belli* such as military attacks. The skeletal machinery for preventing border attacks exists in the United Nations Emergency Force. Continuation of their functions and where possible, strengthening their powers, is a feasible possibility now.

In the long run Arab-Jewish relations will depend less on the fate of the Arab refugees or on Israel's borders than on the nature of Israeli and Arab nationalisms. Both are dynamic and activist; both are strongly influenced by powerful negativist reactions to recent historical episodes. Nor is positive diplomacy encouraged by the wide support that Arabs and Israelis receive from their international supporters: the Soviet Union on the one hand and powerful Jewish influences in Western capitals on the other.

One can hope that in the long run these nationalisms will mellow as their protagonists attain that self-confidence and international maturity which will establish a psychological equilibrium between them. When Arabs have overcome their fear of Western imperialism (after the last Western military outposts have been removed from Libya, Cyprus and Arabia) the fear of Israel will lessen. Indeed, as Arab nationalism becomes more mature and larger numbers of Arabs become educated, the general position of non-Muslim minorities should improve. When the last evidences of Western-imposed military presence have disappeared, the psychological reactions of Arab nationalists to the great powers will alter. Improved Arab relations with the West will probably result in a changing image of Israel. When Western imperialism ceases to be a real or imagined threat, then the image of Israel as a pawn of Western imperialism will cease to have meaning.

The vastness of social change in Israel will not only alter that country's image in the Arab world, but will change its relationships with world Jewry, and consequently with those powerful Western countries in which Jews are believed to wield such influence. Demographically, Israel has already changed from a Western to an Oriental country. Although the country's political, social and cultural elite is still European, an influx of Jews from the non-Western world with a much higher birth rate than their European co-religionists has made the country largely non-Western in population.[8] Ironically, Arabic is now the second language of Israel's Jewish immigrant population, displacing the long popular European Yiddish. True, there is little love lost between Oriental Jewish immigrants and Arabs. The position of Oriental Jews has not been enviable during the past decades. Although Israel's Arabic-speaking Jews are unlikely to be a bridge to the Arab world, they are definitely changing the cultural pattern and outlook and the demographic picture of the Jewish State. Within a generation or two, it will no longer be a white, Western nation. There will be little point in comparing it to white-dominated South Africa, or to *colon*-ridden Algeria in pre-independence days. The strong physical differences that have until recently characterized Israel in its Middle East setting will no longer support the image of the country as an "outsider."

On the other side of the frontiers the Oriental population is rapidly becoming culturally and technologically Westernized. Today there are many sections of large Arab towns that compare favorably in architecture, planning and general appearance of the population with those of Israel. The rapid pace of Westernization has so modernized the appearance of Arab urban dwellers that it would be difficult to distinguish them from inhabitants of Oriental Jewish immigrant settlements. However, lest the reader become too sanguine about the significance of these changes, he should be reminded that Oriental Jews are no less ardent Israelis than are his paler-skinned countrymen. These demographic-social changes affect Arab-Israeli relations in so far as they further weaken the image of Israel as a Western bridgehead. Even after Israel has become transformed to an Oriental state, its Jewish population will remain a minority in a Muslim sea, subject to the same problems that other non-Muslims now face in the Middle East.

Israel's demographic changes are not unrelated to its relationships with Western Jewry. As the cultural gap between Oriental Israelis and Western Jews broadens, the psychological and emotional ties, the close personal relationships between these groups,

[8] According to the *Statistical Abstract of Israel*, 1963, No. 14, p. 110, more than 53 per cent of the country's immigrants during the 1948-61 period were from Africa and Asia. The much higher birth rate of these new settlers has now produced a non-Western majority in Israel.

will also become attenuated. Zionist and many non-Zionist Jewish leaders have already raised the specter of assimilation, especially in America, the largest and most influential diaspora. Many actually fear that with the disappearance of anti-Semitism Jews will also disappear. Recent "alarming" studies indicate that the rapid rate of intermarriage threatens to deplete the Jewish community.[9] Whether or not these warnings are valid, they do indicate that Western, especially American, Jewry is more rapidly integrating into its environment. While this may be alarming to those with a vested concern in maintaining the Jewish community as a special interest group, it harbingers a changing relationship between American Jews and Israel. Although Judaism will remain Israel-centered, the concept of Israel need no longer be that of a political enclave, but of a spiritual Zion, for Jews with security will no longer require the psychological reassurance of an autonomous nation with its own army, laws and other paraphernalia of nationhood. The history of the declining influence of immigrant populations such as the Irish on American foreign policy indicates that from generation to generation ties with the "old country" are considerably weakened. It is little wonder that Zionist organizations have taken alarm at this situation and intensified their efforts to "stem the tide of assimilation."

Israeli organizations and publications such as *Ihud, Mapam, Semitic Action* and the *New Outlook* understand, in varying degrees, the importance of Israel's image to the Arabs and each, in its own way, is contributing to alteration of that image. All urge their government to improve its relations with Israel's Arab minority; all urge greater emphasis within the country's educational system on better understanding of the Arab world; and all have

[9] Eric Rosenthal's "Studies of Jewish Intermarriage in the United States," published in the *American Jewish Year Book 1963*, American Jewish Committee, New York, was much cited in Jewish periodicals here and abroad as evidence of the growing rate of assimilation. Although based on surveys in greater Washington and Iowa, the study concluded that "the Jewish community of the United States is subject to the process of assimilation in such a manner that ethnic and religious bonds that welded the immigrant generation into a highly organized community are becoming progressively weaker. . . . That intermarriage usually spells the end of belonging to the Jewish group is demonstrated by the fact that in at least 70 per cent of the mixed families in greater Washington the children were not identified with the Jewish group."

proposed formulas which they believe will significantly affect Arab reactions to Israel. Despite the fact that these groups are of no present major political significance, they form a vanguard in setting a tone in Arab-Israeli relations which is necessary if social changes on both sides of the frontier are to bring an era of decreasing hostility. Unfortunately, these groups do not have their counterparts in any Arab country, or among the influential diaspora Jewish communities, whose present support for Israel is a primary cause of Arab fears and hostility.

The social changes related to change in Arab-Israeli relationships envisaged above are not likely to result from conscious political endeavor or deliberate planning. They are evolutionary; and the product in large measure of forces beyond the Middle East. To be effective they must be related to changing attitudes toward minorities in general throughout the Middle East. Such changes are subject to an infinite number of variables in international relations both within and outside the region. Consequently, it is impossible to predict when or even how they will occur. But when they have occurred, the Arab image of Israel as a crusader enclave awaiting ultimate liquidation by overwhelming Arab force will have withered away, for Israel will have become part of the Middle East. The description of Israel so fearsomely conjured up by Zurayk and his contemporaries in the Arab national movement will be a spectre of the past.

# XIV.  Arab Socialism

## by Gordon H. Torrey
## and John F. Devlin

*A national, populist, revolutionary movement which strives to achieve Arab unity, liberty, and socialism.*
—Preamble of the Ba'th Constitution

*In our revolution we aim at creating the new society—without classes, capital dictatorship, feudal dictatorship, exploitation, and monopoly, but with social justice and equality.*
—Speech by Nasser at Port Said, December 23, 1961

THE SOCIALISM OF THE ARAB STATES IN THE MID-CENTURY IS A movement of protest—protest against the concentration of political and economic power in the hands of a small ruling class. It is directed against a system which the socialists believe existed to benefit only that class, against privilege and excessive wealth. The post-Ottoman generation of political leaders in Egypt, Iraq, Syria and to a lesser extent in the smaller Arab states, conducted themselves in such fashion as to make the emergence of revolutionary movements virtually certain. Heirs of a tradition which viewed as normal the concentration of political power and economic wealth in an "establishment," these political leaders used the means available to them to stay there. They made the parliamentary systems bequeathed them by Europe into meaningless façades. On yet another plane, the "establishment" identified itself too closely with the former colonial powers.

The "establishment's" control was also very broad, so much so that the young man with political ambitions in the 1930's was faced with a choice of cooperating with the system or spending an indefinite future in the political wilderness. Most chose to conform outwardly to a degree, while complaining bitterly in private. In time, however, the middle class began to grow; the upper class itself absorbed new elements; education and modern communications spread literacy among the people; and new ideas arose among the politically conscious.

As the thirties and forties wore on, a new generation of politically conscious Arabs grew to maturity. Imbued with the same desire for political independence that had animated their elders at the collapse of the Ottoman Empire, the new generation regarded those same elders as reactionary defenders of the *status quo*. To the emerging class of "new men," Arab leaders of the interwar period were insufficiently attuned to the urgency of becoming fully independent of foreign tutelage. Elements of foreign domination remained, especially in the commercial and financial fields. Nor were the leaders eager to promote unity among the Arab states; they stood for a highly conservative economic and social philosophy which would preserve their interests. They represented, in fact, a coalition of merchants, landowners and tribal leaders—the traditionally dominant elements in Arab society, who tended naturally to consider their interests as synonymous with those of the society at large. It was natural, therefore, for the new intelligentsia to demand thorough-going reform in political, economic and social fields, as well as independence and Arab unity.

These malcontents, for the most part were—and are—of middle class origin and comprise a large proportion of the salaried civil servants, the technicians in private industry, university students and military officers. Many of them have received education abroad, and the great majority has become sufficiently acquainted with conditions in the more advanced countries to yearn for similar economic and social advancement in the Arab world. However, since the fruits of political power were secured by the Middle Eastern intelligentsia prior to the attainment of status and financial security, this group has turned from the slow path their Western counterparts followed to seek political and social revolution in an Arabic context.[1] In more concrete terms, the new middle class wants planned economic development with all of its ramifications, a raising of living standards, state control of the means of

[1] See Manfred Halpern, *The Politics of Social Change in the Middle East and North Africa,* Santa Monica, The Rand Corporation, 1963.

production, broad social welfare, land reform, educational expansion and dignity for all, especially in the eyes of other nations.

Giving an impetus to these demands and to the role of the new middle class is the rapidly changing socio-economic structure. The increasing urbanization of the Arab world, albeit far behind that of the West, is expanding the reservoir of malcontents to be activated by the new generation of politically conscious. Also, the very fact of urbanization has brought new problems which cannot be alleviated within the rapidly decaying traditional social structure. The rise of labor unions, the importance of the ever expanding student body and the existence of vast numbers of unemployed and underemployed living in and around the cities have brought new forces to be reckoned with. Arab Socialism was born of these dissatisfactions and under conditions which have left distinctive marks on the body of its doctrine and on its methods.

Since Ba'thist doctrine is the oldest coherent socialist doctrine in the Arab world, it deserves primary consideration. Gamal Abdel Nasser's "Arab Socialism," while not a direct outgrowth and adaptation of Ba'thist ideology, is very similar in its economic and social theories, and these are the only manifestations of socialism which have general influence in the Arab world. Ba'thism is an ideology, much of which is yet to be put into effect despite the establishment of Ba'thist governments in Iraq and Syria: Nasser's "Arab Socialism," is a series of specific moves undertaken to revolutionize the economy and social structure of Egypt. The intriguing attempt by the Algerian revolutionary regime to achieve a synthesis of Marxism and Islam remains confined to Algeria.

The other socialist movements, such as the National Democratic Party in Iraq and the People's Socialist Party in Lebanon, have had relatively little influence even in their own countries.

Bourgeois in origin and composition, nationalist in outlook, strong-armed in action, the Ba'th is a party of paradox and contrast. It dates from 1943, when Michel Aflaq and Salah-al-Din Bitar, Damascus schoolteachers and earlier colleagues at the Sorbonne, founded the Arab Resurrection (Ba'th) Movement. While in France Aflaq, a Christian of the Greek Orthodox Church, became a communist, but had become disillusioned with the Party prior to his return to Syria in 1936. He is the Party philosopher, guiding it along its general path, but avoiding the day-to-day business of administration. Bitar, the same age as Aflaq, is an organizer and administrator. He has served in public office a number of times and was Minister of Foreign Affairs during the two years prior to Syria's union with Egypt in 1958. The little organization played a small part in Syria's efforts to rid itself of French control by printing handbills and pamphlets and by agitating among the students. By the latter part of 1945, the Ba'thists were calling themselves a party, and in mid-summer 1946 they brought out the first issue of the Party newspaper, *Al-Ba'th*. Then in April 1947, some two hundred of the Party faithful gathered for a three day conference—the Party's first—to debate and approve the Ba'th Constitution. Following this conference, the Party entered national politics by participating in the parliamentary elections held that June; Aflaq and Bitar ran and were defeated. Following this, the Quwatli regime suppressed the Ba'th and arrested Aflaq for his open criticisms of government mismanagement. This suppression continued until Colonel Sami Hinnawi overthrew Syria's first dictator, Husni al-Za'im, in August 1949. Aflaq then joined a coalition cabinet as Minister of Education, the only government post he has ever held. In the elections which followed Hinnawi's *coup*, the Ba'th secured its first parliamentary representation, three seats out of the one hundred fourteen in the 1949 Constituent Assembly.

In 1953 Akram Hawrani's Socialist Party merged with the Ba'th after three years of negotiation, and this merger gave the Party a strong political base in Syria, from which, in a few years, it grew to be the dominant political force in the country and finally led Syria into union with Egypt in 1958. During the 1950's the Ba'th flourished in a number of countries. In Jordan it had a brief flurry of prominence which was ended by the fall of the Nabulsi nationalist Government in April 1957. In Iraq the Party grew semi-clandestinely, as all political activity was illegal after 1954, and contributed a minister to the first post-revolution cabinet in 1958. It gained adherents in most other Arab countries but never seemed to take root in Egypt. From a period of desuetude in 1959, the Ba'th emerged to seize power by *coup d'état* in Iraq and Syria in 1963 and still rules in the latter country.

The basis of the Ba'th's appeal is embodied in the Party Constitution. This document is not a blueprint for action or a set of rules by which the Party should function, but rather a picture of what the Ba'th views as the good society.[2] This Constitution has never been amended; the only difference between the first version, printed in Syria in 1947, and later reprints is the addition of the word *ishtirāki* (socialist) to the title at the time of the 1953 Hawrani Socialist-Ba'th merger. The word "socialist," however, occurs frequently in the document itself and is found in the earliest Party literature.

This Constitution envisions a united Arab society encompassing all Arabs from Morocco to Iraq, in which social justice will prevail and political liberalism will persuade the people to choose the Ba'th path. The goal of a just and equitable society, in which extremes of wealth and poverty do not exist, is a cardinal one for the Ba'th—and for Nasser as well. The Ba'th Constitution, for example, calls for the redistribution of land holdings among the citizens on a just basis (Art. 27), for the nationalization of utilities and large industries (Art. 29), for sweeping guarantees of wages, working conditions and old age insurance (Art. 40), for complete free medical care (Art. 39) and for free compulsory education through the secondary level (Arts. 45 & 46). The Constitution is explicit in saying that "the educational policy of the Party aims at creating a new Arab generation faithful to the unity of its nation and the perpetuity of its mission." [3]

There is a second facet of the Ba'thist future which is even more important than its aim of social justice; this is Arab nationalism. The Constitution and the extensive writings of Aflaq and other Ba'thists devote considerable attention to what is called, for lack of a more precise term, "Arabness." "The Arab nation is distinguished by its merits [which are] revealed in its successive rebirths; it is noted for its abundant vitality and creative ability and its capacity for renewal and rebirth." [4] "Arab nationalism for the Ba'th is a self-evident fact which is established without the need for argument or struggle . . . for this reason there is no

[2] An English translation of the Constitution is available in the *Middle East Journal*, XIII, No. 2, Spring 1959, pp. 195-200; the Arabic text in *Nidal al-Ba'th*, I, Beirut, Dar al-Tali'ah, 1963, pp. 172-81.

[3] Ba'th Constitution, preambulatory paragraph to that part entitled "The Educational and Instructional Policy of the Party," *Nidal*, I, p. 180.

[4] Ba'th Constitution, Basic Principles, *Nidal*, I, p. 173.

need to argue whether we are Arabs or not, but it is necessary that we determine and establish [what] Arabism [is] at the present. . . ." [5]

These two aspects of Ba'thist ideology, socialism and Arab nationalism, are inseparable. Aflaq views social progress and a better life for the Arab people as springing directly from a strong and united Arab nation. For him, the classic international socialism of nineteenth century Europe is not suited to the Arab world. Aflaq puts forth his reasoning on this point in an article written in 1946.[6] Western socialism was perfectly correct in taking the form it did because "socialism in the West was forced to stand up not only against capitalism but also against nationalism, which protected capitalism, against religion, which defended it, and against every concept which called for conservatism and the sanctification of the past." [7] The Arab nation, however, lacks the freedom and sovereignty which the Western nations possessed. Every Arab nationalist—for it must be remembered that Aflaq saw his doctrine as applying to the entire Arab-speaking world—should recognize that socialism is the most useful means to revive his nation. Hence, "there is neither incompatibility nor contradiction nor war between nationalists and socialists." [8] "The Arab nationalists are the socialists." [9]

Communism, too, is a system unsuited to the Arab world, a position Aflaq reiterates many times in his writings. Aflaq spells out a number of theoretical and practical differences between Ba'th socialism and communist socialism.[10] Communism explains the evolution of society in economic terms only; it does not give due

[5] Michel Aflaq, "Arab Nationalism and the Nationalist Theory," *Fi Sabil al-Ba'th,* Beirut, Dar al-Tali'ah, 1959, p. 211. *Fi Sabil al-Ba'th* (On the Road to Resurrection) is a collection of Aflaq's writings. It was first issued in 1953, revised and enlarged in 1959 and a version with considerable new material was published in 1963. All references are to the 1963 edition unless otherwise specified.

[6] "The Features of Arab Socialism," *Fi Sabil al-Ba'th,* pp. 200-8.

[7] *Ibid.,* p. 202.

[8] "The Features of Arab Socialism," *Fi Sabil al-Ba'th,* p. 204.

[9] *Idem.*

[10] In *Fi Sabil al-Ba'th,* "Our Position Regarding the Communist Theory" (1944), pp. 195-99, and "Between Our Socialism, Communism, and National Socialism" (1950), pp. 209-13.

weight to the individual; it does not recognize the right to private property.[11] Perhaps most significant to Aflaq, and to his young nationalist, anti-colonial supporters, communism is deceitful because it seeks to tie "the Arab destiny to the destiny of another state, namely Russia." [12] A great point of difference lies in Aflaq's rejection of the Marxist view of the class struggle. For him, too, there is a class struggle, but it is the struggle between the Arab people, on one hand, and everyone who is hostile to them, on the other. These hostile elements may, however, include Arab capitalists, feudalists and politicians who support the division of the Arab nation, as well as others who cooperate with imperialism.[13] Aflaq's class battle is between the Arabs and their enemies, not simply one between the proletariat and the capitalist exploiters.

The Ba'th has been consistent in its opposition to communism from its earliest days. In an election manifesto issued by Aflaq, as a candidate for parliament from Damascus in July 1943, the Ba'th leader claimed to represent "the Arab spirit against materialistic communism," [14] and by 1945 the Communist Party was termed a "pillar of *shu'ubiyah*." [15] As the Ba'th moved into the political arena in the 1950's, a tone of positive neutralism appeared in its statements and attacks on the communists were less noticeable. The antipathy remained, and fear of growing communist strength was an important factor in causing the Ba'thist leaders to seek union with Egypt in 1958. That the sentiment persists is evident in the vigorous crackdown on communists in Iraq after the Party seized power there in 1963.[16] And today, despite their common antipathy to Nasser, the Ba'th has not cooperated with the communists in Syria.

[11] *Ibid.*, pp. 210-11.

[12] *Ibid.*, p. 212.

[13] *Ibid.*, p. 223, "Our View of Capitalism and the Class Struggle."

[14] *Nidal,* I, p. 33.

[15] *Ibid.*, p. 86, *Shu'ubiyah* was a movement in Abbasid days which tended to glorify Persia and debase the Arabs. In the contemporary Arab lexicon, the term signifies any trend which deviates from reform nationalism.

[16] *Middle East Journal,* Winter-Spring 1963, XVII, Nos. 1 and 2, chronology, pp. 115-6. This hostility is reciprocated by the communists; *Mizan Newsletter,* Vol. 6, No. 6, June 1964, p. 14 quotes an article from *Kazakhstanskaya Pravda,* March 21, 1964, which said that in 1963 alone Soviet newspapers and periodicals had published more than 500 articles "exposing the reactionary character" of the Ba'th Party.

In positive terms, then, Ba'th socialism is for the Arabs—for all Arabs but only for Arabs. It has no expansionist aims other than to liberate those areas of the Arab homeland presently under foreign domination.[17] Aflaq is quite specific in stating his belief that "our socialism" can only be realized completely in one united Arab state. This theme is repeated elsewhere in Ba'thist literature. Independence and unity are pre-requisites for the socialist society he believes the Arabs must build. The theme is constant in Aflaq's own writings, in the columns of the Party newspaper, in the stream of statements, pronouncements and anathemas which have flowed from the Party's leaders.

Thus, Ba'th socialism is distinguished from Marxian communism by its rejection of the class struggle[18] and from classic Western socialism by its espousal of insular nationalism. The resurrection of the Arab nation is the chief aim of the Ba'th Party. From this resurrection is to flow all the necessary elements to make this nation great and powerful. This is not a question of merely restoring past glories; "the present experience of the Arab nation is the first and greatest value of this [Arab] nationalism, for it is richer and more valuable than all the stages through which our nation has lived in the past." [19] The Ba'thist mission (risālah khālidah) is to carry out the vitalization of the Arab world and to build a new society.

This nationalist theme is the basis of Ba'thist ideology. It has been a theme with appeal for the young, educated, urban Arab; in many respects it runs parallel to the nationalist ideas propagated by other Arab intellectual leadership, typified by Sati' al-Husri. In the post-war era the Ba'th Party had the advantages of being an organization with little competition beyond the several local nationalist opposition parties existing in Syria, Lebanon and Iraq. Nasser's appearance as a pan-Arab leader in the mid-fifties provided an alternative to the reform-minded. The Ba'th leaders themselves were greatly attracted to Nasser by his success in liberating Egypt from foreign influence. However, they could not fit his pattern of

[17] Party Constitution, Art. 7.

[18] There are other differences as well; the Ba'th ignores religion, for example, but is not actively hostile to it.

[19] Fi Sabil al-Ba'th (1959), p. 212.

personal leadership into their own party system. The fact that the Ba'th was an organization with a true ideology to which the individual could adhere and within which he could work for the nationalist cause was a considerable attraction, and many among the urban intelligentsia joined.

By 1953 the movement had to face the question of whether it should be an elite which would show the way to the Arab world by enlightened example or whether it should go in for a broad membership and fight in the political arena. Aflaq favored the former, while Bitar pressed for expansion. Aflaq's and Bitar's difference on this point—perhaps their only major disagreement—was ultimately resolved in the latter's favor.[20] Aflaq is not a politician, but rather a philosopher as it were, who believes that his doctrines will effect a general spiritual renewal in the Arab world. His writings have from the beginning laid great stress on the spiritual values inherent in the Arab society and depicted them as essential to the success of the Ba'thist nationalist mission.[21]

The enlargement of the Party and its entry into politics brought problems. Even Bitar became alarmed at the bandwagon expansion by 1954. Although the Party required discipline of its members, large numbers were of necessity more difficult to instruct, to guide and to inspire. Until 1954 Party affairs were directed by a Party Council, and there was no distinction between members from, say, Jordan and those from Syria.[22] In that year, however, the Party's growing size forced it to set up an organization pyramid—the National Command in Damascus, or wherever the leaders happened to be, and a Regional Command for each Arab state with sufficient membership to merit it, with branches and smaller divisions as required.

This lack of personal contact with the Party's leaders, of an opportunity to drink from the Party's fountain of knowledge, coupled with the recruitment of a more heterogeneous Party membership, brought a new problem to the Party—the task of making it a truly pan-Arab organization. As long as the Ba'th remained

[20] Gordon H. Torrey, unpublished paper presented at the University of California, Los Angeles, Conference on Radical Ideology, May 31, 1964, p. 17.
[21] See, for example, *Fi Sabil al-Ba'th,* p. 207.
[22] *Nidal,* I, p. 171.

primarily a Syrian party, engaged in politics only in that country, the application of its theories to the rest of the Arab world remained a theoretical exercise. When it did become active and had to face a variety of political circumstances in other countries, it was inevitable that differences should appear. Such differences arose in part out of the difficulties inherent in applying a system developed in the specific context of French-mandated Syria to other countries with different backgrounds. They also grew out of honest disputes over what was the best policy in a given situation, but in some instances they were aggravated by the political ambitions of individual Ba'thists.

Factionalism has intermittently plagued the Ba'th. The Party imposes a discipline on its members, both before an applicant's full acceptance as a member and after he is in the fold. This discipline requires that a member study the Party literature and abide by the decisions reached by Party organizations at all levels. At the same time, the Party is run on democratic lines; each level of the organization elects representatives to the next level, up to and including the National Command. There is, however, allowance for considerable autonomy in the manner in which each Regional Command carries out Party activity in its own country. This very autonomy has provided the means for several important splits in the Ba'th Party.

The first major split occurred in 1959. In that year a national congress of the Party expelled Abdallah Rimawi, then the leader-in-exile of the Jordanian region and a member of the National Command, from these posts and from Party membership.[23] Rimawi fought back; he contended that the congress was illegal and the next year organized a new "national command" and held a national conference of representatives from most Arab countries.[24] Rimawi's attempt to draw the bulk of the Ba'thists away from Aflaq failed, although his group remained in being for a time. He is still active politically but remains outside the true Ba'thist fold. The Iraqi leader, Faud Rikabi, broke away from the Party in the aftermath of its attempt to assassinate Qasim in 1959.

[23] Simon Jargy, "Le declin d'un parti," *Orient*, III, No. 11, 1959, p. 34.
[24] Eliezer Ben-Moshe, "The Test of the Ba'th," *New Outlook*, III, July-August 1960, p. 33.

Another and more serious split occurred when Hawrani broke away after the sundering of the Egyptian-Syrian union in the fall of 1961. Despite the break with Nasser, Aflaq continued to work for a reunion with Egypt, albeit on a more equal partnership basis, while Hawrani strongly supported the new Syrian regime. Finally, the Hawrani faction was thrown out of the Party in 1962. Syria harbors yet another Ba'thist splinter group, the Socialist Unity Party, a pro-Nasser element expelled in 1963.

Another political dilemma caused the most recent Ba'thist split which occurred in 1963. This was the most spectacular and best publicized. It arose out of a dispute between moderate and extremist factions within the Iraqi region of the Party as to how fast the country should be socialized and how exclusively Ba'thist controlled it should be. In the ensuing struggle, leaders of both factions were ousted from the Party by the Aflaq-directed National Command, which assumed direct control of the Party in Iraq. This caused a good deal of resentment among Iraqis, who objected to a Syrian, and a Christian one at that, interjecting himself into Baghdad's affairs. The Iraqi military intervened and the result was that Ba'thist control of Iraq was lost to a military junta.[25]

However, the divisions in the Iraqi Ba'th were only a manifestation of a deep-seated divergence that exists in the Party as a whole. It is a divergence which in part is traceable to the Aflaq-Bitar dispute over the proper role of the Party. Although the Ba'th opted for an active political role rather than for one of education and persuasion, the more retiring and the more forceful schools within the Party have disputed continuously over the years as to how the Ba'th should play its political hand.

This internal conflict goes a long way in explaining the paradox of Ba'thist inconsistency in politics. The Party is torn between fidelity to the idealistic goals and concrete moves designed to seize and hold power. By its Constitution it is committed to a representative system, yet it has a record of strong-arm tactics worthy of the most authoritarian organization. The Party's reaction to the assassination in 1955 of one of its principal sympathizers among the Syrian military, Adnan al-Malki, was a vigorous campaign

[25] Jerusalem *Post*, November 18, 19 and 20, 1963. These events were also widely reported in the Western and Arab press.

against the Syrian Social National Party (SSNP). The SSNP's doctrines of local Syrian nationalism were anathema to the Ba'th which, in collaboration with the army, virtually crushed the SSNP in Syria; over a hundred of its leaders were jailed, two were eventually shot after trial and many remained in jail until 1964.[26]

In Iraq, after the Ba'th seized power from Qasim in February 1963, it wrought swift and summary vengeance on the communists. It also deceived the Kurdish rebels and, according to some sources, prosecuted the war far more ruthlessly than had Qasim.[27] The Ba'th para-military organization, the national guard, came to be disliked intensely by the populace for its excesses, especially in detention centers, during its months in power. Again, in Syria, the Ba'thist-dominated military forces reacted to a *coup* attempt in July 1963 by twenty-seven summary executions, an unprecedented step in Syrian political life, and its suppression of disturbances in Hama in April 1964 cost an estimated hundred casualties.[28]

This is a far cry from the gentle, if utopian, vision of the Party's founders. And indeed the Party is a very different apparatus today from the small group of theoretical revolutionaries who founded it. A brief comparison of the resolutions adopted by the Ba'th at its first congress in 1947 with those approved at the sixth congress in October 1963 illustrates this change. The situations in which the two conferences were held were vastly different. In 1947 the Party was striving to make a name for itself in the turbulent days following the departure of the French and without immediate prospects of exerting influence. In 1963 it was in control of Iraq and Syria and looking forward to still greater progress. Nonetheless, the differences in approach are marked.

The 1947 conference[29] naturally devoted a good deal of attention to foreign influence in the Arab world, declaring itself ready for friendship and cooperation with any country opposed to those

[26] Gordon H. Torrey, *Syrian Politics and the Military*, pp. 282 ff. A general amnesty freed virtually all political prisoners in Syria, New York *Times,* August 30, 1964.

[27] Amnon Bartur, Jerusalem *Post*, July 26, 1963. Bartur says that the Kurds helped the Ba'th to overthrow Qasim, but does not specify in what way.

[28] *Middle East Forum*, XL, No. 4, May 1964, p. 7.

[29] The published decisions are in *Nidal*, I, pp. 185-92.

countries which had usurped Arab land—England, France, Spain, Turkey, Iran and America, the latter for backing the others and supporting Zionism. It called on the Arab League for some prompt steps to speed Arab unity; unifying of Arab armies and diplomatic services, abolition of passports among Arab states and abolition of customs barriers. Domestically, it recognized the difficulty of establishing constitutional regimes but set the achievement of such regimes, as well as full political rights, as the Party's goal.

The steps the Ba'thists urged domestically in 1947 were rather modest ones for a revolutionary party. They wanted reapportionment of taxes, especially those on food and clothing and other necessities; they wanted legislation enacted which would give workers and peasants an income permitting a decent standard of living and proportionate to the profits of the business enterprise or landed estate. Curiously for a group having little connection with the countryside, the Ba'th wanted the government to establish an agriculture ministry, build irrigation works, promote the use of fertilizer and build agriculture schools. They proposed the mobilization of government resources to reduce to the minimum the cost of food and clothing for the masses and the cost of living generally. They called for government control of domestic and foreign trade in order to restrict prices and profits and to prevent exploitation by monopolies.

The statement published seventeen years later on October 27, 1963, at the end of the sixth conference, made a few attacks on imperialism and exploitation but mentioned only Israel and South Africa by name. It affirmed the Ba'th's position in the neutralist third force and saw value in friendship with the socialist world. On the matter of Arab unity, the conference was cautious in the aftermath of the failure of the April 1963 tripartite unity agreement. It called only for a federal union of Iraq and Syria as a first step on the road to full unity. It also stated that it was prepared to accept Nasser's system as a partner in, but not as a foundation for, a unified state. As a party in power, with several months of experience and of problems behind it, the Ba'th discussed the relations of party and government and of party and populace, as well as the problems generated by the establishment of the national guard. It affirmed the right of the people to criticize the Party and made a special point that such organizations as those of labor, students and professional people should not be subject to state control.

The conference decided, moreover, that the socialist goals of the Party should be put into operation immediately. Such a move would have been a reversal of Aflaq's traditional attitude that independence and unity were necessary pre-conditions for the successful implementation of Ba'thist socialism. It represents the strong influence exerted during the conference by the "extremist" wing associated with Ali Sālih Sa'di and Nur-al-Din al-Atassi, Secretaries General of the Iraqi and Syrian regions respectively. Specifically, the sixth conference statement considered the establishment of collective farms on land processed under the agrarian reform measures as a goal to be striven for urgently. The Constitution's aims of free compulsory education and free medical care were reaffirmed and urged by the conference. There were only a few references to industry in the statement and no mention, let alone any threats, of nationalizing foreign companies.

The statement sheds more light on the state of factionalism within the Party than it does on Party policies. But emphasis on doing things rather than expressing pious hopes that they somehow be done characterizes the document. While its language is hortatory, both drafters and readers knew that those who wrote, or at least their Party colleagues, intended to return to ministries in Baghdad and Damascus and put the program into action. That they have not done so is a result of other factors—revolution in Iraq and intra-Party and intra-army rivalries in Syria. In fact, after the upsets and turmoil attendant on the collapse of the Ba'th regime in Iraq, the old Aflaq-Bitar mainstream seems to be once again in control of the Party. The radical wing plays a distinctly secondary role.

Over the past dozen years or so there has been a continued interaction between the Ba'th and Egypt's President Nasser.[30] The Ba'th had been in existence for more than a decade by the time Nasser became the acknowledged leader in Cairo. During his years in

---

[30] A two-part article by Leonard Binder, "Radical Reform Nationalism in Syria and Egypt," *Muslim World*, April, June 1959, pp. 96-109, 213-31, examines some similarities and differences of Ba'thist and Nasserist approaches as they appeared some years ago.

power, he came to adopt and to apply in Egypt—and Syria during the UAR (1958-61)—some of the principal socialist ideas of the Ba'th. A comparison of the two is difficult, for the Ba'th is a movement of ideology which is only now, in a hesitant and tentative way, beginning to apply some of its concepts in Syria. Nasser, on the other hand, is an activist in complete control of his country and has pushed forward with a series of far-reaching socialist reforms, the ideological justifications for which have followed the actual initiation.

This development has mostly come about in the last half-dozen years. For Nasser and his associates, as the *Philosophy of the Revolution*[31] makes clear, seized power in 1952 with no very clear notion of what they wanted to achieve beyond ousting the corrupt Faruq regime. Until 1956, the revolutionary government was concerned with correcting some of the major problems left it by the old regime. Its principal social and economic reform was the Agrarian Reform Law of September 9, 1952, which limited land holdings to some two hundred acres per owner. In other economic areas, it encouraged the movement of foreign capital into Egypt and took a number of steps toward economic development.

This was not revolution and the Ba'th was more than a little dubious about the new administration in Cairo. "The military regime in Egypt is not [apt] to be more successful than others in realizing a unified concept concerning the problem of the Arab people," wrote the Party newspaper in May 1954.[32] Another article in the Party paper, *al-Ba'th,* in July 1954 asserted that Egypt had weakened the struggle against imperialism by agreeing to let Britain retain certain rights and uses in the Suez military base.[33] Less than two years later, however, the Ba'th joined Syrian President Quwatli's campaign of action for a union of Egypt and Syria.[34] As the first contemporary Arab leader to free his country from colonial and reactionary bondage, Nasser became a hero—and one with a dynamic and arresting personality—to many of the nationalist intelligentsia. The Anglo-French-Israeli attack on Egypt in 1956 and

[31] Gamal Abdel Nasser, *Philosophy of the Revolution,* Cairo, Dar al-Maaref, n.d.
[32] *Nidal,* II, p. 255.
[33] *Ibid.,* II, pp. 278-80.
[34] *Ibid.,* III, p. 175 *et passim.*

Nasser's own increasing ambitions to play a pan-Arab role gave him greatly increased stature and prestige in the Arab struggle for unity and for liberation of the Arab homeland. In sum, Nasser turned out to be a militant after the Ba'th's heart in the field of Arab nationalism. The sought-for union was achieved February 22, 1958.

But Nasser and the Ba'thists could not long agree on how to go about reaching the goals of unity and social justice to which both aspired. The Egyptian leader's style of governing—essentially an authoritarian leadership in which one man makes the ultimate decisions—clashed violently with the Ba'th's reliance on a form of party democracy in which many had a voice.[35]

The Ba'thist leaders were idealistically devoted to their long-held belief that unity would automatically solve many of the Arabs' problems. They envisioned a major role for themselves in the United Arab Republic. They saw in Nasser a man whose program was very similar to theirs, who might lead the way to the future they dreamed of and who might even be used for their ends. In a word, they were taken in, and they probably did not realize it until sometime toward the end of 1958.[36] The Ba'th regarded the UAR decree of March 12, 1958, dissolving all political parties in Syria, as not really applying to itself. Likewise, it looked on the National Union in Syria only from the point of its own interests and as incorporating the principles of the Ba'th. If any hopes remained, the elections of 1959 for the various levels of the National Union in Syria killed them; of 9,445 positions, only 250 were filled by Ba'thists.[37]

Yet Nasser has gone further in achieving the same socialist goals of a just society—to which both he and the Ba'th aspire—than the latter has been able to do. A great leveling of position and destruction of privilege has occurred. A gradual extension of state control took place from 1956 on, but the big jump occurred in midsummer of 1961. At that time, all banks and insurance companies in both regions of the UAR were nationalized. Almost a hundred major industrial and commercial concerns were also seized and a further hundred partially nationalized. Maximum individual land

[35] See Charles D. Cremeans, *The Arabs and the World*, pp. 219-29, for a brief survey of Nasser's Arab policies.
[36] Jargy, *op. cit.*, pp. 21-39.
[37] *Ibid.*, pp. 32-33.

holdings were reduced to about one hundred acres. The net effect was to convert what had formerly been a private enterprise economy into a predominantly state-owned one. Further measures against the formerly dominant class were taken in the aftermath of Syria's breakaway from the UAR in September 1961. Nationalization decrees in 1962 and 1963 have put virtually all Egypt's industry and commerce—with the exception of most retail trade—in the hands of the state.[38]

Nasser's "Arab Socialism," as it has been applied in practice, is thus in many respects similar to the ideology spelled out two decades ago by the Ba'th's founders. It differs in one very important, probably vital, respect. For Nasser, the road to achievement of the goals of social justice, of unity and of independence for all Arabs lies in the use of the power of the state which he controls. Egypt's efforts at achieving "unity of purpose" with other liberated Arab states (Iraq, republican Yemen and Algeria at the present time) are conducted on a state-to-state level. There exists no other institution with sufficient life of its own to serve as a bridge among these states. The establishment of an Arab Socialist Union in Iraq and another among Syrian exiles in Beirut is an effort to imitate the already existing Union in Egypt. The Egyptian exemplar was established by Nasser in an effort to provide two-way communication between the presidency and the people. It has little power in its own right and hence cannot usefully serve as a vehicle for political activity as long as all decision-making power lies at the top.

The Ba'th Party is both an elite vanguard and a grouping of reformist elements drawn from the educated strata of the populace, with vitality at all levels. The Party is the vehicle of revolution and resurrection, both within a particular state and in the broader Arab field. Where circumstances have permitted, as in pre-UAR Syria, and in Jordan during the nationalist heyday of the mid-1950's, the Ba'th Party has cooperated with other political organizations and worked through the existing political system. In Syria, the Ba'th, in alliance with army elements, has negotiated with most Syrian political parties of both right and left in efforts to make a more stable government. The Ba'th leaders also attempted to form a liaison with the *Front de Liberation National* (FLN) in Algeria but

[38] Charles Issawi, *Egypt in Revolution,* New York, 1963, pp. 46-75, summarizes the pre- and post-1956 developments.

were rebuffed by the Algerians, who politely refused to receive Aflaq in Algiers in June 1964.

While the Ba'th is ready and willing to be the sole source of political power should opportunity arise, it appears ready to cooperate with non-Ba'thists when the Arab cause requires it. Thus, despite the experience of authoritarian direction from Cairo from 1958 to 1961, when the Ba'th emerged as the controlling force in Iraq and Syria in early 1963, its first major action was once again to seek a unity agreement with Cairo. Although at least some of the Ba'thist leaders viewed the unity talks as a means of relieving Cairo's pressure on their newly established regimes, others—particularly Aflaq, Bitar and their associates—were driven by their ideological beliefs to seek a forward step in Arab unity. In a series of negotiations lasting a number of weeks, Iraq, Syria and Egypt threshed out an agreement which would unite them politically, the Tripartite Agreement of April 17, 1963. The agreement, a lengthy and repetitive document, tried to balance the interests of both Nasser and the Ba'th by providing for a strong presidency and an elected bicameral national assembly in a federal governmental structure. It covered most other fields of governmental activity and, if only a part of its provisions had been carried out, would have constituted a significant step forward toward unity.[39]

Once again the attempt failed and the cause was the same as before. There was no real agreement possible between a party which comes to decisions through a process of internal consensus and an authoritarian leader who took advice but remained unwilling to be fettered by other people's judgments on policy and action. This time the parting of the ways looks permanent. A violent polemic has raged between Cairo and Damascus for the past two years and hostility between the two systems seems likely to persist.

Thus, the chief practitioners of Arab Socialism remain far apart in their day-to-day approach to problems. Nonetheless, the socialist road to a reformed Arab world seems likely to remain the one with the most appeal to the intelligentsia. Whether the Nasserist or the Ba'thist version will eventually predominate is problematic. Much depends on factors not directly related to social and economic problems; external forces and events, and the character and orientation

[39] Text of the agreement is in *Middle East Forum*, XXXIX, Nos. 6 and 7, June-July 1963.

of the new leaders who arise, as they almost certainly will, in states not yet "liberated" from traditional rule. Already, in scarcely a quarter-century, the ideas and concepts formulated in the minds of two Damascus school teachers have led directly to changes of regime in two Arab countries and indirectly to political action elsewhere. These same ideas have also influenced the actions of the region's most powerful leader, Nasser, in applying, however pragmatically, socialist remedies to cure the ills of Egyptian society. Socialism seems destined to play an integral part in reform and revolutionary movements throughout the Arab area for some time to come.

# XV.  The Objects and Methods of Nasserism

## by George Lenczowski

NASSERISM HAS SOMETIMES BEEN USED AS A TERM WITH NEGATIVE connotations, especially by President Nasser's foreign critics. However, there is no intrinsic reason why it should not be used objectively, exactly as the terms "Marxism," "Leninism," or "Jeffersonian democracy" are being used. There is no doubt that Nasser's impact upon the Arab world has been of major proportions and that he has been identified in the public mind with certain goals and procedures. To clarify what these goals and procedures are in the spirit of impartial inquiry is the purpose of this article.

When, on July 23, 1952, Colonel Nasser's Free Officers overthrew King Farouk's Government, they were only one of the several forces which prior to that date challenged the very foundations of the existing *status quo*. Of these, the Moslem Brotherhood was by far the most powerful. By contrast, Nasser's organization was untested and its ideological stand so vague as to be virtually nonexistent. It was little more than an emotion-charged protest movement of younger officers, directed against the corruption, abuses and inequalities of the royalist-oligarchical regime. Initially, Nasser's group did not even regard itself as ready for the assumption of governing responsibilities, and invited an old-time politician, Ali Maher Pasha, a nationalist untainted by corruption, to head the first cabinet of the Revolution. Yet it did not take long for the Revolutionary Command Council to change the concept of its role in the society: from a mere watchdog of virtue it easily evolved into the position of actual ruler.

As is often the case in underdeveloped countries, it was easier to effect the military *coup* than to stay in power. To entrench itself, the RCC had to dispose of a number of actual or potential enemies. In the first place, the old parties were invited to purge and reform themselves but, having failed to do so, were banned. Next came the turn of the Moslem Brotherhood, which was first wooed and later destroyed. Thirdly, the RCC dealt decisively with its own inner dissensions: the initial front-man of the Revolution, General Mohammed Naguib was removed from the top position of the Republic to be replaced by a man who had always been the real head of the Free Officer movement: Nasser himself. By the beginning of 1955, all the competitive political forces were dispersed, intimidated or destroyed, and the RCC remained as the sole master on the scene, with Nasser's undisputed leadership over it. Furthermore, his position had been strengthened by the conclusion of two agreements with Britain (in 1953 and 1954) which settled the problem of Sudan and that of the evacuation of British troops from Egypt.

What were the objectives of the revolutionary government? No simple answer is possible because they underwent an evolution influenced by domestic and international developments. With a perspective of twelve years to aid us in our analysis, it is possible to distinguish four phases in the growth of the Egyptian Revolution: the phase of "Egyptocentrism," 1952-1954; the Pan-Arab phase, 1955-1958; the Domestic Socialist phase, 1958-1961; and, finally, the Pan-Arab Socialist phase, from 1962 onward.

I. EGYPTOCENTRISM

During the phase of "Egyptocentrism," in the period 1952-1954, the RCC was primarily concerned with the identification and eradication of the evils of the old order. These were described as imperialism, feudalism and monopoly capitalism. However, the remedies proposed by the new rulers were so general and vague as to appear as slogans rather than as a real program. They could be summed up as: (a) the establishment of a strong national army; (b) the establishment of social justice; and (c) the establishment of a sound democratic society.

While thus the regime's program was lacking precision, its early reform legislation addressed itself to three concrete issues of immediate pragmatic import: the land question, civic equality and economic development. The laws of the late summer of 1952 provided for the agrarian reform (maximum 200 feddans of land per owner), abolition of titles and privileges and encouragement of foreign capital investment by reversing the ratio of domestic to foreign shareholding decreed by the earlier anti-foreign legislation. It was evident that private profit-seeking was not yet viewed as an evil and that even foreign capital was considered as potentially beneficial, provided it shunned monopolistic practices.

In all this Egypt provided the central focus of attention and endeavor. Nasser and his colleagues had as yet no strong sense of Arab mission. The much-quoted three "concentric circles" which Nasser described in his *Philosophy of the Revolution* in 1954 do not seem to invalidate this finding. These circles—the Arab, the Islamic and the African—and especially his reference to a historical role "in search of a hero" in the Arab world—have often been invoked as a proof of Nasser's Pan-Arabism. While there is no doubt that at no time in his career did Nasser conceive of Egypt as living in isolation from the rest of the Arabs, it should be pointed out that to him Egypt was to be the *center;* i.e., the point of special concentration of effort. All three circles were treated as concentric around Egypt, and Egypt was to make the most for *itself* out of this fortunate central position. This conception of Egypt stood in contrast to the idea that, let us say, the Syrian and Jordanian pan-Arabists have had of the role of their respective countries in world affairs. To them the only major reality that counted was the "Arab Nation" of which their peoples were component parts and to which they should owe an undivided loyalty. In contrast to Egypt, the African concentric circle was meaningless to them. They were also reluctant to appeal to the broader Islamic solidarity: the latter, if given undue emphasis, was apt to dilute the feeling of Arabism and, in addition, might be used by the reactionary elements as an anti-revolutionary weapon.

Nasser's original view of Egypt as the center has never been rejected during the subsequent history of the Revolution. What has been changing is the amount of attention paid to the purely domestic scene as contrasted to the broader arena of the Arab, Afro-Asian and world politics.

## II. PAN-ARABISM

The beginning of the Pan-Arab phase may thus be traced to the moment when Nasser projected himself from the purely domestic role of Egyptian reformer into the role of an all-Arab leader. The moment in question was the formation of the Baghdad Pact in early 1955. This initiative gave to Nasser an opportunity to step into the role of the "hero" he referred to in his book. Calling the alliance a "foreign pact" likely to draw the Arabs into the cold war, and branding Nuri's Government of Iraq as a traitor and imperialist stooge, Nasser scored a major success with a responsive audience throughout the Arab world.

Having thus tested his powers on a wider forum, Nasser soon found another opportunity to address a multinational audience. What had been merely a negative reaction to someone else's action in Baghdad became elevated in Bandung (spring, 1955) to the level of a crystallized political philosophy, that of "positive neutralism." According to Nasser, "positive neutralism" reflected the feelings of the Arab peoples everywhere; his government was a spokesman for these feelings; if there were other views voiced by some Arab governments, they did not represent the true popular will. Thus Nasser's Arab policy began to drive a wedge between the governments and the popular masses. The official Cairo propaganda shifted its focus from earlier attacks on Egypt's evil past to an offensive against reaction and dependence on imperialism in the Arab world as a whole. Although hints about the nefarious role of the kings were not lacking, it was not yet a concerted anti-monarchy drive. The reticence in this respect was dictated by tactical considerations: Nasser was willing to accept alliances with certain royalist regimes. Foremost among these was Saudi Arabia. This paradoxical cooperation between revolutionary Cairo and patriarchal Riyadh stemmed from their hostility toward Hashimite Iraq and Great Britain, though the motivation was different in each case. It was especially in Syria that the Egyptian and Saudi policies supplemented each other: Cairo waged relentless psychological warfare while Riyadh supplied the funds to influence Syria's politics.

The second royalist ally of Egypt was Yemen. For reasons less clear than those of Saudi Arabia, Yemen's emerging dominant figure, Crown Prince Mohammed Bader, launched a policy of close cooperation with Egypt and the Communist bloc countries. Another instance of an alliance with the royalists was the moral, political and partly military support given by Cairo to the Imam of rebellious Oman. Struggle against British dominance in the peripheral areas of the Arabian Peninsula provided the common denominator.

Nasser's pragmatism in choosing his allies was not restricted to the royalist camp. In Iraq, in Syria and in Jordan, covertly or overtly, pro-Nasser forces frequently made common cause with the Ba'ath socialists and even communists in opposing the pro-Western regimes or leaders. The Soviet-Egyptian arms deal of 1955, followed by the Suez crisis of 1956, made the policy of neutralism hostile to the West popular among wide strata of Arab public opinion. By the end of 1956, Nasser's prestige as the chief exponent of Arab unity and anti-imperialism had skyrocketed. His portraits were displayed in barber shops of Amman, coffee houses of Damascus, grocery stores of Jiddah and the *suqs* of Libyan Tripoli. Cairo's *Voice of the Arabs* was listened to avidly throughout Arab lands. And, side by side with this, Egypt's military attachés in the Arab capitals were busy establishing footholds in the armies of the countries to which they were accredited.

The proclamation of the Syro-Egyptian unitary state in February 1958 constituted the legal culmination of the drive for Arab unity. It was followed by an act of federation between Yemen and the United Arab Republic on March 8. But the political apogee was reached on July 14, 1958, with the revolution in Iraq which put an end to the Hashimite rule. Simultaneously, pro-Nasser forces were engaged in armed rebellion against President Chamoun of Lebanon, with the United Arab Republic supplying arms and instructors to the rebel forces while a renewed attempt at a *coup* was made in Jordan. By mid-July it looked as if the old order, including the separate Arab sovereignties, were to be swept aside in one major wave of militant pan-Arabism. The Arab world was in the throes of revolutionary ferment, with Nasser's shadow cast over an area ranging from the Zagros to the Atlantic, and Egypt's domestic reform relegated to a secondary plane. However, the pan-Arab dream stopped short of fulfillment. The military intervention of the United States in Lebanon and of Britain in Jordan saved the sovereignty of these two countries. On the other hand, the victory of Abdul Karim Kassem, dictator of Iraq, over his pro-Nasser associate, Colonel Abdul Salam Aref, put an effective end to the drive for Iraqi-Egyptian union so long as Kassem stayed in power.

By the end of 1958, the pan-Arab offensive was checked in the most advanced and promising sectors. Furthermore, the absorption of Syria, accompanied by the wholesale demise of its former political leaders, acted as a memento to all vested political interests in the Arab world. For Nasser and his associates it was clearly the time to sound tactical retreat and to have a closer look at the internal situation of their enlarged state.

III. THE DOMESTIC SOCIALIST PHASE

The exact opening date of this phase is hard to determine. It may broadly correspond to the duration of the United Arab Republic, with its culmination reached in the summer of 1961. Following the setbacks to the pan-Arab offensive, it was natural for Nasser to concentrate on making the UAR a going concern. By the end of 1958, the official "line" in Cairo was as follows: Egypt's Revolution is not for export. Let bygones be bygones. From now on, the UAR will have only one Arab policy: to serve as a point of attraction by the force of example and by the success of its own development and reform.

Putting one's own house in order had two aspects: one was the working out of the right relationship with Syria; the other—attending to the domestic problems, mostly economic—in Egypt. By 1958-59 the initial vague references to social justice had given place to a crisper slogan of a "socialist, cooperative, democratic society." Planning and development of the public sector of economy were on the rise in Egypt, with heavy accent on industrialization. The economic *dirigism* was accompanied by the tightening of police controls, expansion of bureaucracy and the "streamlining" of political procedures typical of one-party developing countries. Furthermore, the oversupply of "diplomaed" intelligentsia and the personnel policy requirements in the army produced their own dynamics which led the ruling group to search for new placement opportunities. Such opportunities were partly provided by the sequestration of British, French and Jewish enterprises following the Suez crisis. But there still remained a substantial native private sector of the economy, owned and managed by members of the class which looked with nostalgia upon the free and easy days of the pre-revolutionary period. Consequently, when in July 1961 a large-scale nationalization of banks, insurance companies and major corporations was ordered by a presidential decree, it appeared like a logical step, socially and economically, in a regime whose tendency toward totalitarian controls had been obvious for some time past.

The assertion that revolution was not for export had, however, one flaw: it had to be exported to the Northern Region (Syria) if the state was to preserve its unitary character. For three and a half years Syria's economic organization substantially differed from that of Egypt. Syria's bourgeoisie, though eliminated from power, was still there, owning the means of production and presenting a potential threat. How long could a revolutionary-authoritarian regime like Nasser's allow such differences to invite dangerous comparisons between Syria's relatively liberal *laissez faire* and Egypt's politico-economic regimentation? To control this potential source of disaffection, and to keep an eye on competitive leftist movements (the Ba'ath and the communists), the Egyptian security apparatus was obliged to penetrate Syria in both the civilian and the military sectors. All of these moves were accompanied by the stepped-up internal propaganda which increasingly tended to equate union with revolution. Union between the two regions, the argument ran, could never be real unless both of them underwent a similar revolutionary experience in the socio-economic sphere, not to speak of the obvious required identity of the political organization. From this followed a logical chain of reasoning: to oppose union was to oppose the sacred cause of Arab unity, hence to commit treason; but because union and revolution were to be treated as an indivisible whole, to oppose the revolutionary economic measures was also treason.

The July 1961 nationalization decrees, which were to apply to both regions, were the last drop which filled the cup to overflowing. From that time on, an influential circle in the Syrian Army, chafing under the Cairo-sponsored manipulation of personnel and arms, joined with a group of deposed conservative politicians to shake off the Egyptian rule. On September 28, 1961, this coalition carried out a *coup* and, having arrested and deported Nasser's "viceroy," Marshal Abdul Hakim Amer, proclaimed Syria's separation.

IV. THE PAN-ARAB SOCIALIST PHASE

Syria's defection was not only a blow to Nasser's prestige but also a serious setback to Arab unity. While Syria's conservative separatists were branded by Cairo as traitors and imperialists' stooges, their action stimulated a rethinking of the whole problem of Arab unification. The outcome was the adoption of a new formula: to succeed as a living reality, Arab unity must be based on solid foundations. Mergers of states with deeply contrasting socio-economic and political structures can only lead to superficial unity which will be vulnerable to any attack of inimical forces. To attain real unity a basic prerequisite must be fulfilled: the countries in question have to undergo a thorough revolutionary change in the socialist direction. Once this is achieved, unity will be a natural result and its exact form—unitary state, federation or close cooperation—will be a matter of secondary importance.

The first task then was to secure a thorough revolutionary transformation. It was clearly Egypt's mission to define and clarify the doctrine of this transformation, so as to set the example for others to follow.

The Congress of Popular Forces, convoked by Nasser in the spring of 1962, adopted, in July, the "National Charter," a document setting forth the ideas and principles of Arab Socialism. The gist was as follows: to attain the objectives of freedom, socialism and unity, the Arab Nation must resort to revolution and not evolutionary reformism. In this revolution Egypt constitutes the nucleus. It has to assume leadership and pioneer on the path of progress, in accordance with its historical legacy of pre-eminence. Politically, the army constitutes the people's vanguard. Dictatorship of any single class is rejected. Instead, social harmony is sought on the basis of an alliance of the "working forces." This is to be reflected in an all-embracing organization, the Arab Socialist Union, and in the assignment of half the seats in it, as well as in the future National Assembly, to farmers and workers. The Egyptian

Revolution, to succeed, must establish ties and assure interaction with the revolutionary liberation movements in the Arab world as a whole. Imperialism must be fought as an implacable enemy (including Israel as imperialism's tool), but the methods of struggle must be adjusted to the changed methods of imperialist penetration. The latter does not appear any more in the form of overt aggression but in the form of indirect infiltration via the "palaces of reaction" and via the sponsorship of the divisive political parties under the guise of democracy. True democracy means the sovereignty of the people and cannot be separated from socialism. Arab Socialism must not follow any old-fashioned rigid theories (such as dictatorship of one class) and must be adapted to local conditions. Its aim is not only to redistribute the national wealth but, primarily, to expand the base of it. This must be done scientifically, through national savings, modern technology and total planning. Production will be carried on by both the public and the private sectors, with the public sector being responsible for the overall planning. Both sectors will be subjected to control by the people, and "popular councils should have authority over all production centers." Arab Socialism does not believe in nationalizing the land. It allows private ownership free of feudalism. Foreign private capital is viewed with "dark doubts." Foreign government aid is welcome provided it has no strings attached to it. It is, in fact, regarded as a tax that the advanced countries with a colonial past must pay to compensate their former victims of exploitation.

The objectives of foreign policy are described as struggle against imperialism, support of liberation movements, nonalignment and positive neutralism, determination "to liquidate Israeli aggression" in Palestine and to oppose Israel's infiltration of Africa, opposition to racial discrimination, support for the pan-African movement and Afro-Asian solidarity, maintenance of the bonds with the Islamic world and loyalty to the UN Charter.

The section on Arab unity reiterates the views presented earlier in this article as characteristic of the fourth, Pan-Arab Socialist phase. It makes clear explicitly that (in contrast to the previous phase), the Revolution *is* for export and that the UAR will not be deferred from her mission by "the outworn argument that this would be considered an interference in the affairs of others." The

UAR, in fact, has the "duty to support every popular, national movement" but she will leave "the maneuvers of the struggle to the local elements."

When, within less than nine months since the adoption of the Charter, socialist revolutions occurred in Yemen, Iraq and Syria, it appeared as if the prerequisites for unity were being fulfilled. In Iraq and Syria, revolutions were effected under the aegis of the Ba'ath Party, whose advocacy of Arab unity and socialism was of long standing. It was, therefore, logical that without much delay both Ba'athist governments sent high-level delegations to Cairo to conclude a unity agreement with Egypt. Although their negotiations with Nasser resulted in the signing of the Declaration of the Union Accord on April 17, 1963, whereby it was agreed to establish a Federal State to be composed of the Egyptian, Syrian and Iraqi Regions, its implementation was to be delayed pending a twenty month transitional period. During the first five months the Federation's constitution was to be drafted and, together with the presidency, submitted to a referendum. Even more important than the formal delay in setting up the new state were the serious differences which arose in the course of the negotiations between Nasser and the two Ba'athist delegations.

These differences centered on the conflicting concepts of the union and the state. While Nasser strove for a dominant and central position for Egypt, the Ba'athists insisted on equality of the three regions. On the other hand, Nasser's concept and practice of personal political leadership clashed with the Ba'athist system of collective leadership. And lastly, while the Ba'ath wanted to preserve its identity as a party in any larger political front, Nasser's aim was to have such a front entirely dependent on the will of the supreme political leadership, with obliteration of the organizational identity of its component parts.

Under the circumstances, disputes over the interpretation of the Union Accord arose on the morrow of its signature. The abortive pro-Nasser *coup* in Damascus in July did nothing to relieve the tension. By the early fall of 1963 it was clear that a voluntary union among the three countries in question was not possible so long as each of them was ruled by the government then in power.

This situation, no doubt disappointing to many an Arab nationalist, reflected a new and more fundamental development that took place in the Arab world, namely the emergence, in the 1960's, of competitive revolutionary centers which put an end to the exclusive role of Egypt as the fountainhead of Arab nationalism and socialism. This centrifugal trend was accentuated by the appearance of Ben Bella as the sole master of the Algerian Socialist Revolution.

## The Structure of Power

Political power in Egypt, since the *coup* of 1952, was initially concentrated in an eleven-man Revolutionary Command Council. In the formative stages and until the removal of General Naguib by the end of 1954, the RCC seems to have acted as a collective body with Nasser serving as virtual chairman but no more than that. By the end of 1955, such events as the Baghdad Pact, the Bandung Conference and the Soviet arms deal had caused Nasser to grow in stature with a corresponding shift in the balance of power within the RCC. As a leader whose charisma with the masses and the military was now an accomplished fact, he was in a position to establish a more direct contact with his popular base without having to rely on the intermediary of his closest associates. Thus from a chairman of *primus inter pares,* he emerged as an undisputed boss. At the same time, he has demonstrated extraordinary skill in handling this group of erstwhile comrades: with only three exceptions, he has succeeded in keeping this group in a state of loyalty and cohesion through more than twelve years of his Revolution.

Today Nasser's power may be said to rest on a combination of organizational and psychological factors. These could be listed as: (a) the Army, whose present hierarchy is entirely of Nasser's making; (b) the security services; (c) Nasser's charismatic appeal to the masses, which works regardless of the zeal or apathy of an average Egyptian for his revolutionary program; and (d) the ideological weapon which has to all practical purposes pre-empted the stage and deprived any competitive ideology from seriously contesting the field.

In the face of these realities of power-wielding, the formal structure fades into relative insignificance. In terms of major decision-making, it did not matter whether Nasser's Egypt had at one time or another a National Assembly, a single government-sponsored political organization or a constitution. Yet, there seems to be a law of politics which prompts any regime issued from a revolution to seek formal legitimacy and Nasser's behavior in this respect has not been an exception. Under his aegis, Egypt and, later, the United Arab Republic, has had three constitutions adopted since the Revolution: in 1956, 1958 and 1964. All three emphasized the socioeconomic concerns of the government and gave the monopoly of political action to a single organization called the "National Union" in the first two documents and the "Arab Socialist Union" in the third. It was this single organization (the name of "party" was carefully avoided) which was given the exclusive right to nominate candidates for the National Assembly.

## The Challenge of Economic Development

From the very beginning, the Government of the Revolution was committed to a policy of industrialization and development. The most spectacular single project has been the construction of the High Aswan Dam, whose first stage was completed in May 1964. Deepening and widening of the nationalized Suez Canal, establishment of a steel plant in Helwan and development of the largely state-owned petroleum industry to the point of reaching a virtually self-sufficiency, could be listed as other better-known major projects. Otherwise the industrialization process was progressing on a broad front in a variety of sectors, with the state playing the primary role.

Every time that the state takes upon itself the tasks previously performed by free enterprise, one is tempted to inquire into the results and to compare the performance of each. To draw such a comparison would exceed the purpose and limits of this article. We will therefore limit our remarks to the listing of a few problems that Nasser's regime has encountered in its drive for development. In the first place, one should observe that, as pointed out earlier, the regime has not been giving undivided attention to domestic reform and development and that much of its energy and part of its resources have been channeled toward the political issues outside of Egypt. One may wonder, therefore, about the cumulative effect of intervention in Syria, revolutionary propaganda in other Arab countries, massive military presence in Yemen, arms aid to some liberation movements and intensive participation in African affairs upon the course of domestic development. One may also pose the question of the effect of arms-for-cotton deals with the Soviet bloc on Egyptian diversification of agriculture, inflow of convertible currencies and food deficits. Furthermore, it is permissible to distinguish between two kinds of state intervention in the economic process: in one case the state invests capital in major ventures of public utility or industrial infrastructure for which private capital is not available; in another the state takes over (with or without compensation) the existing profitable enterprises, usually for socio-political reasons, rational or emotional. While on purely economic grounds the first kind may be perfectly justified, the second may prove costly or even deficitary. This in turn is linked with the availability of managerial and entrepreneurial talent. For socio-political reasons the class that traditionally supplied such skills in Egypt is being systematically uprooted. While the regime possesses already a number of sophisticated managers in its bureaucracy and is producing more, it is not certain that it can prevent a lag between the departure of one class and its replacement by the new one.

Last but not least, the regime's program for development exceeds the country's resources to finance it. The regime has resorted, therefore, to massive reliance on foreign aid. While Soviet assistance, technical and financial, has been primarily channeled toward the Dam construction and secondarily toward some other industrial projects, the United States aid has largely centered on grain and food deliveries, mostly under the Public Law No. 480 program. By mid-year 1964, the cumulative total of the U.S. assistance to the UAR had reached the figure of $1,199,655,000. The magnitude of this aid can perhaps be best measured by the fact that up to 60 per cent of the flour consumed in Egypt comes from the United States. Two other substantial foreign sources of aid are the International Bank, which helps finance the development of the Suez Canal, and West Germany, which is engaged in a variety of technical projects.

In political terms, the securing of funds from such antagonists in the cold war as Russia and the United States must undoubtedly be called a success. Not without some justification, Nasser is in a position to point out that this is the result of his policy of positive neutralism and his strong insistence on absolute sovereignty of his decision-making, even if in some respects it displeases the givers.

*Conclusion*

To sum up our inquiry, we may ask: is the Nasser-led Egyptian Revolution just another manifestation of the awakening of the ex-colonial underdeveloped world or does it have specific characteristics which would justify a special term of "Nasserism"? The answer appears to be that it is both. On the one hand, Nasser's objectives of anti-imperialism, social justice and development, have been common to other Arab and underdeveloped countries. So have some of his methods: the military-reformist authoritarianism, the elimination of opposition, the reducing to impotence of the traditional and upper-middle classes and the state intervention in the economic process. On the other, there are elements of substance and style in his policies that are new and original, though by now no more exclusive to him. Among these we may mention his "positive neutralism"—a term coined in Cairo and only later adopted by imitators, his view of Egypt as having a special mission due to its central position within the Arab, African and Islamic circles, his bold and risky challenges to Western supremacy—such as the arms deal with Russia and the seizure of the Suez Canal, and his reliance on massive economic aid on a state-to-state basis from both the East and the West. There is also something specific, almost monumental, in his style; his strivings have always aimed at great achievements: the Aswan Dam, the sovereign control of Suez, Arab unity, leadership in Afro-Asia and support for liberation movements anywhere between Angola and Cuba. He has also contributed heavily to one of the most perplexing distortions in the twentieth century in helping to spread two ideas: that imperialism and capitalism should be equated, and that imperialism is practiced only by the West but not by the Communist powers. The socialism he has introduced is not of his own invention inasmuch as, within the Arab world, the Ba'ath Party has preceded him in its doctrinal formulations. But, in terms of its bold application in practice, he has also been a pioneer. He has not created a true one-party state because such political bodies as he has tried to set up at one time or another have never been genuine parties, but mere appendages to the already existing power structure.

It has been said that one of his primary claims for distinction has been his search for dignity. If we assume that poverty, corrupt government, foreign domination and general retardation have produced among his people an inferiority complex mixed with frustration, it is possible that his courage and determination in challenging the past evils have put into motion a psychological compensatory mechanism apt to restore the feelings of self-respect. But we should beware of over-simplifications. There is perhaps too much of a propensity in the underdeveloped areas to interpret national dignity in terms that would sound alien or immaterial not only to the citizens of the advanced countries, but to the people of education and culture regardless of their geographical location and national identity. Recovery of dignity is often thought of in the ex-colonial world as being achieved through such measures as sover eign violations of a binding international agreement, confiscation of foreign property, expulsion of a foreign correspondent, refusal of a work permit to a badly needed technician or delivery of a militant speech full of personal invective against a foreign leader.

Contrasting with this is another type of dignity, more commonly adopted in the West. It is the dignity of a self-reliant individual, capable of self-criticism and free to criticize his government and vote it out of power; an individual not bound by any official ideology, not expected to applaud his leaders in mass meetings and not branded as traitor if he dissents; practicing patience and courtesy toward his fellow citizens if he is in public service; and having a sense of independence because the state is not the only employer.

Does the present generation of revolutionary-authoritarian leaders in the developing countries understand this difference? Does Nasser? And if so, does he consider the second type of dignity a luxury not suited to his time and place? Or is it perhaps that, in contemporary Asia and Africa, these individualistic values are expected to be replaced by the social concept of dignity whereby an individual can hope to find self-respect only through the communal achievements?

# XVI.   U.S.A. and UAR:
# A Crisis in Confidence*

## by John S. Badeau

DURING RECENT CONGRESSIONAL DEBATES ON AID LEGISLATION many harsh things were said about the United Arab Republic and its President. One Senator stated that "Col. Abdel Nasser . . . has been responsible more than any other single individual for keeping the political cauldron boiling in the arid, strife-torn Middle East . . . pouring oil on whatever brush fires break out." President Nasser has been equally sharp and critical. Early in 1964 he publicly described American foreign policy toward the Arab world as "not based on justice but on the support and consolidation of the base of aggression, Israel, and we cannot, under any circumstances, accept it."

To be sure, much of this may be dismissed as political talk for the public ear. Nasser, no less than American Senators, has a constituency which periodically must be stirred up and marshaled for support. There is thus little new in the current skirmishing between Arab and American spokesmen—but those who follow U.S.A.-UAR relations closely feel there ought to be. For this increased tempo in verbal attacks comes during a period of notable improvement in relations, when both the United States and the UAR, as a matter of basic policy, have been trying to get along with each other.

For both parties the change began in the aftermath of the Suez affair. By its prompt support of the United Nations and its refusal

* Reprinted by special permission from *Foreign Affairs,* January 1965. Copyright by the Council on Foreign Relations, Inc., New York, New York.

to back the Israeli-Anglo-French invasion, the United States gave practical proof of its impartiality in Middle East quarrels which threatened the peace of the area and the world. This was followed by a quiet mending of relations in the closing days of the Eisenhower Administration. Economic aid to Egypt was cautiously reinstituted and a franker exchange of views took place. President Kennedy supported and expanded this policy, identifying the Middle East as an area vital to American interests. He sought to develop relations with Egypt around points of mutual interest, while recognizing that the United States had, and would continue to have, sharp differences with Nasser.

In making this approach, the United States paid particular attention to economic assistance. Whatever else the revolution in Egypt stands for, it is the most vigorous attack on the perennial problems of poverty, disease, ignorance and privilege ever seen in the ancient Valley of the Nile. With a burgeoning population (doubled since 1936), severe limitation of arable land (3½ percent of the country's total area), and limited foreign exchange earnings (chiefly the cotton crop, Suez Canal tolls and tourism), it is obvious that the UAR cannot forge ahead with desperately needed modernization and social advance without substantial foreign assistance.

Here was a point of mutual concern on which closer American-Egyptian relations could be built. On its part, the UAR needed to develop a healthy and progressive society without being captured in the process by the Soviet bloc. But a socially stable and progressive Egypt was also in the interests of the United States, one of whose basic Middle East policies is to contribute wherever possible to tranquility through social progress in this vital region. Political and economic chaos in the Valley of the Nile would have repercussions in the surrounding area. Both in its own right, and as a major influence in the Arab world, the sound economic progress of Egypt is a desirable American objective. American economic assistance, chiefly through the P.L. 480 Food Program, was therefore increased.

Egypt's response to this approach opened a new era in U.S.A.-UAR relations. A cultural agreement was signed in 1962. In 1963, after 11 years of negotiation, Egypt entered into an Investment Guarantee Agreement with the United States, aimed at stimulating and protecting American business interests. On several occasions, notably at the Economic Conference in Cairo in the summer of 1962, the UAR played a moderating role in containing African and Asian extremists. Nasser opposed the Soviet resumption of nuclear testing and shifted his policy away from supporting Gizenga in the Congo. While maintaining diplomatic relations with Cuba, the UAR displayed little enthusiasm for Castro and took a reasonably sympathetic attitude toward President Kennedy's showdown with Khrushchev. And for the first time in some years, the controlled press in Egypt gave a fairly objective, often sympathetic, account of American actions.

Against this background of cooperation, the shrill crescendo of bitter accusation between American and Egyptian leaders strikes an ominous discord. A popular Egyptian proverb says, "One day it's honey—the next onions." After the good diet of the past three years, are American-Egyptian relations in for a ration of onions? Under the present Administration, the United States made its most determined effort to protect its interests in the Near East through a reasonable rapprochement with the UAR. Are all such efforts bound to be fleeting? What is it that interrupts them just when everything seems to be going well?

The answer is not to be found so much in specific policies of the two countries as in the atmosphere within which these take place. At the end of the First World War an American observer reported that "Before all else [the nations of the Near East] need renewed confidence in each other and in us, and in our honest purposes of good." That is as true today as it was 40 years ago. The day of honey in Arab-American relations so easily changes into a day of onions because there is mutual distrust of each other's "honest purposes of good." Actions in themselves relatively minor become objects of deep suspicion because they are seen as cloaks for "imperialism," "neo-colonialism," "pan-Arabism" or the personal ambitions of some Arab ruler. The crisis is often a crisis of confidence, generating a fog of suspicion which chokes good relations and makes it difficult to negotiate a lasting solution to differences.

It is a crisis in confidence which currently threatens American relations with the UAR. Although the mutuality of interests continues, the United States is wondering whether in the light of recent events it can trust the UAR to follow a reasonably consistent course of cooperation—or will it undercut vital American interests in the Arab world at its own whim? And can the UAR trust the United States to pursue its present course with continuity—or will the erratic winds of changing administrations and election pressures continually blow American foreign policy off course? It is doubt about these fundamentals of the American-Egyptian relationship which has created a crisis between the two nations.

One reason for such doubts is the very success of recent policy. Each party now finds itself playing an important role in the national interests of the other—a role in which the "capacity to hurt" is large. American food makes a massive contribution to the well-being of Egypt and is a resource on which the UAR national budget is currently based. While the country could get along without it (as the aftermath of Suez shows), the withdrawal of our food sales would create a serious economic problem. Moreover, the attitude of the United States influences both government and private credit resources in Western countries upon which the UAR now depends for its badly needed foreign currency assistance. Thus the UAR is nervous about anything which might suggest a sudden shift in American policy and scrutinizes carefully and suspiciously every American statement, fearing the worst.

But the United States also is nervous about Egypt. The UAR and its President are the single most powerful force in the Arab world. With the largest and most modernly equipped Arab army, the most powerful and sophisticated propaganda system and wide appeal among the Arab masses, President Nasser has a potential which cannot be neglected by any nation having interests in the Near East. He has the power to harm American interests to a considerable degree—as the response to his call for liquidating the American air base in Libya shows. It is not simply a matter of power and ambition; Nasser typifies the socially revolutionary and politically self-determining forces which are at work in most countries of the Near East. If these forces, under the spell of Nasser's leadership, are aroused against American interests in Libya, Jordan and Saudi Arabia, they can cause much trouble, even if they might not in the end totally destroy the United States' position.

But this mutual fear is more than a current mood, bred by recent experience. There are, in fact, good reasons for the United States and Egypt to suspect each other—reasons which have a long history. Each nation has a bill of particulars against the other, drawn from the experiences of the last decade. It is this which forms the reservoir of suspicion from which a crisis of confidence is so easily drawn.

## II

On Egypt's part, the first count against the United States is the *unpredictability of its policy*. American-Egyptian relations since the Revolution in 1952 amply illustrate this. In the opening stages of the new régime, America was closely and hopefully identified with it, believing that a change in social and political conditions was long overdue in the Valley of the Nile. This led to a "honeymoon" policy, when sympathy and identity of interests seemed high.

In 1955 this cordial relation abruptly changed, due to Egyptian arms purchases from the Soviets. Failing to secure military equipment from the West on acceptable terms, Nasser turned to the Soviet bloc. The American reaction was a reversal of policy, which now set itself to contain and separate Egypt from its Arab neighbors. This was the policy of "isolation"—a long cry from the "honeymoon" which preceded it.

This policy failed. The United States was unable to isolate Egypt, the Israeli-Anglo-French invasion of Egypt brought Nasser to the summit of his influence in the area, and it became clear that some new approach was needed. In the aftermath of Suez, America therefore shifted to a line that was "cautious but correct," gradually reinstituting aid and seeking at least minimal normal relations.

Under President Kennedy, this was reinforced and expanded to become a policy of "selective cooperation" built on mutual interests. In no sense was this a return to the "honeymoon," with uncritical support of all UAR policies. Rather it was based upon a sense of mutual needs and a willingness to concentrate on these instead of on the many disputes which had soured past relations.

Thus in less than a decade the United States has followed four different policies toward Egypt. While each is defensible in terms of the conditions which produced it, the effect on the Egyptian is to create the impression that American actions are unpredictable, not built upon clear principles—indeed, not even built upon a consistent view of America's own interests. It is this penchant for change in the American course which makes the Egyptian reserved and suspicious of us, especially during a period when relations are good.

A second cause of Egyptian suspicion is the rapid rise of American power, particularly in and near the Middle East. Prior to the Second World War, the American presence in the Arab world consisted chiefly of missionaries, educators, archeologists and a limited number of businesses, petroleum being the largest. The United States was a threat to no one; it had no bases, no troops, no fleets, and it displayed none of the panoply of power Arabs expected from a great nation.

This changed after the war. Beginning with President Truman's commitment to the defense of Turkey and Greece in 1947, the United States played an increasing role in the area. Military bases in Morocco, Libya, Turkey and Arabia, the powerful Sixth Fleet always just across the horizon, support for the military establishments of Iran, Turkey and Greece, the landing of Marines in Lebanon—these were disturbing proofs to the Arab that the United States had become a military presence which could interfere with actions of the Arab states whenever it chose. What Great Britain once was, the United States has now become—the policeman of the world. Therefore the spectre of American might *in the Middle East* always lurks just off-stage and Egyptians are convinced that at some unexpected point it will step from the wings to play the dominant role in their affairs.

This fear is fed by a third suspicion—that the United States is too often in league with the forces of "imperialism and neo-colonialism." What the Egyptians mean by this is not (despite the paragraph above) that America will deliberately seek to create a Middle East empire. It is that we are damned by our association with the British and the "reactionary" Arab régimes. As to Britain, many Arabs believe that the present remnants of its historic position in the Middle East are supported by the United States. While at the time of the Suez invasion in 1956 the United States joined in condemning (and thus terminating) the Anglo-French invasion, within a few days we froze Egyptian assets in America, refused to sell food and drugs to Egypt, and ended the CARE program. Obviously, it is argued, America was prepared to support Britain as far as it dared.

This identification with "imperialism" is given more substance by our interests in and association with Arab régimes which the Egyptian considers "reactionary." By this he means the monarchies of the area and their governments which he claims do not represent popular consent or the interests of the people. The Egyptian argument is that these régimes are based upon an economic and political élite who keep power against the best interests of the common masses by cooperating with the foreign power having a stake in the country. He believes that the very character of the régimes in Jordan, Saudi Arabia, Iran and Libya (to name the current lot) drive them into subservience to Western, therefore American, power. This is the "neo-colonialism" against which the non-aligned world so frequently agitates as a threat to its untrammeled independence.

These three causes for distrust are brought to a focus in the problem that most continuously and deeply besets our relations with the Arab world—the question of Israel. There are many aspects to this tangled affair, but as regards American foreign policy the heart of the matter is that the Egyptian (and most of his fellow Arabs) believes that Israel exercises a veto power on American policy toward the Arab world. Whatever understanding of the realities of Arab life there may be in American circles, and however logically American interests can be served by at least an even-handed policy toward the Arabs, the Egyptian is convinced that when the cards are down Israel and its supporters can force the United States to make their interests paramount. Thus the Egyptian believes that no balanced American policy toward the Arab world can be permanent. Sooner or later it will run counter to Israeli interests, and when that happens, the United States Government is powerless to hold to its course.

So runs the Egyptian indictment. But Americans have equally deep suspicions of the UAR. Most basic is the conviction that Egypt and its President are compulsive meddlers in the affairs of their neighbors. Both openly and secretly they stir up strife, support dissident movements and seek the overthrow of régimes of which they disapprove. Even Egyptians recognize this and express themselves in one of Cairo's many jokes about the régime. According to the story, when President Nasser went to Algeria . . . [in the spring of 1963], he took with him a number of movie films, one of his favorite forms of relaxation. Among these was "Mutiny on the *Bounty*." After seeing the picture, the President sent a cable to the Foreign Office saying, "Contact the mutineers on the *Bounty* immediately. Tell them we support their cause and any attack on them will be considered an attack on the UAR!"

During the past . . . years there have been five instances of UAR meddling which particularly disturbed Americans. The first was Egypt's support for the *coup d'état* which overthrew the Imam of Yemen. What began as modest help to Republican forces against the Royalists ended with full-scale military occupation of the country. Egypt eventually had nearly 40,000 troops in the Yemen. A second instance was the dispatch of UAR arms and technicians in support of Algeria in its border dispute with Morocco—and this at a time when Cuba was also getting into the act.

The third incident was the supply of small arms to the Government of Cyprus during the current civil war on that unfortunate island. While any government has the legal right to sell arms to another government, it seemed that Greek Cypriots had ample quantities of weapons on hand, both for their regular and irregular forces. What reason had the UAR to contribute to an already over-abundant supply except the desire to fan the fires of conflict between Greek and Turkish Cypriots? And why did Nasser welcome Makarios so warmly to Cairo . . . unless the UAR is more interested in perpetuating than in calming the Cyprus disorders?

The fourth instance is perhaps the most serious. In February 1964, President Nasser, in a public speech heard throughout the Arab world, called for the ending of British and American base rights in Libya. The response was an immediate public furore in Libya which came dangerously near to ending in the abdication of the King. Once again Egypt was interfering in the affairs of its neighbors, and in a form directly challenging an American interest.

Finally, there is the current Egyptian campaign against the South Arabian Federation and its British sponsors. Here is an area remote from the UAR, without visible impact on Egyptian security interests. Whether the Egyptian offensive is a diversionary ploy in the Yemen affair or a more general stirring up of trouble for trouble's sake, it only confirms American opinion that the UAR is always minding someone else's business.

This continuous "keeping the pot boiling" by Egypt causes serious problems for the United States. Not only does it have a number of specific interests in the countries involved, but its policy has been to promote tranquility among Middle Eastern states. We believe that disputes, small in themselves, run the risk of inviting outside interference and so spreading into a major conflict. We do not want to see our friends in Arab countries threatened by Egyptian meddling and we do not intend to have world peace shattered by small-nation disputes.

The second set of American complaints against the UAR is related to the first. Egypt's ability to involve itself in affairs throughout the area is based in part on its military and propaganda strength, and this deflects money from urgently needed economic development. While not massive as modern armies go (about 150,000 men for a population of 28,000,000), Egyptian forces are the biggest and best-equipped in the Arab world. Their weapons and aircraft are by far the most sophisticated. Egyptian secret activities abroad in the form of subsidies, weapon supply and agents are large and continuous. These efforts are supported and extended by propaganda including subsidies to newspapers, writers, conferences, foreign students studying in the UAR and an extensive multilingual radio program.

All this is expensive. It may be argued that all nations incur such expenses; they are accepted in our chaotic modern world as a necessary part of "national security" which costs us all so much. But the point for Egypt is that it cannot afford the role of a dominant or dominating power in the area and at the same time win its internal fight against ignorance, poverty and backwardness. Remarkable improvements have been made in Egyptian life under Nasser's régime, but it is still touch and go as to whether the Egyptian economy can permanently bear the burden. Why does the UAR insist on incurring a high bill for activities abroad when at least some of this money is so desperately needed at home?

A third general cause for American suspicion toward Egypt is the continuing concentration of political power in personal hands. This is what the American means when he speaks of "dictator-ship"—not so much a theory of government (as Fascism or

Nazism) as a practical situation in which the fate of society and individuals is determined by one man or a small group of men upon whom the citizenry has no form of restraint.

It was to be expected that in the early days of the Revolution Colonel Nasser and his associates should become the *de facto* center of power in the country. But if a revolution is to be anything more than a *coup d'état,* it must eventually broaden its base, diffuse its power and build a rule of law. None of these things appears to have happened yet in Egypt. Laws are promulgated by Presidential decree, there is no provision for a "loyal opposition," and expressions of criticism of government policies are only possible within the very narrow limits set by the Government itself. The press is firmly controlled. At times private citizens are under sharp surveillance (as during the 1962 French spy trials) and "guilt by association" plays a large role.

All this does not add up to a police state in the full pattern so familiar in Communist countries. But it does have a profound effect on society, generating an atmosphere of unpredictability and curtailed liberty. In so far as the American sees world issues as involving the principles of freedom and responsibility, he is suspicious of the character of the Egyptian régime and the direction it has thus far been traveling.

This suspicion is related to another American question about the UAR, namely its relation to the Communist world. The more extreme statements that Nasser is at least a crypto-Communist and that Egypt is in fact, if not in desire, a Communist satellite can be dismissed as uninformed and wishful thinking. But whatever its intentions, the UAR, as Americans see it, has put itself dangerously in fee to the Soviet system. The Egyptian army is equipped from top to toe with Soviet weapons. This makes the nation entirely dependent upon Soviet good will for military spare parts and replacements. In fact, the Soviet monopoly on the Egyptian régime's chief instrument of power—its military establishment—gives the Russians an absolute veto on certain Egyptian policies if they care to use it. Whatever the UAR's dedication to independence may be, its freedom of action in relation to the Soviets is more sharply limited than it is in relation to the free world.

Added to this is the belief that Soviet and UAR policies in the

Middle East too often coincide. A major Soviet objective has been to dispossess the Western powers of influence in the area, thus opening the way for Soviet action. The UAR would appear to serve this through its attack on the British position, foreign bases (which are all Western) and non-revolutionary Arab states with which the West has close relations. Thus, while Egypt does not intend to be a Soviet satellite, its own activities sometimes aid and abet Soviet interests and cause problems for the United States.

Finally, there is Israel. Depending on the knowledge and emotional commitment of the American, his attitude ranges from seeing in Nasser the dragon who will devour Israel as soon as he is strong enough, to the more sober recognition that the UAR's continued hostility to Israel is the keystone of the Arab attitude which refuses to consider even a remote possibility of peace discussions. This concerns many Americans who are in no sense Israeli protagonists. In so far as the Arab-Israeli dispute is a constant source of tension and conflict, its lack of solution is a constant threat to tranquility, progress and stability in the Middle East. Many Americans want it settled, not because they favor Israel or the Arabs, but because they are thoroughly weary of alarms and excursions which periodically set the world's teeth on edge. If the UAR would exercise its leadership in the Arab world for a gradual rapprochement with Israel, everyone would breathe easier.

Accusation and counter-accusation—how much of it is strictly true? Only a detailed study of each issue would answer this, and then it would be seen that there is confusion as to facts and highly questionable judgments in the interpretation of them. But one thing is clear, when all the mythology has been extracted from the mutual causes for suspicion, a hard core of fact remains. Egypt has sound reasons for mistrusting the United States, and the United States cannot help but mistrust it in return. The crisis in confidence is real, not artificial, and it is the chief factor which must be taken into account by both countries if they desire to continue reasonably cordial relations to their mutual benefit.

Can confidence be restored? Given the causes for suspicion recounted above, it may be argued that this is impossible; the gulf is too wide and has been deepened over too many years to be bridged now. This is certainly true for the immediate future. Both parties need to understand and admit that the restoration of confidence is a slow business and that no sudden change in foreign policies will bring it about immediately. For one thing, national as well as personal characteristics are hard to change. Egypt is a revolutionary society and nothing the United States can do will alter that fact. All the problems of dealing with its ebullient and frequently embarrassing activities will continue and must be recognized as part of the given situation. On its part, the United States will not change its character as a leader of the free world with interests that frequently run counter to Egyptian desires. No matter what Egypt thinks or does, America will not place its own and its partners' security in jeopardy by turning a blind eye on any Egyptian activity which causes tumult in the Near East or appears to strengthen the Soviet position.

This is to say that both countries will get along better only if each is more realistic about its capabilities of easily and quickly influencing the other's course of action. Americans are prone to think that they can play God in Near Eastern (and other) affairs, shoring up or bringing down régimes, or by threats and economic pressure forcing the UAR government to take actions which it judges to be against its basic national interests. And Egyptians equally exaggerate their limited ability to put pressure on the United States through propaganda, appeals to revolutionary groups in other countries, or agitation against American positions such as Wheelus Air Base and the petroleum interests at the head of the Persian Gulf. Each country can damage the other, but neither can force a basic change in policy unless it is prepared to resort to overt action—and in this the United States is in the stronger position.

If this fact is accepted, it means that differences and clashes of interest between the United States and Egypt will continue for some time. The problem is not to wipe these out (which is impossible) but to curtail and contain their power to threaten a reasonable relationship between the two countries. For this both sides must be prepared to take some positive steps. For the Egyptians, there must be a greater appreciation that the public image they create in the American mind largely determines what it is possible for the U.S. government to do. The United States is a democracy, which Egyptians do not fully understand. Neither the Secretary of State nor the President can sustain a policy toward Egypt (even when it is in the best interests of the United States) without some Egyptian help in creating a climate of favorable public opinion. When this climate is unfavorable, it is not because (as alleged by Egyptians) the American press is controlled by pro-Israeli interests or American Senators . . . are captives of the Jewish vote. It is because of what the Egyptians themselves do. They can now do several things which will help their position.

One is to display more dedication to carrying out their word. Failure to make even token troop withdrawals under the Yemen disengagement agreement has seriously shaken American faith in President Nasser's *bona fides*. Actions taken against foreign companies in Egypt despite earlier agreements and promises have the same effect. In general, Egypt must work to correct the impression of undependability which its actions have generated.

Egypt can also affect the American attitude by emphasizing accomplishments rather than propaganda as its implement of influence in the Arab world. The sound development of the Valley of the Nile economy with resulting success in raising living standards will do much more to win Egypt a good reputation in the Middle East and abroad than strident and vicious radio broadcasts. The real measure of the Egyptian Revolution's place in history will not be the extent to which it can outdo other Arabs in invective, but the degree to which it can stand upon its actual accomplishments of a better society. The Egyptian image as a responsible Arab world power has been badly damaged by its unceasing and raucous broadcasts.

Again the American attitude will be affected by the efficiency with which the Egyptian social and economic plans are carried forward. Great changes for good have taken place in Egypt, but great wastage of human and economic resources has also taken place in the process. American economic assistance has been large; but it is difficult to make the case for its continuance unless the Egyptian developmental process is tightened and foreign adventures curtailed in the interest of internal development. Economic conditions in Egypt are not as bad as many foreign observers would like to believe, but they are considerably worse

than the Egyptian official admits. If the American is to be induced
to continue helping in the remaking of the Egyptian system, he
must be given more confidence in the process.

Then there is the difficult matter of Israel, which creates a continuing and most exacerbating strain in UAR-U.S. relations.
Americans cannot expect Egypt to change its basic attitudes on
this, any more than France can expect the United States to change
its attitude toward Red China. But there are several things Egypt
can do to ease the situation and thus create confidence in America, particularly in non-Zionist circles. One is to let its actions
speak rather than its words. The Egyptian policy toward Israel
over the past few years has, in fact, been encouragingly moderate.
Nasser's public eschewal of aggressive military action as an answer
to the current Israeli utilization of Jordan waters is a case in point.
The trouble is that Presidential speeches often outrun Presidential policies. The Israel dispute is unnecessarily dragged in on
every occasion and vague verbal attacks on Israel are taken at
their face value in Congress and by the American public.

Even more important would be some steps by the UAR toward alleviating the arms race with Israel. It is the American
conviction that this can be done without imperiling the basic security of the United Arab Republic. Acceptance of international
safeguards in the development of atomic power and some willingness to consider means by which the arms level can be frozen at
its present position would create a very favorable world reaction.
Even if Israel did not respond, or respond fully, Egyptian leadership in this would go far to encourage the great mass of Americans
both in and out of government who want only to see peace in the
Middle East.

But the task of creating confidence is not Egypt's alone; the
United States must also be prepared to make some changes. The
first is a greater consistency of approach. American foreign policy
toward Egypt has been so erratic largely because Americans—like
Egyptians—react rather than act. They do not recognize that it is
possible for two countries to oppose each other on specific issues
while maintaining a continuing and mutually profitable relation.
It is too often an "all or nothing" policy. Either American wheat
buys Egyptian compliance to an American viewpoint, or there
will be no American wheat. This assumes that the object of Amer-

ican aid is to "bring Egypt to heel," and that when this fails the only alternative is pressure totally to stop the aid program. This seldom works, and particularly it does not work with President Nasser. If the United States desires to protect such national interests as involve the UAR, it must be prepared steadily and quietly to pursue a policy that does not fluctuate like the stock market with every political crisis. American policy must be aimed at maintaining a relationship with Egypt, not on seeking pretexts to sever it.

This means that the United States must be more clear-sighted in defining for itself and the UAR what its vital interests are. There is a confusion in the American mind—even among policymakers—between American interests and what Americans consider desirable. The latter is as broad as the moral values of the particular observer and includes a free press, the parliamentary system, private enterprise—or even the whole gamut of the American political system. Desirable as these may be to the American, they are not *per se* American interests, involving the essentials of national security. It is these latter which are the central concern of foreign policy and the American approach to the UAR must be made consistent with them.

It is as difficult for the United States to decrease suspicions generated by its policy toward Israel as it is for the UAR in the same situation. But the attempt must be made if American interests in the Arab world are not to suffer needlessly. The United States—like the UAR—has certain commitments in the Arab-Israeli situation from which it will not retreat. These include recognition of Israel as a sovereign and continuing member of the international community of nations and support for and collaboration with the United Nations in dealing with questions arising from the Arab-Israeli dispute.

Arabs need to understand and respect these commitments, as Americans must do. It needs to be made clear both in Congress and in sections of the general public that the American commitment to Israel is *limited*. Our commitments are not based on the assumption that in every and all circumstances we will come to Israel's aid. Nor is Israel (or any other Middle East state) the chosen instrument of the United States in its policy toward the area. The basic consideration must always be what serves *Ameri-*

*can* interests in the Middle East. And this must be so regardless of its effect in helping or hurting either Israel or the UAR.

This principle is understood in policy-making circles in Washington and, in general, action accords with it. The difficulty lies in the sensitive domestic political situation. Often it is felt that Israel and her protagonists must be placated by public statements, even though these do not herald a shift in American policy. It is too much to expect that all politicians will resist the temptation to drag Israel into their election campaigns as a vote-catching device, but at least responsible government spokesmen can take more care as to the place and content of their speeches. It was unfortunate that President Johnson's first policy statement on the Middle East was made before an organization identified with Israel, just as it would have been equally unfortunate if it had been made to a pro-Arab group. It would also help if American policy decisions involving Israel could be kept out of election campaigns, thus underscoring their character as considered moves based upon American national interest and not merely election gestures.

Difficult tasks are evidently involved for both parties. Many will say, "Why bother to attempt them, when the differences between the two countries are so continuous and exasperating?" The answer is that both Egypt and the United States need each other; their realistic national interests demand reasonably cooperative relations. This is why, despite the strains and vagaries of policy during the past decade, there has never been an irrevocable rupture. In each period of bad relations, as the point of no return approached, both parties paused, took a new tack and tried to repair the breach. In the aftermath of the Soviet arms deal the United States did not succeed in isolating Egypt and possibly bringing about its downfall; and Egypt, despite strenuous efforts during the same period, did not permanently hurt American interests in the Arab world. Both found their capabilities more limited than they thought and their mutual interests more powerful than they had admitted. They therefore gradually returned to a policy of fostering better relations.

It is these mutual interests which form the basis of an enduring relation between the two countries. Despite suspicions, clashes and differences in policy, the United States and the United Arab

Republic have concerns in common on which a reasonable co-operation can be built. Egypt wants to develop in independence, without becoming either a Western or a Soviet satellite. Similarly the United States, now increasingly recognizing the inevitability (and often the utility) of the non-aligned position of many nations, is concerned to see Egypt independent. Egypt wants a better and more stable social system, with a rise in living standards for the masses of the Nile Valley. Here again American and Egyptian interests coincide; a stable Egypt is very much desired by the United States, for a major catastrophe there would have repercussions throughout the entire Arab world. To improve its economic situation, Egypt needs continuing ties with the West; even if the Soviet connection were to be increased vastly, the Soviet bloc cannot do what needs to be done for the Egyptian economy. And all of Egypt's foreign cultural, intellectual and technical traditions are of the Western world. With them the Egyptian feels at home. To make this Western connection secure in both its economic and cultural aspects, Egypt needs good relations with the United States.

So long as the United States has vital interests in Arab lands and the United Arab Republic has a role of influence and leadership, the two countries cannot escape doing business with each other. The question is whether they can be sufficiently mature, clear-sighted and patient to work out gradually a consistent and mutually profitable relationship.

# XVII. The U.S.S.R. in the Near East: A Decade of Vicissitudes

## by Uri Ra'anan

FEW OBSERVERS COULD HAVE FORESEEN IN 1954 THAT THE U.S.S.R. and its East European allies were about to embark upon ten hectic years of courtship, during which they would lavish some $1.5 billion in military assistance and an even larger sum in economic aid upon the Near Eastern objects of their desires.[1] Had they envisaged such a possibility, fewer analysts still would have believed that such feverish attentions would lead only to endless flirtations and incessant demands, interspersed with emotional tiffs and coy glances in other directions, but not to any stable or lasting attachments.

Of course, it remains an unproven assumption that even the most sanguine dreamers in Moscow ever expected seriously that the other powers would permit the Russians to enjoy the delights of conquest in this much-wooed region. Actually, Soviet writings and statements (1954-56) indicated aims of a more "modest" and negative kind, i.e., the denial to the West of the resources and, above all, of the strategic assets of the Near East. Failing that, the U.S.S.R. seemed prepared to settle for some form of acceptance by the West of Soviet membership in the Near Eastern concert of powers. Even if such relatively limited goals were envisaged in Moscow, however, sober reality has fallen well short of Russian expectations.

The West, after all, still enjoys unhampered access to the raw materials of the region, although at a somewhat higher price than

[1] For the purposes of this analysis, the Near East includes the countries of the North African Maghreb.

before. Indeed, it seems difficult to believe that any local régime would ever wish to deprive itself permanently of its natural West European market for those exports, especially oil, from which most of the Near East's foreign currency income must necessarily be derived. As for the strategic aspects, land and air bases near the Soviet borders are no longer quite so vitally important to the West in the age of the ICBM and Polaris, while the maritime approaches to the region are, more than ever, controlled by the U.S. Sixth Fleet. Khrushchev's military policy, with its disdain for conventional—especially surface naval—power, no doubt undermined Russia's capability in the area of matching the U.S. with a counter-striking force. Thus, partial Soviet successes in destroying both the effectiveness of the original Baghdad Pact and, with it, the attraction of the whole concept of military pacts with Near Eastern countries, cannot be regarded as much more than a temporary and psychological setback for the West.

Whatever palpable hits the Russians may have scored should, in fact, be sought in the diplomatic and tactical sectors rather than in the economic or strategical fields. For instance, there is little doubt that, in the Near East, the U.S.S.R. has played with some limited effect upon the differences between the various Western powers, although of course, Moscow did not create these differences. Thus, during the Suez campaign the Soviets tried very hard to lure the U.S. into an American-Russian partnership for the purpose of expelling Britain and France from the region. They succeeded, however, only within the narrow confines of the UN parliamentary scene, while being firmly prevented from establishing a Russian beachhead in the Near East. In fact, the West as a whole has never accepted the U.S.S.R. as a full and legitimate Near Eastern power. As a consequence, the Soviet freedom of manoeuvre has been severely circumscribed. The Russians have been made painfully aware that any attempt to intervene directly and with physical force in the Near East would bring a united West into action. Soviet attempts to play up U.S., U.K. and French antagonisms have had to be confined to diplomatic feelers, since, outside the UN, the U.S.S.R. has never been admitted to discussions between the great powers at which the Near East was a major subject.

It is unquestionable, however, that Moscow has been able to

register some worthwhile achievements by exploiting temporary constellations in which Russian interests and those of certain local régimes in the Near East happen to run along parallel lines. In this way the U.S.S.R. found it possible to embarrass and upset the West: thus, for reasons of their own, Cairo and Algiers were prepared to act as conduits for Soviet arms to various Congolese rebel groups (1960 and 1964), to Makarios, to the Angolans, to Somalia and to other sensitive areas; the same and other Near Eastern leaders readily and vociferously joined the Soviet chorus of denunciation against "imperialism" in Cuba, Africa, the Dominican Republic, Vietnam and elsewhere (Afro-Asian Solidarity Conferences, exchanges of visits with Soviet and Chinese officials and the UN provided the scenes for such outbursts); above all, Moscow derived the utmost tactical and propagandistic advantage from its alignment with irredentist elements which desired to alter the existing territorial division of the region.

The question remains, however, whether such limited, transient and essentially negative gains have really been commensurate with Soviet efforts, to what extent they have been neutralized by constant tensions between the U.S.S.R. and its newly-gained friends, whether they could not have been achieved at a cheaper price and whether the Russians can, or wish to, meet the continually rising demands of various Near Eastern recipients of Soviet aid. It must also be asked whether the concessions which Moscow eventually made in the ideological arena, at the expense of local Communist parties, have really paid off and whether Soviet zigzags over such issues as the Kurdish-Arab conflict have not usually ended up by alienating both sides.

In this context it may be instructive to re-examine the methods by which the U.S.S.R. gained entry into the region a decade ago; such an analysis can throw light upon the inherent contradictions faced by all great powers in evolving their Near Eastern policies. As the Russians attempted to replace the West as the predominant force in the area they eventually confronted the same serious dilemmas.

In 1955 the Soviet Union enjoyed tactical advantages in the Near East precisely because it was an outsider. The West—in effect the "custodian" of the region—was committed to the maintenance of tranquility in the Near East. Thus it was obliged to combat elements opposed to the established balance in order to defend the existing *pax occidentala*. Automatically the West became identified with the territorial *status quo* and, to a lesser extent, with the political and social *status quo*. Thus, the "revisionist" elements, i.e., those attempting to revise the existing territorial division or power structure of the region, had to realize from the beginning that they could not hope to gain enthusiastic support or encouragement from the West. This held true equally of the Jewish *Yishuv* in Palestine prior to 1948 during its struggle against the British Mandatory authorities, of the radical Arab nationalists from 1948 onwards as they tried to reverse the Israeli victory and to eliminate the newly-established Jewish State, of the Egyptian *junta* after 1954 when it tried to wrest Near Eastern hegemony away from Nuri a-Said's Iraq, and of the Kurds when they revolted against Arab rule.

Yet, paradoxically, the West could not become too ardent in support of those local elements whose posture was essentially defensive and whose attitude, therefore, was basically pro-Western. Desiring to maintain its position throughout the region and to have equal leverage everywhere, the West could not afford to be drawn into active participation on one side of a local conflict, since by so doing it might forfeit its acceptability and its "presence" on the rival side. Thus, Western interests seemed to demand a policy of relative neutrality, of even-handed approach, toward local disputes. This innate ambivalence seriously hampered the effectiveness of Western policies at the time. Local leaders who were dissatisfied with the existing distribution of power and territory knew that they could not gain Western support, but soon they also realized that massive Western force, in all likelihood, would not be employed against them, at any rate as long as they stopped short of actually invading their neighbors. Such radical, irredentist politicians in the Near East, therefore, were antagonized but not deterred by the West, especially since they found that they could exploit the mutually contradictory policies which the U.S., the U.K. and France pursued (in spite of their Tripartite Declaration of 1950).

In contrast to the West, the U.S.S.R., just because it had not established an active Near Eastern "presence" at that stage, had nothing to lose by giving complete backing to one single element in the region—namely, irredentist leaders. In this way Russia could make sure of winning over one group, while it hardly mattered if, by so doing, Moscow alienated some other Near Eastern states, since it had no physical footholds to endanger in any case. Having no responsibilities or commitments in the area at that time, the U.S.S.R., unlike the West, did not have to fear the embarrassment of being required to take action in order to quench dangerous, hot local wars. By fanning such disputes, therefore, the Russians could aggravate instability within the region, gravely inconveniencing the West and score immediate gains in the capitals of irredentist states without in any way having to foot the bill. Thus the U.S.S.R. was able to back Arab claims against Israel, Egyptian attacks upon Iraqi hegemony and Kurdish demands for autonomy. This was a game which, in its initial stages, could hardly be lost since no Western power with major commitments in the Near East could possibly afford to outbid an "irresponsible" outsider like the U.S.S.R. in a competition for the favor of irredentist elements. After all, the West could hardly ally itself with forces desiring to overturn the existing Near Eastern balance, the preservation of which was a vital Western policy objective.

At that stage Soviet policy made adroit use of the then prevalent Western susceptibility to "pactitis"—a weakness with which the memory of John Foster Dulles has become associated, somewhat unfairly. The West, in its endeavors to contain Soviet expansion, was attempting to augment its security by establishing bases within the immediate vicinity of the Soviet frontiers since this was then the most practical way of rendering Soviet territory accessible to Western non-conventional might. In this manner the West could hope to neutralize the Soviet preponderance of ground forces. Such a policy could only be implemented, however, by winning over the regimes whose territories were to sustain these bases; for this purpose, it was useful to extend political and military support to these régimes within the framework of military pacts or alliances. The countries which found such alliances most attractive were naturally those with the largest stake in the *status quo* (Pakistan being a possible exception). It was thus logical that states like Turkey, Iran and Iraq should be drawn into the framework of a Near Eastern military pact, threatened as they were by irredentist claims emanating from the Russians, the Kurds and the

Syrians and by the rivalry of Egypt. In turn, however, this development still further exacerbated the feelings of restless leaders in Cairo and Damascus since it was their traditional rivals who were thus receiving preferential treatment and arms from the West.

It was precisely this state of affairs which enabled the Soviet Union to "jump over" the Northern Tier (Turkey, Iran and Iraq) and to align itself with resentful Near Eastern rulers, such as those of Egypt, Syria and even Yemen. The Soviets resorted to the obvious method of achieving this objective by offering Russian arms to these irredentist states in order to compensate them for the Western weapons given to their rivals. There is little doubt that it was considerations of this kind which gave birth to the famous Czech-Egyptian Arms Deal of 1955 and to subsequent similar transactions through which the U.S.S.R. gained entry into the region.

It will be noted immediately that the Soviet motivations analyzed here were of a markedly non-ideological nature; considerations of this type could be expected to guide any traditional power pursuing a "classical" foreign policy within a framework of *Realpolitik*. It was, in fact, only by removing ideological blinkers and by deciding to follow precisely this form of practical and realistic policy that Moscow was able to achieve the necessary elasticity for a diplomatic breakthrough in the Near East. Previously, during the 1947-49 period, and even for some time thereafter, the Zhdanovite "two camp" theory, with its simplistic division of the world into Communists and their enemies, prevented the Soviet Union from taking full advantage of existing antagonisms within the region. By 1952 Stalin was beginning to put new stress upon the importance of "contradictions" within the Western camp, emphasizing that such a situation offered great opportunities to an adroit Soviet foreign policy. However, he died a few months later. Malenkov who, at the Nineteenth CPSU Congress in 1952, had expounded Stalin's new tenets, attempted to apply such a flexible policy to the Near East. In the new régime's foreign policy platform of August 1953, Malenkov put forth feelers to Egypt and other states in the region, but few concrete steps followed.

In Moscow the local scene was still viewed largely through the distorted lens of the dialectic, as if the lessons of the nineteenth century European class struggle could, with some tactical alterations, be applied to the Near East. Much weight was still placed upon the fortunes and prospects of the local Communist parties. Unlike the Chinese who, at that particular time, were following a rather undoctrinaire approach, the Russians treated the "national *bourgeoisie*" of the ex-colonial countries as fundamentally two-faced and unreliable, so that any alignment with it could only be of the most tenuous and transitory nature. The independence of the new Afro-Asian nations was still regarded as something of a sham. Moscow also did not believe that any statesman could really pursue a line of genuine neutrality between East and West. Thus the U.S.S.R. was better able to exploit the "contradictions" between London and Washington than those between the West and Afro-Asia. Moscow had not yet liberated itself from the classical two-stage theory of colonial revolution, which meant, in fact, that the "national *bourgeoisie*" in Afro-Asia was supposed to expel the colonial powers by means of a temporary alignment with the local Communists and then to sit by while the latter prepared a "second revolution" against their erstwhile allies. Moreover, such naïve doctrines were kept alive by a notable lack of objective knowledge in the U.S.S.R. about the Near East and the ex-colonial world in general.

As a result of all these defects, Moscow missed great opportunities, failing to reap any advantage, for instance, from the grave Iranian crisis; Mossadegh's struggle against the West was just not taken seriously enough by the Russians. It was not until 1954-55 and, more noticeably, after the Twentieth CPSU Congress in 1956, that Soviet "Eastern" scholarship was seriously revived to the point of being permitted finally to make some factual contributions to Moscow's interpretation of the contemporary Near Eastern scene. It was only in the sixties, however, that some scholars, especially in the Institute of World Economics and International Relations, really were able to reach this point. The man who encouraged this development at the Twentieth Party Congress by his scathing denunciation of the paralysis imposed upon Soviet "Eastern" sciences, was, significantly, a "Near Easterner" himself—Anastas Mikoyan.

The basic factor, however, which rendered possible gradual abandonment of outworn doctrines and a major departure in Soviet policy toward the Near East, was the ascendancy of Nikita

Khrushchev in 1954-55. Khrushchev's dynamic, restless and some-what adventurous concept of world affairs found the Near East to be a region of irresistible temptations. Consequently, from 1955 until 1959 Moscow was able to spark some startling, although momentary, flashes of success in Egypt, Syria and Iraq. Without ever achieving a full physical "presence" in the Near East—in the form of protectorates, bases or combat contingents—the Soviet Union was able to vault over Western barriers and to establish a very active diplomatic "presence" in the region, based upon ex-tensive arms deals, training of local armies, economic aid, inces-sant exchanges of delegations and vociferous support for the territorial and political demands of anti-Western régimes. During this period the propagandistic output of missions and solidarity conferences of various kinds was voluminous. Such showy, if superficial and fleeting, gains could be registered by exploiting local antagonisms through the undoctrinaire application of a classical *Realpolitik,* as has been noted earlier.

While still enjoying the initial advantages of a complete outsider to the region, the U.S.S.R. had been able to exploit the West's dilemmas and difficulties in order to gain entry into the Near East. However, very similar dilemmas soon became Russia's heritage as her own stake in the Near East increased. Suez in 1956, the 1958 Iraqi-Lebanese-Jordanian crisis and other fever peaks soon proved that, while it was one thing to exploit local disputes in order to embarrass the West and ease the Soviet path into the Near East, it was quite another to permit such antagonisms to reach the point of hot conflict once the U.S.S.R. had penetrated the region. The moment Moscow acquired a tangible stake in the area, includ-ing local diplomatic alignments, sizable aid investments and Soviet-trained and equipped Near Eastern armies, it became obvi-ous that it might be harmful to permit local wars to break out. The West, after all, still controlled military footholds in or near the region and, moreover, still dominated the maritime approaches to the Near East by means of the U.S. Sixth Fleet, while the Northern Tier still barred the way to massive invasion from the Caucasus. Since the West was bound by definite moral and treaty commitments to prevent acts of aggression within the region, it was clear that the Western powers were both able and obliged to put a rapid end to local outbreaks.

If the U.S.S.R. incited and abetted Near Eastern irredentist leaders to launch an attack upon their neighbors, the chances were great that the West would quash such conflagrations and, in so doing, would crush those elements which had relied upon Soviet protection. In that case Moscow faced an unpalatable choice between staging a nuclear confrontation with the West or standing by helplessly, watching Soviet investments going down the drain, Russian-trained armies being defeated and Soviet weapons being demolished—with consequent disastrous loss of prestige. Moreover, such Western intervention would have the effect of bringing back Western land forces to a region in which the U.S.S.R. was attempting to eliminate the Western physical presence. There was no conventional way of deterring the West since, as has been noted, Khrushchev's policies did not provide the U.S.S.R. with an effective, conventional striking force for use in the region. Therefore, Moscow had no acceptable policies in case of local conflagration; consequently, Soviet interests required that the escalation of local conflicts be stopped short of the point of actual outbreaks. Whenever events outran Soviet control, Moscow's embarrassment became obvious, as during the Suez crisis when the immediate Soviet reaction to Anglo-French intervention in Egypt was . . . to evacuate Russian military equipment and experts. Only after it became apparent that U.S. pressure was causing London and Paris to falter did the U.S.S.R. begin to rattle its rockets.

As the author has attempted to show elsewhere,[2] Khrushchev had not possessed the foresight, in the initial stages of his Near Eastern offensive, to provide for such contingencies. The very attraction of Soviet military assistance to countries like Egypt and Syria lay in the fact that Russia claimed to be abstaining from any demand for political "strings." Yet the "strings" imposed by the U.S. in return for its military aid—a constant theme of Soviet propaganda attacks—actually consisted of no more than a commitment that recipients would use such weapons only for defense and internal security and not for aggression against neighbors. Having fulminated *ad nauseam* against Washington's "strings," Moscow could not very well impose similar limitations of its own. In the absence of such restraints, however, Moscow had no con-

[2] "Tactics in the Third World: Contradictions and Dangers," *Survey*, October 1965.

vincing leverage to control the future actions of Soviet military aid recipients or to avert local wars which might prove dangerous. While Russia could always threaten to cut off the supply of spare parts and ammunition to recalcitrant recipients, such action was certain to be interpreted by proud and touchy Near Easterners as a flagrant breach of good faith. Consequently, Moscow had to tolerate their adventures or risk losing, at one blow, all the political assets it had accumulated and the large investments it had made.

The fact remains that the Russians never cared to put the issue squarely to the test. Thus the Iraqi Army, in several campaigns, employed Soviet arms against the Kurds in spite of Moscow's open discomfort; after all, Russia had been attempting to court the Kurds for a long time. Egypt brought Soviet weapons into some disrepute, under humiliating circumstances, during a prolonged and unsuccessful war against primitive Yemenite tribesmen. After supporting the Egyptian expedition for years, Moscow began to evince embarrassment at the whole affair, yet fighting continued for many months longer. Algeria and Morocco could not be prevented from coming to blows at a time when both countries were in possession of some Soviet arms and when the Russians were trying to woo both Rabat and Algiers. For that matter, the U.S.S.R. gave veiled indications of concern lest miscalculations by Arab recipients of Soviet hardware should produce a showdown with Israel, thus precipitating Western intervention in the area. In none of these instances, however, did Moscow prove to have decisive influence upon the Near Eastern capitals on which it had lavished so much assistance and support; nor did the Russians dare to cut off aid completely as a means of ensuring compliance with their wishes.

Clearly, the prevalence of local rivalries and disputes within the Near East, which initially had eased Russia's entry into the region, presented Soviet foreign policy with very serious problems during subsequent stages. This was true above all of the more permanent and enduring conflicts which mark the Near Eastern scene. Quite apart from local clashes, however acute, which were basically limited to one specific locale or to one particular moment, the region was and is dominated by three major cross-currents: (1) Existing states, whether they were reconstituted from ancient en-

tities (like Syria, Iraq, Egypt, Yemen and Israel) or are of more
artificial origin (like Jordan, Kuwait and the Sudan) have managed gradually to instill in their populations some sense of loyalty
and identification; while this feeling varies widely in depth from
country to country and is obviously stronger in historic units, it is
now a real and important force throughout the Near East. (2)
Across the frontiers of most of the established states there extends
another force which is fundamentally inimical to their continued
separate existence: that is the pan-Arab unity movement, reinforced by Islamic sentiments, which clashes with the concept of
an aloof, independent Syria as much as pan-Germanism once
opposed the idea of an independent Austria. (3) Within many of
the Near Eastern states there exist ethnic or religious minorities,
above all the Kurds in northern Iraq, whose aspirations are both
potentially disruptive of existing political units and incompatible
with the final aims of pan-Arabism.

It is obvious that these three forces are mutually exclusive, although very occasionally there have been brief, tactical alliances
between Cairo's pan-Arabism and the Kurdish national movement
for the purpose of overcoming a mutual enemy in Baghdad. No
great power has ever been able to align itself for any length of
time with more than one of these three political currents. Generally
speaking the West has found it easiest to cooperate with elements
which accept the established states and their frontiers and which,
therefore, support the regional *status quo*. Consequently, the two
rival forces—Cairo's Arab unity movement and the Kurds—have
been inclined to look for counter-support from outsiders, including the U.S.S.R. Occasionally, however, local rulers who were
basically in favor of the territorial *status quo* have found themselves so hard-pressed by their opponents that they were prepared
to accept assistance from any source, including the Soviet Union.
This occurred in 1957 when radical elements in the Syrian Army
turned to Moscow because their country was simultaneously pres-
sured from Baghdad, Ankara and Cairo. It happened again in
1958-59 when Kassem's revolutionary régime in Iraq faced strong
hostility both from the West and from Egypt and sought temporary
Russian protection. Thus, in the early years of the Soviet Near
Eastern offensive, Moscow had a wide choice of potential friends;
what should have been apparent, however, was that *status quo*

supporters, Nasserites and non-Arab minorities should be considered mutually incompatible elements. The U.S.S.R. could penetrate the Near East by exploiting one or several of these forces, but it could not remain friendly with all of them over any period of time.

Thus, Nasser's identification with the Arab unity movement a decade ago brought Egypt into conflict with the Western-backed territorial *status quo;* consequently, Cairo's and Moscow's aims temporarily coincided. Yet the full achievement of Egypt's aspirations would clearly mean the end of Syrian and Iraqi independence and the suppression of those elements in Damascus and Baghdad which had had separate, friendly dealings with Moscow; simultaneously, it would mean the end of Kurdish hopes. Moreover, all the powers, including Russia, would be bereft of serious leverage when left face to face with one huge Arab empire ruled by one single, proud and touchy leader. Therefore, Moscow could not support Cairo without inner reservations. Similarly, the Kurdish struggle for autonomy might be useful to the Soviet Union because of its divisive repercussions in the region and because the Kurds, having been abandoned by the outside world, might be forced, however reluctantly, to have recourse to the U.S.S.R. On the other hand, it was impossible to back the Kurds fully, because to do so would not only run counter to Cairo's pan-Arab aspirations, but would be unacceptable to most of Russia's friends in Baghdad. Again, it was in the Soviet interest to help a reasonably friendly Syria or Iraq to maintain its independence against Cairo's attempts at domination; yet Nasser's staunchest opponents in these two countries are either friends of the West or supporters of the Ba'ath —a movement which is as hostile to the U.S.S.R. as it is to the West. Obviously, therefore, any long-term policy for the Near East which Moscow could evolve either had to be full of inconsistencies and contradictions or it had to alienate many potential allies in order to maintain firm friendship with one particular Near Eastern force.

Soviet dilemmas in the face of conflicting ethnic aspirations were intensified by a typically Near Eastern phenomenon—the coincidence between religious, ethnic and political lines. For instance, minority groups such as the Kurds and the Greek Orthodox Christians were often prominent in the local Communist parties;

the outstanding Near Eastern Communist leader, Khaled Bagdash, is of Kurdish origin. Here again, Moscow was in difficulty: support for such minority enclaves in a predominantly Arab and Moslem area like Syria meant abandoning hope of winning over the masses; courtship of the latter, however, meant alienating the most sympathetic minority elements.

The almost insoluble nature of these problems found clear reflection in the zigzags of the Soviet line on the question of Arab unity. In the immediate post-war period the U.S.S.R. had regarded pan-Arabism and, especially, the Arab League with deep suspicion as creations of British "imperialism." This attitude changed in 1954-55 when Egypt and Syria began to invoke pan-Arab arguments against Iraq's accession to Western defense arrangements; Cairo and Damascus attached the Baghdad Pact as a betrayal of Arab solidarity. Having exploited this situation adroitly to penetrate the region with its famous Arms Deal, Moscow enjoyed a short honeymoon with the Arab unity movement. Disillusionment followed in 1957-58 because of developments in Syria. For a short while it seemed as if pro-Soviet elements in the Syrian Army and government might bring the country into alignment with the U.S.S.R., but then anti-communist elements, headed by the Ba'ath, used the pretext of Arab unity to rush Syria into union with Egypt as a way of avoiding Moscow's embrace. (Later the Ba'ath was to become as hostile to Cairo as it was to Moscow.) At the time the U.S.S.R. was obliged to accept the situation with resignation and to recognize the new United Arab Republic. However, the Russians had now experienced some of the drawbacks of Arab nationalism and were thus forewarned by the time of the Iraqi Revolution, later in 1958, when events began to take a similar turn. After the pro-Western Nuri a-Said régime was overthrown in Baghdad, the new ruler, Kassem, seemed to be leading the country along distinctly radical paths. At that point, regarding Kassem as a potential rival, Nasserite elements attempted to force Baghdad into union with the UAR. Kassem naturally resisted this attempt, the success of which would have meant his removal. Since the West regarded his régime with hostility, he felt that in order to survive he had to resort to the help both of Moscow and of the local Communist party, at least for the time being. The U.S.S.R. was determined that Iraq should not witness a repeat performance of the Syrian debacle and, therefore, strongly opposed Cairo's efforts to overthrow Kassem and to absorb his country in the name of Arab unity. It was this factor which brought Cairo and Moscow into serious conflict in 1959, although, overtly, the clash was triggered by Egyptian measures against important communists in Syria after the creation of the UAR.

In spite of massive Soviet military and economic assistance to Cairo and the dependence of the Egyptian Army upon Soviet training and spare parts, however, the U.S.S.R. was unable to make Nasser desist from interfering in Iraq. Moreover, he publicly defied Moscow over the issue of the treatment of local communists. For that matter, once the immediate threat to his régime diminished in 1960, Kassem, another beneficiary of Soviet aid, gave recognition to a tame communist faction and took steps against the orthodox communist leaders supported by Moscow. Furthermore, he used his new Soviet weapons to launch a military offensive against the Kurds.

While, therefore, Moscow clearly found itself at odds with pan-Arabism after 1958-59 and was to remain distinctly cool toward the movement until 1963, the Soviet attitude toward Nasser personally remained ambivalent. It could be said that Moscow found some use for Nasser's tactics, but disapproved of his strategy. In other words, Cairo's offensives against other régimes in the Arab world were, in the short run, regarded as helpful to Moscow—as long as they were not too successful. Where Egyptian pressure was applied against pro-Western régimes, as in Jordan and Lebanon, the U.S.S.R. was content. Where Cairo's pressure was brought to bear on a radical ruler, such as Kassem, the immediate effect, as has been noted, was to drive him closer toward the U.S.S.R. and the local Communist party in order to protect himself. Moscow, however, regarded it as unacceptable if Nasserite pressure persisted to the point of undermining and destroying a "promising" régime such as Kassem's. It is this Soviet ambivalence toward Nasser's tactics and strategy, which may explain in part why Moscow continued to give aid both to Cairo and Baghdad in spite of the setbacks suffered in the two capitals from 1959 to 1961. Moscow continued to support Nasserism wherever its immediate impact was injurious to the West, as in Africa; on the other hand, the U.S.S.R. happily recognized the new Damascus régime in 1961 when Syria broke away from the UAR and reasserted its independence. At the same time, Moscow printed and broadcast polemics against Nasser's ideology of Arab Socialism. Soviet references to Arab unity were full of reservations.

By 1964, however, there was a distinct change in Moscow. The victory of the Ba'ath in Syria and Iraq during the previous year had produced régimes which were virulently anti-communist; Baghdad had even sent Soviet advisers and technicians packing, although only temporarily. Nasserite attempts to overthrow the Ba'ath were thus highly acceptable to Moscow. Soviet hostility to Iraq continued even after Aref toppled his erstwhile Ba'ath collaborators in Baghdad, since Aref himself had been associated with the massacre of Iraqi communists in 1963. Hence, by 1964-65 the U.S.S.R. found unfriendly régimes entrenched throughout the area, except for Cairo and Algiers. Consequently, Moscow was ready to give more wholehearted support, even ideologically, to Nasserism. It was noticeable even at this stage, however, that Khrushchev, while visiting Egypt in the spring of 1964, still carefully differentiated between unity of the "progressive" Arab masses and a "reactionary" Arab nationalism—attacking the latter (mainly because of the irritating presence of Aref during Khrushchev's visit).

As has been shown, Soviet considerations regarding the Arab national movement were based mainly on issues of *Realpolitik* rather than ideology. The U.S.S.R. felt (from 1957 to 1963) that there were important advantages in being able to play off rival régimes in the region against one another. Therefore, Moscow had nothing to gain from the forcible creation of a united Arab empire under one proud and stubborn leader. Some of these considerations were possibly shared by other great powers. However, by 1964 the Russians realized that the original pan-Arab tide was beginning to ebb away with the passage of years; even in "artificial" countries like Jordan, loyalties to the state were gradually instilled in parts of the army, the civil service and some sections of the middle class. As for Iraq and Syria, these were, after all, ancient entities with deep local pride and Syria's experience proved that even avowedly "Nasserite" elements did not necessarily wish to subject their local autonomy to Egyptian rule. Thus, there was no longer much danger that support of Cairo would necessarily lead to the creation of an Arab empire. In principle, the U.S.S.R. has never been over-enthusiastic at the prospect of seeing large confederations, units or empires arise in the immediate vicinity of the Russian frontiers. After all, it was Yugoslav support for some form of Balkan confederation which helped to precipitate the Soviet-Yugoslav conflict in the 1940's. However, even if the Soviet attitude toward Arab movements must thus be regarded as having been motivated mainly by traditional considerations of power politics, ideological factors cannot be disregarded altogether.

The U.S.S.R., after all, still was and is a Communist power and, at least until the early 1960's, had not yet abandoned plans for recreating some kind of global communist authority which should coordinate communist tactics in individual countries. It was obvious that persistent and total Soviet disregard for the interests of local Communist parties must undermine such attempts and, as the Sino-Soviet dispute intensified, considerations of this kind became more important to Moscow. Thus the Russians were bound to pay some attention to the fortunes of the local Communist parties, even though Soviet policy in the region as a whole was predicated upon alignments with monolithic non-Communist régimes, which expected the fate of the local communists to be totally subordinated to their dictates. Not that the U.S.S.R. could have estimated very highly the chances of an actual communist takeover anywhere in the Near East, except, perhaps, for a very brief period in Iraq during 1959. Moreover, it is more than doubtful whether Moscow thought that such a takeover would be advantageous to its interests. Being deeply conscious of Western military domination of the approaches to the region and assuming, no doubt (especially after the 1958 Western landings in Lebanon and Jordan), that the West would react decisively to any such threat, Moscow probably considered an alignment with non-communist régimes to be preferable, for the time being, to an actual communist seizure of power.

Altogether, communist strength in the Near East, except, perhaps, for occasional exploits by the Tudeh in Iran, has not been at all impressive. The Egyptian Communist party—or parties to be exact—has been fragmented and faction-ridden. The Algerian CP has been heavily impeded by memories of its initially very dubious attitude toward the FLN's national liberation struggle. The Iraqi

CP indulged in irresponsible adventurism and butcheries in Mosul and Kirkuk during the 1959 crisis, burdening itself with blood feuds; consequently, it had only itself to blame if its own ranks were decimated by massacres four years later, in 1963. The Syrian CP, ably guided by the only major personality among Near Eastern Communist leaders, Khalid Bagdash, has never achieved enough of a mass following to constitute a decisive force, although its adroit manoeuvres from 1954 to 1957 seemed, for a short while, to bring it close to success. Since, with the exception of the Lebanon, none of the Arab countries have enjoyed long periods of multi-party democracy (one-man leadership, especially of the military type, being the rule), the Soviets must have realized from the beginning that the local Communist parties were likely to be suppressed together with all other political opposition.

It is hard to believe, therefore, that the periodic persecutions endured by Syrian or Egyptian communists, which were neither unexpected nor unprecedented, could have been the real cause of Khrushchev's anti-Nasser outbursts in 1959 and 1961. As noted previously, it was power considerations rather than ideology which motivated these developments. On the other hand, there is no doubt that the repeated anti-communist measures of régimes which apparently depend on Soviet aid, was a matter of embarrassment to the Soviet leaders. Moreover, the Russians found that they could not remain indifferent to the fate of local communists without alienating them. Thus, in 1959 Khaled Bagdash started to take his complaints against Nasser to Peking, a clear threat to the monopoly over the Near Eastern CP's enjoyed by the U.S.S.R. until then. As the Sino-Soviet dispute grew more heated, both Moscow and Peking tended to measure success or failure by the number of individual Communist parties which each could win over. Thus it became apparent that the Russians could not go on entirely disregarding the claims and interests of the Near Eastern communists.

It was not until the last days of 1963, however, that Khrushchev attempted to find a consistent ideological formula which might square the Near Eastern circle. In his "interviews" with Ghanaian, Algerian and Burmese editors, he evolved a new thesis of "revolutionary democracy," clearly meant to fit Near Eastern realities. According to this formula, which was developed and extended during 1964, the one-party régimes governing newly-independent countries were to receive Soviet ideological endorsement as well as additional economic and military aid, provided they not only maintained their anti-Western posture, but also ceased overt persecution of the local Communist parties. In return, the local communists would be encouraged not only to support the régimes in power, but to enter into a united front with them. Moscow went so far as to tell Communist parties to merge with the official party organizations of the local régimes, thus abandoning their separate frameworks. In two countries the new line was actually implemented. In Algeria the CP started to merge with the FLN and undertook also to publish its newspapers jointly with the FLN. In Egypt the various communist factions had for some time been deprived of overt recognition from Moscow (for instance, the Egyptian CP was not officially mentioned among the parties participating in the 1960 Moscow gathering of 81 Communist Workers' parties). Early in 1964 Nasser was encouraged by Moscow to release individual communists from jail, in return for which a major faction of the party came out in support of Nasser's Arab Socialist Union. Some of the more prominent communists received minor posts of public responsibility, primarily in connection with the organization of the Egyptian press.

As the author has attempted to show elsewhere,[3] there was considerable resistance to Moscow's new policy, especially from Khaled Bagdash and his Syrian CP. He objected to the Soviet endorsement of Nasser's régime (Moscow had stated that Egypt was now genuinely on the "path to socialism"). Bagdash protested that military dictatorship could not be genuinely "socialist" and should not receive Soviet ideological support. Sections of the Lebanese CP and one faction of the Egyptian CP apparently voiced similar objections. However, during 1964 the Soviet leadership bludgeoned the Near Eastern Communist parties into acceptance of the new line, pointing out that Nasser and Ben Bella were no longer actively suppressing individual communists and that the latter should, therefore, be content. A gathering of Near Eastern communists held in Central Europe late in 1964, finally gave approval to the new line, although with significant reservations (for instance by requesting "democratic freedoms" for

* "Moscow and the Third World," *Problems of Communism*, January-February 1965.

Egyptian communists). Presumably this meant that the newly-freed communists should be permitted to organize. After Khrushchev's ouster, however, and especially in the fall of 1965, there were reports of renewed communist objections to Khrushchev's 1964 line. There is no sign now of any Soviet attempt to bring pressure to bear on the Near Eastern communists as Khrushchev had done. A freer hand for Bagdash, however, is fraught with danger since it must cause friction with régimes in power.

This slight retreat from Khrushchev's wholehearted embrace of various Afro-Asian régimes went hand in hand, late in 1965, with a new trend of increasing retrenchment in Soviet foreign aid. The Czechs, openly, and the Russians, in slightly less overt fashion, showed signs of disillusionment with the meager results of a decade of economic, technical and military largesse. Although Aswan, for instance, was an undoubted propagandistic showpiece, it was more than doubtful, as has been noted, whether the U.S.S.R. was gathering any lasting political returns from this and other expensive items. It is perhaps no coincidence that a change in the nuances of the Soviet approach could be noted after June 1965, following the *coup* in Algeria, which clearly came as a shock to the Soviets and their allies. Moscow had been prepared, in the previous year, to sacrifice the Algerian CP because Khrushchev believed in the durability of Ben Bella's régime and considered his friendship worth gaining. Consequently, Khrushchev had been prepared to override the objections of the patrons of the Algerian communists—the French CP—and of some Near Eastern communists, and to go ahead with this policy. Yet, by mid-1965, the U.S.S.R. found that these sacrifices had been worthless since Ben Bella suddenly disappeared into the black of night and the new régime of Boumedienne struck ruthlessly at the communists, in spite of their promise to "merge" with the FLN. While Moscow preserved diplomatic silence, loud complaints were heard from other East European capitals and from the West European CP's, who voiced regrets at the mistake made in 1964.

Similarly, in Egypt Khrushchev had gone a long way during his last months toward underwriting Nasser and Arab Socialism ideologically, in the belief that a decade of Nasserite rule had proved the régime's durability. However, in the second half of 1965 the Moslem Brotherhood plot in Egypt, significantly supported by small sections of the military and of the security services (which were subsequently purged), seemed to show that here too one-man rule precariously depended upon . . . one man! The new Soviet régime, therefore, could hardly conclude that Khrushchev was right in thinking that Near Eastern rulers were necessarily stronger and more lasting allies than are the weak local Communist parties. Of course, Khrushchev's successors maintained to the full their diplomatic friendship with Cairo and soon attempted to woo the new ruler of Algeria; however, there appeared to be more willingness in Moscow to respect the interests of the Near Eastern Communist parties and less readiness to write them off.

In the foreign assistance field, while dutifully disbursing the major aid agreements which Khrushchev had made in his last year, the new Soviet rulers showed little willingness to undertake new sizable commitments. At the most, they were prepared to write off some past debts—an act of realism, perhaps, rather than of generosity. Late in October 1965, after enlarging upon the sacrifices which the Soviet people had made in order to help developing countries, a *Pravda* editorial explained that it would be a mistake to "level" the gap between the advanced socialist countries and the developing areas; on the contrary, Africa and Asia should favor the further advance of the socialist countries since, only in this way, would the U.S.S.R. and its allies be able to assist them effectively in the future. A Soviet pamphlet told the developing countries that disarmament was in their interest, since it would leave the *West* with larger resources for foreign aid! This was obviously a hint that they should expect assistance from the U.S. and Western Europe rather than from the U.S.S.R. and Czechoslovakia. Moscow also revealed new interest in Afro-Asian regional development schemes and in *multilateral* aid; both would clearly reduce the pressure which aid recipients could bring to bear on the U.S.S.R. In a revealing analysis of foreign affairs, a Czech journal explained the need for retrenchment, bluntly accusing the developing countries of greed in demanding economic and military assistance from the Communist countries.

Perhaps the U.S.S.R. and its allies found it possible to treat Near Eastern aid recipients a little more sternly since the Chinese had clearly failed to make significant inroads into the area. The UAR had steadfastly supported Moscow against Peking over issues such as Soviet participation in Afro-Asian conferences, the Test Ban Treaty, etc. Most other Near Eastern countries behaved similarly, with the occasional exception of the erratic Syrians, while the new Algerian régime maintained a cautious neutrality. As far as the local Communist parties were concerned, not one went over to Peking in spite of obvious resentments at the line laid down by Khrushchev during his last year. One unimportant splinter in Egypt accepted Peking's lead and a few very insignificant elements did so elsewhere. It was only among some militant and adventuristic elements in the ranks of the *non-communist* youth (e.g., the Palestine Liberation Organization), that Peking was able to gain a little influence. Thus, by 1965 the Soviets could feel relatively safe in ignoring Chinese rivalry as a major factor in their Near Eastern policy.

The fact remains, however, that if China did badly in the region, and the West, perhaps, did no more than hold its own, the U.S.S.R. had also failed to achieve any significant or lasting successes. Over a whole decade of concentrated and expensive effort, Russia was able to do little more than temporarily "vibrate in unison" with certain Near Eastern régimes. Even then, such alignments lasted only as long as it suited the interests of Moscow's various local partners. While annoying to the West, this phenomenon brought no tangible or permanent gains to the Soviet Union. For all the great powers alike, the Near East has remained a touchy, recalcitrant and difficult area.